EXCLUSIVE LIMITED EDITION

Thank you for ordering this Exclusive Limited Edition. It has been specially published for those of you who don't want to wait to find out Why YOU Are Your Ultimate Relationship, and also for my colleagues for their endorsements.

If you are moved to share with me, I would be honored to hear about your experience of the journey to discovering Your Ultimate Relationship.

InnerAlignmentMethod.com

Why **YOU** *Are*

YOUR ULTIMATE RELATIONSHIP

Find What You Really Want by Discovering What You Already Have

Dear Gabriel,
   Welcome to the fountain of YOU!

Warmly,
Ron

Ron Levy, MS, LMFT

YUR
PUBLISHING

ISBN: 1939325005

ISBN 13: 9781939325006

Library of Congress Control Number: 2013921457

YUR Publishing

Calabasas, CA

InnerAlignmentMethod.com

Cover: DeSimone Design

DISCLAIMER

This book is intended to assist people in creating extraordinary lives. While its contents are for informational and even transformational purposes, they are not intended to be a substitute for professional medical advice, diagnosis, or treatment. If you suffer from depression or any other medical and/or psychological condition, you should seek out appropriate advice from your physician or other qualified mental health professional in your area. I do not recommend disregarding professional medical advice or delay in seeking treatment because of something you have read in this book.

The views contained herein are solely those of the author and should not be construed as the views of any other person or organization, or an endorsement of any specific persons, organizations, products or procedures.

**What people are saying about Ron Levy and
the Inner Alignment Method:**

Ron Levy has succeeded at something I thought would be impossible: Making the personal growth he facilitates in his private practice available through a book! *Why YOU Are Your Ultimate Relationship* is a guide that is both fun to read and inviting to apply. In it, Ron describes an ongoing process of self-discovery and connection, laid out with such clarity that putting it into practice is irresistible. Each step is sized just right to promote the progress of an interested explorer. It's like having a treasure map, only the treasure turns out to be the fountain of YOU! I'm keeping this close by to continue my inner exploration and healing.

Joan Newton, Granada Hills, CA

Why YOU Are Your Ultimate Relationship by Ron Levy offers a way to progress in these uncertain times by encouraging a vision of an enriched state of living with practical ways of growing in that direction. Levy describes his Inner Alignment Method and gives explicit instructions for practicing simple exercises that lead to healing. In his gentle way, Levy encourages releasing old patterns and improving life by connecting with oneself lovingly, compassionately, and respectfully. Through real-life stories, he teaches how to reach out to others, while growing and building a solid internal relationship.

This authentic, warm, and loving book is valuable to me as a psychologist as it describes a useful therapeutic technique with excellent examples. It also offers an enhanced way of life through becoming comfortable with "not knowing." Not knowing provides freedom from clinging to any one perspective or belief, and allows us to greet new ideas with interest and enthusiasm. I recommend this book highly for those seeking to enrich their lives.

Rie Rogers Mitchell, Ph.D., A.B.P.P.

Professor Emeritus

California State University, Northridge

Past-President, International Society for Sandplay Therapy

Ron's process is the most organic, in-the-moment, proactive, truly unique and heartfelt therapy I have ever encountered, and it has changed my life profoundly. I tried many different types of therapy and therapists, yet nothing came close to helping me grow and find my true power as much as Ron's work has. It is truly a blessing. Once we find the relationship Ron teaches us to find, we are free. I would not be where I am today had I not discovered I AM.

Mitch Stone, Malibu, CA

This book is filled with profound life truths that are easy for anyone to absorb. While it is overflowing with great information, the reader cannot help but see and experience themselves and the world differently as they read through each chapter. *Why YOU Are Your Ultimate Relationship* literally teaches people how to love - themselves, each other, and the world. I thoroughly and highly recommend this book to anyone wanting more peace and joy in their lives.

Jeanne T. Blackstone, West Hills, CA

Why YOU Are Your Ultimate Relationship is outstanding - easy to read and accurately represents a client's true experience of the healing process in the Inner Alignment Method. I love the natural flow, from how to do the work to the practice exercises with precise instructions. The spirituality of the work comes through the pages with such gentleness that it can easily be received by everyone.

As a psychologist, I would highly recommend this book to my clients – and to everyone – to accelerate their progress in releasing old patterns of behavior and gaining rapid insight about how to improve their lives, and connecting more fully with all parts of themselves in a loving and respectful way. The payoff will be exponential when they begin to feel the freedom and joy that come from such an authentic self-experience.

Vickie B. Bert, Ph.D., Westlake Village, CA

Ron Levy's *Why YOU Are Your Ultimate Relationship* is a game changer! I have read numerous self-help books throughout the years. While many others have given me insight into my psyche in a very intellectual way, Ron Levy creates a living, breathing road map, a barometer from which I can always determine what's going on in my psyche in real time. I have never read a book that has affected me to the degree and depth that this one does. Since reading *YUR*, my compassion for myself and those I share this planet with continues to grow; I continue to sharpen my ability to listen to my inner voice in all moments of my life, creating the space for true growth, artistic expression and infinite potential! I highly recommend this book for anyone who really wants to discover who and what they are all about!

Andrew M. Schoenberg, Las Vegas, NV

Ron Levy has a natural and intuitive understanding of the dynamics of the human psyche and soul – as well as an insight into the deep yearning within us all to become whole. He is no less than a master guide who teaches his clients how to navigate the confusing labyrinth of family and cultural conditioning in order to arrive back at who we truly are.

Judith Diana Winston, Santa Monica, CA

The Inner Alignment Method as described in Ron Levy's *Why YOU are Your Ultimate Relationship* is a very original and brilliant method of self-discovery and healing. I have read and studied many other personal growth books, and none of them has approached self-healing in such a dynamic, foundational way. The book contains simple processes and tools for discovering who we truly are, and how we can relate to ourselves and others with greater compassion and understanding. My own work with the Inner Alignment Method has provided the key that has allowed me to cultivate a deep inner awareness and relationship with myself, which continues to grow and thrive every day!!!

Amy Komie, Thousand Oaks, CA

Beautifully written, with simple directions for implementing this model for self-healing. Ron's wonderful book outlines in such a clear and easy manner how one can develop the skills they need to address their own personal issues without always needing a therapist to talk to. This model helps people see very clearly why they are experiencing and feeling whatever it is that they are experiencing and feeling. There is very little I have read that can help a person do this. In my opinion, Ron's book is breaking new ground and pioneering a whole new way for us to work with our thoughts and emotions without feeling "wrong" for having them.

James Hopson, Los Angeles, CA

You are not a drop in the ocean—
You are the entire ocean in a drop.

—Rumi

—To the Infinite Child Within Us All—

CONTENTS

Part IV: LIVING *Your Ultimate Relationship*

Inner Alignment and the Realm of the Children

INTRODUCTION:

YOUR PATH STARTS HERE...

What if you had a roadmap to navigate all of life's obstacles and challenges—a clear pathway with simple directions to take you straight to the life you want? *Why YOU Are Your Ultimate Relationship* lays out that roadmap for a journey to the most empowering place you could ever reach: that of a profound relationship with yourself.

It may seem an odd concept to have a relationship with yourself; a relationship takes two people, not just one, right? But such a perspective denies that you and I are always talking to ourselves, carrying on an inner conversation, at times beyond our awareness. *Why YOU Are Your Ultimate Relationship* shows you how to chart this new territory—your own inner landscape—and gives you access to healing at the source of your being, for a new future and an extraordinary life.

In more than 30 years of practicing psychotherapy, I've found that people often seek help because of challenges they are having in their relationships with others. Whether their issues involve a romantic partner, boss, children, friends, or coworkers, everyone wants to have satisfying and fulfilling relationships with the people in their lives.

I repeatedly hear from clients that their obstacle to having gratifying relationships is *someone* or *something* that needs to be fixed. Even when the issue is their own health or finances, either some other person or circumstance is the cause of their problem, or they blame themselves for that problem. Regardless, everyone wants me to help them change their situation, the other person, or themselves, so they can finally put an end to their emotional pain.

But I don't guide my clients and the people who attend my workshops to fix or change anything. Instead, I teach them how to connect with themselves and become the source of their own answers. Equipped with the practices and tools I give them, they begin a journey to bring forth their truest, most authentic self. As their facilitator, I guide them in discovering and experiencing who they already are—people fully capable of living extraordinary lives. In the process, I am always profoundly moved when I witness my clients' and students' transformations as they discover their own ultimate relationship—the one each of us can have with ourselves that in turn creates a more meaningful connection with everyone else.

You too can discover and develop *your ultimate relationship* with the Inner Alignment Method, using a set of tools and practices I call Inner Alignment Training. I also refer to it as *Inner Alignment Method Training (I AM Training)*. You will learn how the relationship you once had with yourself has become fundamentally misaligned, and how to bring that relationship into a state of healthy alignment. I AM Training makes *you* the source of power in your life, and with practice, you'll step into that power. You'll never again have to blame another, feel like a victim, or be dependent on others as the source of your happiness.

Developing and living your ultimate relationship is the goal of I AM Training. As you develop your inner alignment, you resolve the issues that have held you back by healing the wounds that lie underneath. You establish a strong foundation of integrity within yourself and find that all of your relationships become more satisfying and fulfilling as a result. You have a direct and ongoing experience of your closest friend, trusted teacher, and guide—*YOU*.

Who is this extraordinary you? It is you in your most liberated and unconditioned expression—what I call your *Infinite Child*. This boundless, loving presence is your essence, and the source of all your power in life. But that Infinite Child has been locked away and silenced, waiting for someone to arrive with the key that will open the door. In I AM Training, you learn how to develop what I call your *True Adult*, who will open that door and welcome your Infinite Child into the world. You as a True Adult become the bridge for your Infinite Child to find full expression, so you can begin living your life as *who you truly are*.

So, who are you truly? You'll discover the answer as you learn how to live as a True Adult, in alignment and profound relationship with your Infinite Child.

Throughout this book, you will be given practical guidance and tools for developing your ultimate relationship. In the process, you will transform your history of struggles and hardships into a deeply meaningful connection to who you are and to your life's purpose. You will also have the opportunity to sit in on therapy sessions with my clients and see how they use I AM Training to create lives that make their hearts sing. Through their experiences, you will discover your own connection to the Infinite Child within you and begin to experience a strong, solid relationship with yourself. I will also share my own experience of discovery as I became a student of my greatest teacher, the Infinite Child within me, to develop this method. This is the same source of profound connection to all that is, which you will discover within yourself.

Congratulations! You are about to unlock the door, open it, and invite the magnificent, whole, and empowered being that you are—and have always been—into your life.

Inner Alignment Method Training is the key.

▲

Here's what to expect as you set out on your life-altering journey to create a new relationship with yourself and, in that process, with everyone around you.

In *Part I: Discovering Your Ultimate Relationship*, I cover the basic ground of the Inner Alignment Method and show you how I developed it in my personal and professional life. You will learn how the relationship you originally had with yourself as a child was thrown out of alignment due to your circumstances, leaving you powerless and driven by a need to protect yourself at any cost. You will also learn a listening skill that enables you to realign with and welcome your Child into an enduring relationship with you as a True Adult for fulfillment in every area of your life.

In *Part II: Developing Your Ultimate Relationship*, I introduce you to the cornerstone practice for developing a strong and solid inner relationship: the *Child–Adult Conversation*. I also provide you with a foundational tool, the *Inner Alignment Chart*, designed to increase self-awareness and strengthen your inner relationship. Both the Conversation and the Chart will be demonstrated by my clients when you sit in on their sessions. You will also get a chance to use these tools in areas of your own life where unresolved issues have prevented you from finding complete fulfillment.

In *Part III: Deepening Your Ultimate Relationship*, I go into greater depth to show you how Inner Alignment Training is used to resolve important life issues. You will join more of my clients in session as they grapple with problems in committed relationships, at work, and in raising young children. You'll be able to participate in the process my clients undergo, learning in a way that is both experiential and practical. At the end of each chapter, activities are provided to help you attain results in each of these areas of your own life.

In *Part IV: Living Your Ultimate Relationship*, I expand the scope of your ultimate relationship, showing you what it looks like to go from surviving to thriving—and even evolving—in your everyday life. As you deepen your relationship with your Child of the Infinite, the internal noise of negativity, fear, and judgment of yourself and others is cleared out of your system. Your Infinite Child then guides you toward ongoing enlightenment and an extraordinary experience of being alive. ("Child of the Infinite" is the self-reference given to me by my own Child of the Infinite, and while I use the terms "Child of the Infinite" and "Infinite Child" interchangeably throughout the book, I most frequently use the less cumbersome term, "Infinite Child.")

In the Epilogue, I explore how living in alignment with our own Child—which connects us with the Children in everyone else—is the ultimate solution for current challenges in our communities, our nation, and our world.

Are you ready to start living your life on a scale of intimacy, power, and fulfillment that you never thought possible? If so, you've picked up the right book.

As you step onto the path and begin the journey, I welcome you to yourself—the person you will get to know and love as you discover and live *Your Ultimate Relationship*.

Part I

DISCOVERING *YOUR ULTIMATE RELATIONSHIP*:

Inner Alignment Method

(I AM)

CHAPTER 1

A RELATIONSHIP WITH YOURSELF

"**I** feel so angry, so frustrated… so *powerless!*"

My client, Melanie, is expressing her feelings about her relationship with her partner, Eric.

"Every time we try to work out our disagreements, things get worse; we never seem to get anything resolved." Pain and hopelessness fill her voice. "Last night, I got angry about something Eric said and tried to talk with him about it. After six years together, you'd think we could clear things up by talking."

Melanie pauses and looks down for a moment before continuing. "But it just got worse. So I gave up and went to bed; he slept on the couch. But I couldn't sleep. I lay there awake, being tossed around by my feelings for most of the night. In the morning we tried to talk again, but we both got defensive and I ended up confused and frustrated… I just don't know who to blame—him or myself!"

Melanie takes a deep breath and sighs audibly. Looking at me, she says, "No wonder couples give up and decide to split up… or stay together and go numb. I don't know how long we can go on like this."

She begins to sob softly.

The Relationship Trap

What Melanie is describing is the reason so many people come into therapy—the frustration and despair they feel as they face painful conflicts in important relationships in their lives. So often, I hear this lament: *When we try to work out our conflicts, either nothing changes or things get worse.* It doesn't matter if my clients are struggling with a romantic, business, or family relationship. Sooner or later, they find themselves ensnared in painful conflicts from which they can't escape—a situation I call the *relationship trap.*

Attempts to work on relationships always fail when the goal is to change the other person. Fingers get pointed, and a rigid "me vs. him-or-her" attitude results. Both partners become further entrenched in their positions—*I'm right, and you're wrong!*—the all-too-familiar blame game.

Maybe you've experienced a similar dynamic in your own relationship or in a relationship you had in the past. The painful pattern of blaming and trying to change the other is enacted relentlessly—even if you've read all the books, attended all the seminars, and had years of therapy. Regardless, you still struggle. So often, it seems the more effort you make to change things, the more tightly shut the trap becomes. After a while, you find a way to ignore your feelings, pretending that everything is okay. Eventually, you become resigned and settle for a life of disappointment—a victim of what you felt helpless to prevent.

The relationship trap can happen with your romantic partner, coworkers, business colleagues, friends, and even your children. Eventually, all human relationships are subject to the trap of blaming and attempting to fix, which never gets better, only worse.

But there is a way out of the trap... only the way out is actually "in." By shifting your focus off the other person and putting that focus—not blame—on yourself, you can begin to develop an empowering relationship with yourself: *your ultimate relationship.*

It all begins with you.

4

Your Ultimate Relationship

Your ultimate relationship, the one you're about to develop with yourself, will be the most gratifying and far-reaching relationship you can have in life. Why? Because having this relationship with yourself will lead to more gratifying relationships with everyone else in your life.

Yes, *everyone!* Your spouse or significant other, your boss, your parents and family members, your children . . . and everyone with whom you come into contact. When you have a strong and solid relationship with yourself, you can resolve issues with others. You can escape from the trap of endless conflict that has kept you resigned to never finding the happiness you want and deserve.

You will also realize a number of other benefits as you develop a relationship with yourself:

▷ You will discover new inner resources that strengthen you from the inside out. You'll find that you can seek assistance from others, including therapists, life coaches, and spiritual teachers, but you will retain your own authority while benefitting from their guidance.

▷ You will heal and evolve, learning from life's circumstances, breakdowns and "mistakes," and will open yourself to your highest potential.

▷ You'll experience a new kind of independence that allows you to connect with others without requiring something from them to make you happy. Instead, you will be complete within yourself.

Sound magical? It is. But before learning more about the benefits of having a relationship with yourself, you may want to know how such a relationship is even possible. For many of us, the inner world is unexplored and uncharted territory—a land of mystery that stirs up uneasiness, discomfort, or fear. But your inner relationship is nothing to fear, as you are about to experience. The bridge to your personal source of wisdom and power is already in place. It's simply waiting for you to cross, moving into alignment and an extraordinary life.

You will find that growing and developing your inner relationship is similar to cultivating a relationship with any other person in your life. In all relationships, getting to know the other person takes time. You may each feel awkward at the beginning, but as you spend time together, you become more comfortable and grow closer. It's the same when that other person is *you*, and you want to become closer to yourself.

But beyond just spending time and getting comfortable, cultivating a close and flourishing relationship with anyone takes some work. Falling in love does not ensure that your love will be sustained over time. Just as you need support to sustain a love relationship with another person, you also need support to build and sustain your relationship with yourself. Training in the *Inner Alignment Method* provides that support.

Inner Alignment Method

The Inner Alignment Method is an original approach to life mastery based on a new understanding of human experience. It enables you to discover your ultimate relationship and develop it into a solid and dependable part of your life. You learn to open an inner channel through which honest and wise communication flows. You also practice establishing strong inner boundaries and a structure to continuously upgrade your life—all vital elements for achieving your ultimate relationship.

In I AM Training, you begin by taking the spotlight off everything out there and turning that spotlight inward. Instead of trying to change other people and circumstances (the outer world), you make a 180-degree turn inward, focusing your efforts for change on what is going on within yourself.

To say "the answer lies within" is almost clichéd—you've heard it so many times. But the Inner Alignment Method gives you a clear map of your inner landscape, leading you directly to the source of your answers. You begin by gaining access to relevant information about your past that you had long forgotten. You

6

discover that all of your reactions to life's challenges stem from wounding experiences in your childhood and the set of beliefs you acquired as a result of those experiences. Here are some examples of those often unconscious beliefs:

> ▷ *I don't matter.*
>
> ▷ *No one really cares about me.*
>
> ▷ *I don't get/deserve to be seen, heard, or respected—in short, connected with.*

Those or similar beliefs, along with the coping methods you established long ago to make life work in the face of such beliefs, are all still living within you. They are unconscious programs that, without any choice on the part of the real you, have been automatically creating your life. Such programs always block intimacy, which is the key to your happiness. However, intimacy can make you feel vulnerable. If the other person in your interaction or relationship appears disinterested, or worse, expresses a negative reaction to you, you can be unconsciously reminded of those early experiences of rejection and the feelings of having no value or interest to others—again, that you don't deserve to be seen, heard, or connected with.

As you learn how to free yourself from your unconscious, programmed beliefs, you'll find that you naturally and safely allow yourself the gift of intimacy with others. However, we must first begin with what got in your way.

It all started when you were a child, expressing your authentic experience to your parents or other caregivers. Whenever they responded with negativity or even disinterest, you felt rejected by them, assuming they must know the truth about you. You experienced that truth as: *being you* is undesirable. When this happened enough times—or even one time—a protective part of you stepped in and suppressed or hid those vulnerable parts of yourself. You did this so that you would be less likely to put yourself in a position of potential rejection in the future. In so doing, you lost touch with who you truly were. Instead you began to live a programmed reality in which it was dangerous to share yourself with others. Intimacy (in-to-me-see) was, and still *feels*, dangerous.

What happened next was that over time, inadvertently, you continued to experience recreations of that wounding experience with other people. For example, as others sensed that you were holding parts of yourself back, *their* wounds led them to interpret your caution to mean that you didn't trust *them*. They felt pushed away and undesired by *you*, so they became more cautious and less vulnerable with you. You, in turn, felt them holding back, which triggered in you a sense of being mistrusted or kept at a distance. This then fueled your original feelings of being undesirable, resulting in your feeling unsafe in relationships. And thus, the negative cycle has continued.

With Inner Alignment Training, you will learn to separate from all your early programming and observe your survival strategies that, whether you realize it or not, you have put in place to help you cope.

You will discover that those coping strategies evolved from feeling powerless as a child, based on the reality that your parents, other caregivers, teachers, and religious authorities—the "Big People"—had all the power. They could affect both your happiness and your pain based on whether you met their expectations or not.

Now, even as an adult, you may still be living by your experiences as a child. You think that in some way others still have the power over whether you feel happiness or pain. When you believe that others are somehow responsible for your experience, you give away your ability to create your own happiness. Consequently, you experience an undercurrent of dissatisfaction that undermines any possibility of a truly happy life.

I AM Training gives you the power to heal your childhood wounds and clear out those unconscious programs so you'll no longer find yourself running endlessly in circles, recreating your painful past. As this new relationship you are developing grows, so does your inner strength, your natural integrity, and the beautiful experience of being more freely yourself. In addition, you will start to experience the peace, joy, and fulfillment you had never thought possible, and it will feel entirely natural.

In order for you to grasp what this new understanding is all about, I'm going to introduce you to the model and the structures that make up the basis of the Inner Alignment Method.

The Inner Alignment Relationship Model

The Inner Alignment Method is based on a model of inner relationship that consists of two structures: the *Child* and the *True Adult*. When these two structures begin to align with each other, you will start living in a state of integrity that ushers in a new, profound experience of yourself. This is your ultimate relationship: able to resolve all your issues, to upgrade all of your relationships.

Let's look more closely at the Inner Alignment Relationship model. The Child is comprised of three aspects: Infinite Child, Hurt Child, and Coping Child. You first experience yourself as an Infinite Child—the you who arrived at birth, pure and timeless. This aspect of your Child exists in an energetic reality within which everything is connected. Your Child of the Infinite is the part of you that guides you in a process of ongoing enlightenment that continuously evolves you. It is through your Infinite Child that you become the embodiment of the spiritual notions that God is everywhere and that the universe works in strange ways to assist your ongoing awakening. What some call "magic" and "miracles" become everyday experiences that emerge from your growing relationship with your Child of the Infinite.

During childhood, the inevitable trauma and wounding of life left you feeling hurt and alone, without any ability to make things right. You were still an Infinite Child, but at times your experience was interrupted by those painful events that shifted you from your infinite state into a hurt state.

In reaction to such trauma and powerlessness and in the absence of a reliable Big Person, the Coping Child is created to protect the Hurt Child. A Child trying to be an adult, the Coping Child—also referred to as the *Little Adult*—is required to manage life in the best way he or she can. As you grow into adulthood, your Coping Child, or Little Adult, increasingly takes charge of your life. Over time, your Little Adult is the aspect of your Child you come to think of more and more as "me."

But as a Little Adult, you are hardly a mature adult. Rather, you are a child striving unsuccessfully to be an adult—hence, a little adult. (When I use the term *Child*, I may be referring to the Infinite Child, Hurt Child, the Coping Child/ Little Adult, or all three.)

The second structure in the model—the *True Adult*—is you as the powerful recipient of your Child's thoughts, feelings, and intuitions. As a True Adult, you act as an empty vessel, receptive and aligned with your Child in all of his or her separate aspects—Infinite, Hurt, and Coping. From the empowered perspective of a True Adult, you free your Little Adult from running your life and welcome back your Infinite Child—the source of your wisdom. As a True Adult, you create a new relationship with your Child that he or she will always be able to count on. From then on, as a True Adult, you will always have a direct connection with your Infinite Child—a trusted guide pointing you in the right direction, an inner guru (gee-you-are-you) connecting you with your deepest truth.

You will soon discover how these two basic structures, *Child* and *True Adult*, come into alignment to enhance your life in every area. As you progress in your training, these terms will naturally become more and more familiar to you.

Emerging as a True Adult

Right now, any struggles you are having stem from not yet having had the opportunity to develop your True Adult in those particular areas of your life. This has created a fundamental misalignment within you. But once that misalignment is addressed with Inner Alignment Training, you as a True Adult and the separate aspects of your Child will begin to align. This alignment forges a new relationship in which you are no longer run by your Little Adult's focus on coping.

In the coming chapters, you will learn how to create alignment as you heal your Hurt Child, free your Coping Child, and emerge as a True Adult. You'll discover how to relate to yourself in a way that enhances your learning and growth. Rather than a rigid adjustment, the process is like a gentle massage, moving those structures into alignment.

Your inner alignment carries over into all of your relationships. As a True Adult aligned with your Child, you will develop the ability to recognize the Child in others and will thus be able to communicate with everyone more easily, clearly, and compassionately. As the bond deepens between your Infinite Child and your True Adult, you will discover an experience of your oneness with humanity—your fundamental connection to all that exists. I use the term *Realm of the Children* to refer collectively to the Child in every person. The Children form an energetic network of wisdom and guidance, always moving in the direction of greater unity and harmony for all.

Through I AM Training, you become a True Adult by welcoming your Infinite Child into your life for the relationship you've been waiting for—your ultimate relationship. As your Little Adult gratefully surrenders all impossible efforts to run your life, the noise inside your head quiets, leaving you calm, centered, and receptive. You as a True Adult then enjoy an ongoing flow of communication with your Child of the Infinite. From this sacred connection, a deep confidence and inner peace will emerge, creating harmony within—and thus, harmony without.

▲

What's Next...

In I AM Training, you connect to your childhood experience with an awareness that leads to a deeply personal and profound relationship within yourself, with others, and with all of life. In chapter 2, you will learn how I discovered the Inner Alignment Method and developed it as a unique therapeutic—even spiritual—training for life mastery.

CHAPTER 2

MY ULTIMATE RELATIONSHIP

The Inner Alignment Method—its model, practices, and tools—came directly out of my personal life experience. From as far back in childhood as I can remember, my Infinite Child's presence was constant, guiding me internally with wisdom and clarity, especially in times of stress or challenge. I never thought of that presence as separate from me, but rather embraced what I now call my Child as my own inspirations, feelings, and thoughts.

Later in life, as a practicing psychotherapist, I often listened to my wiser inner voice when working with clients. Then, while in session one day, I was guided to lead my client to the same direct relationship with her Child that I'd always had with mine. This was the birth of the Inner Alignment Method and Training.

The Discovery

I'd been practicing psychotherapy for a number of years when my client Samantha arrived for her weekly session. I could see she was in a highly conflicted emotional state. Early in the session, she began to describe a severe trauma from childhood involving parental punishment. But hers was no ordinary punishment. Samantha's mother, clearly suffering from severe, unhealed wounds of her own, had repeatedly pushed and held Samantha's head under the sudsy bathwater. She threatened to drown the small child as a consequence for what she'd perceived as unacceptable behavior.

Minutes into recounting this incident, Samantha began to tremble and gasp, "No, Mommy! Stop! Please stop!" Her distress grew as she slipped further into reliving the trauma, and soon she was shaking and crying uncontrollably.

I remained calm, but found myself interrupting her frequently to ask questions about what she was experiencing. I was perplexed by my response. As a therapist, I'd been trained to encourage people to connect with and express their feelings, not to interrupt them in the midst of those feelings. Such deep emotion, I'd been taught, was a sign that a client was opening up and that the therapy was working. Yet my instinct—my Infinite Child—was telling me something very different, which was to interrupt Samantha to separate her from the feelings she was experiencing.

I trusted my inner direction and continued interrupting her, but I still questioned myself, wondering whether perhaps I was personally uncomfortable with her suffering and trying to make myself feel better by stopping her.

Again, I checked inside for guidance and received a clear message coming to me in the voice of my Child: *This is not about your feelings. She is actually reliving her early trauma, and her feelings are as real for her now as they were back then. You need to help her to shift out of her experience, not allow her to be retraumatized.*

I responded to my Child, saying inwardly, *But she knows she's in my office having a therapy session with me, not back in that bathroom with her mother.*

My Child came back: *No, she doesn't know that. The horrible experience is happening again for her right now, just as if she'd traveled back in time and is still that small child with her head being held in the soapy water.* My Child was insistent and continued guiding me with more specific direction. *Don't stop her from feeling her feelings, just tell her to move into a different seat.*

Again I responded inwardly, to my Child, this time emphatically: *I don't fully understand what you're telling me to do. I have to figure it out first.*

My Child replied: *I know exactly what I'm doing. Just listen to what I tell you and I will guide you every step of the way.*

At that point, I no longer questioned what I needed to do. Gently and calmly, I said, "Samantha, I'd like you to move over into this other chair, and then we'll continue."

Samantha emerged, as if in a fog, out of her nightmare, just enough to move over to the chair I'd indicated. There she sat, staring back at the now empty seat she'd just left.

Guided by my Child, I spoke. "In that chair over there—where you were just sitting—that is *you* as a little girl," I said, gesturing toward the empty chair. "In this chair now, you are an adult—no longer a child. That little girl over there was just speaking about a horrific event in *her* past."

By emphasizing that she, as an adult, was separate from the little girl who'd just relived the memory, I was able to help Samantha get some distance from her torturous past that had come to the surface to be healed. For a brief moment, she was able to separate from the abusive experience with her mother and enter a state I later came to call *healthy separateness*. The physical movement to another chair had helped her to gain distance from the memory she'd been reliving, and she was no longer submerged in it.

I continued speaking. "Sitting here as an adult, you know that what happened back then with your mother is not actually happening now. But for the child who experienced it, it was happening all over again."

Samantha nodded, still somewhat dazed.

I continued, "Right now, I'd like you, as an adult, to look over at the chair where that little girl sits, scared and shaking, because she just relived that terrifying event. When you are ready, tell her that you know how horrific and traumatic it must have been for her."

With my prompting, Samantha spoke those words to the terrified child she imagined sitting in the chair across from her. As she addressed the child in

15

the other seat, she was able to separate herself from her childhood experience even further, no longer trapped in reliving the trauma. She had broken out of the prison of a memory that had tormented her throughout her life, and she was free to discover a new perspective on what had happened so long ago.

When Samantha appeared to have stabilized in her new objectivity, I had her move back into the first seat, again guided by my Child. I watched as she immediately went deeper into the horror, reliving again the traumatic event. I waited until I received my Child's guidance, directing me to have Samantha move again to the other chair. I then supported her in continuing to separate from her traumatic experience and telling the little girl in the other seat that she could imagine how horrible it must have been for her.

After switching seats back and forth several times, Samantha gradually reached a calmer state and was able to share with me, objectively, about her experience. "This is weird, but fascinating," she murmured softly, as if to herself. "I understand… why I've been so afraid of everyone my whole life." Now, in a stronger voice, she continued, "I feel… somehow… lighter and freer." Our session was complete.

Samantha was now aware of the past in a new way, no longer trapped in reliving it over and over again as a helpless child in an adult's body. She was able to see that her current self-judgments, guilt, and self-abuse were Little Adult methods of coping with the terrible pain she'd suffered in childhood.

When Samantha was able, as a developing True Adult, to achieve enough separateness from her Child's trauma to connect with and receive her Child's expression, something new and profound occurred within her. Her Child now has a reference for a safe Big Person, one who can stand beside her in this excruciating memory. She is no longer alone.

Moreover, Samantha now has a reference for being a separate True Adult for her Child whenever painful memories surface. With each session, her True Adult's presence fills her, replacing the need for her Child to go into Little Adult reactive coping mode. Now, the safe and loving Big Person who had been missing from her childhood will always be with her. Samantha's world has changed forever.

After what Samantha and I went through together, I knew my way of doing therapy would never be the same again. With deep gratitude and respect, I acknowledged that I now had a brilliant advisor available to sit in on all of my sessions—my own Infinite Child. Through my inner guidance, I discovered an extremely effective way to show my clients how to connect with their own Child for a new kind of inner relationship that would empower them to heal and to lead extraordinary lives.

Childhood—An Energetic Connection

As a young child, I recognized that my inner voice, my Infinite Child, was energetically connected to everyone else. Later, this energetic link existed for me as a vast reference from which I received wisdom and guidance—the Realm of the Children. I knew myself to be part of a larger whole, where all the Children dwell, yet at the same time, I knew that I, like everyone, was unique in my individual expression.

But as a child, I was also painfully aware that most of the Big People around me—parents, other close adults, teachers—acted as though they were *cut off* from others and even from themselves. Their disconnection baffled and disturbed me. I wanted people to experience more harmony and connection, which I knew to be their underlying truth.

My Hurt Child

My early experience of the inevitable disconnection we all undergo in childhood was deeply wounding for me, as it is for us all. Every time I felt the truth of the connection we all share being denied by the Big People I depended on, I felt crushed. I experienced their denial of our essential connection as an almost unbearably painful loss—the result of which I later came to call the *Hurt Child.*

My first conscious memory of such disconnection—and the deep wounding that resulted—occurred when I was 4 years old. One day in the backyard of our home, my father and I were standing before my grandfather's favorite lemon tree, sharing a close moment of intimacy and love. My grandfather loved lemons, and whenever he visited, he would trim the lemon tree, a special family ritual. What happened next may seem minor, but for me as a child, life changed in that moment.

Feeling such a close bond with my dad, my small arm wrapped around his leg, I suddenly felt a sharp jolt of energy. The jolt shook my whole body with a frightening sense that my father was leaving me. I looked up and saw him gazing into the distance. I remember tugging on his pants, shaking him, and crying out, "Daddy, don't go! Don't go! Stay with me, stay!" My desperate cries didn't stop my feeling that he was in some way leaving me, in a way that would forever change our connection. Although he hadn't moved physically, within moments he was gone, and I felt he could no longer hear or feel me.

I continued crying out for him until he responded abruptly. "What? I'm here!"

But it was too late. I had lost him and was no longer feeling the loving connection we'd shared just moments before. I knew something had changed between us. I felt deeply sad and painfully alone.

What had happened? Early wounding always involves a painful experience of disconnection from the Big People we depended on and felt especially close to. I believe that my father, standing with me before the same tree his dad always tended, had re-experienced in those moments the trauma of his disconnection from his own father. He in turn disconnected from me, his own young son, because of the painful feelings about father–son connection that were being stirred up for him. It was as though he had gotten zapped by his programmed belief that a father

18

and son cannot have a direct, deep, meaningful connection with one another. Consequently, he was no longer able to feel our connection or to hear me crying out for him. In front of the lemon tree, our relationship had changed.

The following story illustrates how our Infinite Child is energetically connected to everyone else, and responds naturally to the suffering of the people around us.

Gift of the Infinite Child

As a young child, I felt keenly in touch—as are most, if not all, children—with the emotions of the Big People. However, I was perhaps more consciously aware than others that the Big People's reactions weren't personal. They were always about them, not about me.

I felt my kindergarten teacher, a single woman in her late 50s, was unhappy. As the winter break approached, I sensed her growing anxiety. In my mind, I saw her going home to a dark and empty house, fearing she might not survive the holidays.

One night, I announced to my parents, "We have to get Miss Hogan a diamond ring and a diamond bracelet." I didn't know why the jewelry was needed, but I knew it was somehow the right thing for my teacher to have before she left for the break. I was so insistent that my parents agreed to take me to the store to see what we could find. But as diamonds were not in the family budget, they only let me buy a rhinestone ring.

On the last day before the winter break, I gave the gift to Miss Hogan.

"Oh . . . you didn't have to get me a present," she said as she began to open the small package.

"You don't have to open it now," I said, thinking it might be better if she were in her home, alone, when she opened it.

She continued, "I *want* to open it now." When she saw the sparkly ring, her anxious face changed dramatically. I could feel her melt inside as she put the ring on her finger. *I may be able to make it through after all,* she seemed to be saying to herself. I felt her wanting to cry, as she looked at me and put her hand to her heart. She shook her head and looked down at the ring.

"I wanted to get you a real diamond," I said apologetically, "but my daddy said it was too much money, so you don't have to wear it."

She smiled, her eyes tearing up. "Oh, don't you worry, honey, I'll be wearing it."

On the first day back from vacation, I was surprised to see the ring on her finger—after all, it wasn't real, and I didn't want her to feel obligated to wear it. I went up to her desk and said, "You're wearing the ring…?"

"You bet I am," she responded, positively glowing as she held out her hand to show me. I could feel the comfort that the ring—and the love of a little boy—had brought her through the lonely weeks of the winter break.

There were many other incidents that demonstrate how my Infinite Child informed my young life, as is true for all children before their fundamental inner alignment is lost. The following story is about another one of those incidents.

A True Adult in the Sandbox

Because I listened so naturally to my Child of the Infinite, I would often have a perspective that included the big picture of whatever was happening in any given situation. Later, when I created the model for the Inner Alignment Method, I identified this perspective as the *True Adult.*

I was beginning to experience myself as being part of a larger team, and so, when any conflict arose, I wanted to make things work for everyone. The following story of playing with my classmates in a sandbox on the school yard illustrates how that perspective impacted me and those around me.

Our teacher had become upset with us because too much sand was spilling over the side of the box and onto the ground. She gave a stern warning about keeping the sand in the box, but once we were playing, no one remembered and nothing changed. After she issued several threats to take away our sandbox privilege if we didn't stop, I decided something needed to happen or we'd lose our favorite activity. I didn't want to be the only one cleaning up, so I came up with a plan that would include everyone. I formed a clean-up committee to return any sand that spilled outside to the box, hoping the other kids would follow our lead and be more careful.

At home, I asked my dad for help with my plan. Together, we went through the garage and considered different tools that could motivate the clean-up committee and make the task fun. We decided I would bring a special "magic brush" to school that only the committee kids would be allowed to use to clean the sand off their clothes after they had scooped up the overflow and gotten it back into the sandbox.

Back at school, the magic brush worked nicely for a few days, until the novelty wore off. After a while, my classmates, not surprisingly, wanted to play rather than clean up. However, by that time, we all had become more careful, and the overflow problem was no longer an issue. Soon we were all enjoying our sandbox play without any further threats from our teacher.

All young children are able to feel when there is a "disturbance in the force," as I did in this sandbox adventure. By listening to my Child's inner voice, connecting me to all the Children, I was able to play a part in creating unity and alignment in my environment—an example of how a True Adult responds to any conflict or disturbance. Even as young children, we all have the capacity, although rarely expressed, to take on the perspective of a True Adult.

Adolescence:

A Bridge Between Worlds

We all have wounds that stem from the inevitable, painful experiences we have had with the significant Big People in our lives. In my own history, each time I tried to connect with my parents more deeply, I felt powerless to create the connection that I wanted with them and that I knew, deep down, they wanted with me. As difficult as it might be for some people to believe, all parents, on a soul level, want to share a flow of love and positivity with their children. Having been wounded themselves, however, they are largely limited to re-enacting what they experienced with their own significant Big People.

As I grew older, my Little Adult continued to try to protect my Hurt Child from further pain by doing what all Little Adults do: my Little Adult pushed my Hurt Child's pain down. In this way, he could maintain a workable existence and avoid any chance of being swallowed up by my Child's feelings of sadness over the loss of a meaningful connection with the Big People.

At the age of 9, I began training in the martial arts, rapidly excelling. Later, in high school, recognized as a martial artist, I was approached by a school bully to teach him karate. At first I refused, but relented when he promised me, with tears in his eyes, that he'd stop being a bully if I worked with him. I took him on as a student, and soon, others noticed the dramatic changes in him and wanted me to teach them karate as well. In order to accommodate them, I turned my parents' garage into a studio, putting up a large mirror, weapons rack, and a bag for kicking and punching practice. Within a short period, I had acquired over 20 students, and was holding individual and small group lessons.

Teaching karate, first to my classmates and then to students from the community, helped me deepen my connection to my source, my Infinite Child, who has guided me so unmistakably my whole life. My teaching became a vehicle for me to further my own personal growth and awareness. Further, I found I was able to "hear" the Child in each of my students as they communicated with my Child, showing me what they needed in both their training and in their lives. My Child saw what was stopping them from discovering their full capacity, both inside and outside of the studio. He then gave me clear guidance for how to encourage the expression of the truth in each one of my students.

Dark Night of the Soul:
A True Adult Speaks

When I was 16, I experienced what I might describe as a dark night of the soul. Late one night, I was sitting alone in my bedroom staring at the wall on which I'd posted photos of my students. I began feeling a gnawing sensation of disappointment and futility over the reality that there was so much more I wanted to bring to my students about what was possible for them in their lives. But something was missing. Words began to emerge, powerfully, from deep within me: *It's not working! It's just not good enough! What am I going to do? I just don't know…*

I turned out all the lights and sat on my bedroom floor in the dark, feeling hopeless, frustrated and confused. Within moments, I was sobbing. I wanted my students to discover their true power and deeper connection with themselves, something I knew, from my own experience, was also possible for them. I knew that additionally, there is a deeper connection that is available between each of us, and with all of humanity. But I didn't know exactly what that meant or how to bring it to them.

The words continued to form as I cried out despairingly, "It's just not working fast enough…. They're not getting it…. I need them to understand more, to get it more deeply."

"It makes sense that you're so upset and crying," I responded to myself, objectively, as if speaking to someone else. I began to feel somehow calmer and more confident as I recognized the truth in the words that came to me. "It's so important to you that your students experience themselves and each other as who they truly are and what they are capable of. You know there is so much more available for them, and you feel that what you're doing just isn't enough."

A sense of relief washed over me, as if a locked door had just been opened and I could see the light inside. However, once again, my anguish was spoken out

loud through the pained voice of my Hurt Child. "I don't know what's missing....
How can I get them to get it... to discover who they truly are?"

The calm, objective voice came back, once again validating the feelings that
had been expressed. "How painful and confusing it must be for you, when you
know there's something missing and you want your students to discover who
they truly are."

The conversation continued between my Hurt Child and the "someone"
who was hearing my anguish and then responding to me, *through* me. I was having a live, *verbal* conversation, not just in my head, but out loud. My dark night
of the soul had faded and my Child felt a ray of hope.

Looking back on that night, I realized that the calm, validating voice
responding to my Hurt Child had been my own, coming through me as a True
Adult. I came to know that this True Adult aspect of myself is guided by my Infinite Child, who always knows what my Hurt Child needs to hear.

The conversation between my Child and me as a developing True Adult
lasted only about 20 minutes, yet it seemed timeless. Gradually, I experienced a
lifting of the burden I'd been carrying, and in its place was a feeling of peace and
awe. "Thank you for hearing me and talking to me about this," my Hurt Child
said out loud to me as a True Adult. I could feel in my being that a profound
change had taken place. While I had no idea why this change had come about, I
sensed that my questions would be answered. I could relax and trust that somehow, because of this conversation, whatever needed to happen with my students
would happen naturally.

That night in my room, I experienced my first *Child–Adult Conversation*, a
phenomenon that would become the cornerstone practice of the method I later
developed as the Inner Alignment Method. As I'd sensed, it wasn't long before I
was guided in specific ways to more effectively interact with my students.

An incident occurred within a week after my dark night of the soul, as I
was talking with one of my students about his problems at home and at school.

Suddenly, I felt a shift within myself, as if the clouds obscuring my view had parted, allowing me to see what my student, Andy, needed to hear in order to find his own solutions. It occurred to me years later that what I had been for him in that instance was a True Adult, connecting him to his own deeper wisdom, just as I as a True Adult had done for my own Child days before.

As a teacher, I had reached a new level in my ability to listen, in each moment, to my Child's guidance. While I had always engaged my students in exploring their inner worlds as a metaphor for their lives outside the dojo—what happens in their lives shows them what's happening inside of them, and what's happening inside of them shows up in their lives—we all accelerated in our growth through our interactions with one another.

Soon students began to come in asking specifically for "talk lessons" during which they would have a more focused opportunity to address the challenges going on in their lives. Through authentic conversation, I found myself assisting them to free themselves from the negative self-judgments that had slowed their progress both in karate and in their lives. My students began to value themselves, feeling freer from the judgments that had kept them from knowing and living their truth.

Transition:
Karate to Therapy

Looking back, I see that I had been teaching my students to develop themselves as True Adults and to strengthen each of their connections with their Child. As a result of our talk lessons, they found themselves quite naturally relating more effectively and harmoniously with their parents, siblings, and everyone with whom they interacted. Not surprisingly, all my students were seeing improvements in their relationships with others, their grades, and their overall confidence, reflecting how much better they were feeling about themselves.

At one point, I had over 25 students training with me in my garage studio, all referred by word of mouth. In addition to individual and small group lessons, which always included a talking component, I held weekly "fight nights," events at which many of my students would come together for sparring matches.

I continued to teach valuable life lessons as part of my students' training. Increasingly, our fight nights became opportunities for group sharing and explorations of life. I taught everyone about the importance of having respect for themselves and each other, and that it didn't matter who won or lost a match, because we were all furthering our skills while assisting one another in our growth and development as authentic people and natural leaders.

With each fight night—large group lesson—my students became more open and vulnerable, exposing their deepest and innermost feelings. I was teaching them how to be in charge of their lives: to support and share themselves with one another while being true to themselves. They continued to recognize how just being and discovering who they are, through their sharing, provided great value for everyone. As their training progressed, their lives improved rapidly, as did mine.

More and more, my martial arts classes were becoming psychologically therapeutic. One day, a student's mother asked to sit in on her son's lesson. With his consent, she was welcomed. When the lesson was over, she pulled me aside and remarked, "You are doing in-depth psychotherapy with my son."

Nervously, I asked, "Is that okay?"

She replied, "I've been in therapy for many years, and I'd say you are better than most of the professionals out there."

She told me of her friend, a therapist who traveled the world training other therapists. She arranged for the three of us to meet the next time her friend was in town. Over lunch, Louise, the therapist trainer, grilled me intensely about what I'd done with her friend's son. Even though I was concerned about being in trouble in some way, I could only answer her questions honestly and directly. When lunch was over and all her questions were answered, she peered deeply into my eyes, paused, and with great gravity pronounced, "You are a healer of souls."

At first I was shocked, but quickly realized that this woman was pointing to what I'd been doing with my students all along. It was a relief to experience being validated by someone with such professional stature, rather than to find myself in hot water for doing therapy with my students.

The clarity and insight I gained by working with my students, their parents, and others led me to pursue a career as a psychotherapist. While working on my graduate degree in counseling psychology, I began seeing my first clients as a trainee in 1984. Later, I became a Licensed Marriage and Family Therapist (LMFT). Since then, I've been practicing and developing what I discovered so long ago as a teenage martial arts instructor—the Inner Alignment Method.

I often say about my job as a therapist, "I just work here!" To me, the "job" I'm doing is listening to my Infinite Child, who is connected to the Infinite Child in each person I meet. So in that sense, I'm basically just being true to myself. This means listening to my Child and everyone else's Child as they guide us all to the highest quality of life that we are available to experience.

▲

What's Next...

In the next chapter, I will introduce you to the Infinite Child who lives within you so you can begin to develop a relationship with the most amazing guide and most enlightened master you are ever likely to encounter. You will also discover how you became disconnected from your Child, who has been trying to reconnect with you ever since. By becoming aware of *your ultimate relationship*—the one you have with yourself that connects you with all of humanity—you can start living your life by the guidance of your Child of the Infinite.

CHAPTER 3

CHILD AND LITTLE ADULT: A FUNDAMENTAL MISALIGNMENT

I AM Training invites you to get to know yourself in a new way. You begin to see yourself not just as a single identity, the person you think of as "me," but rather in terms of the components that make up your identity. These components are the two structures of the Inner Alignment Relationship Model: *Child* and *True Adult*. These two structures give you the necessary clarity to empower yourself and transform your life. In any area of struggle, your Little Adult, rather than you as a True Adult, has been the only presence available for your Hurt Child. For a child to be responsible for another child is a terrible burden; this dynamic can never truly work because it is a fundamental misalignment of one's inner structures.

Avoiding struggles in your life requires inner alignment: the presence of a True Adult who can step in on behalf of your Hurt Child. But until now, only a Little Adult has been available. With Inner Alignment Training, you acquire the ability to shift this fundamental misalignment that has been causing your problems, and learn what it means to step into your life as a True Adult. Only then can you connect with your Infinite Child and effectively create a powerful, joyous reality.

In this chapter, we will take a closer look at your Child, as both *Infinite Child* and *Hurt Child*. You will also learn how your *Coping Child*, or *Little Adult* gradually stifled the other two aspects of your Child and took over the responsibility of running your life. Along the way, as your Hurt Child's feelings were suppressed, you also lost touch with your Infinite Child's presence in your life. Inner Alignment Training addresses the misalignment that has left your Child out of the picture. It enables you to establish a new relationship with yourself and claim your true identity and power to make your life your own.

But first, I invite you to meet your Child.

Meet Your Child

You began life as an *Infinite Child*, the *you* who arrived on the planet as a pure expression of the Source. You experienced, moment by moment, all that was occurring in utero as well as what was happening outside of your mother's body. Like a radio receives information through waves, you received everything going on around you through energy, absent concepts or constructs of reality. Like a sponge, you soaked in all the information in every moment. You made no attempt to judge, interpret, or make sense of anything; you just purely received and experienced life—as a Child of the Infinite.

That infinite aspect of you remains eternal, regardless of your chronological age, yet it has been largely invisible and unnoticed. Since most people experience themselves as their Little Adult, they don't get to experience their

Infinite Child their vast source of energetic guidance available to them in each moment—very often. They may get a glimpse of their Infinite Child through intuition, inspirations, spiritual experiences, or dreams. They might also experience their Infinite Child through the arts, such as a piece of music or a story, poem, or movie that evokes deep emotion and makes them feel connected to other people.

While infinite, energetic information cannot possibly be held all at once in your conscious mind, you do have this source of unlimited capacity within you. Your Child of the Infinite is this energetic phenomenon. With I AM Training, your Child of the Infinite is able to communicate with you directly through both verbal and energetic interaction.

Because the Child connects experientially, getting to know your Child is a process of receptivity and discovery, not of questioning or analysis. Think of the Infinite Child as your higher self, your soul, the still, quiet voice within, your inner guidance, or your bridge to the cosmic consciousness or the field of infinite possibility. You might also associate your Infinite Child with expansion, timelessness, a source of oneness with all of life, divine wisdom, and joy. Another way to think of your Child of the Infinite is as the source of the answers that lie within.

Sound like God? Well, that's not far from the truth, but the Infinite Child is not limited to organized religion. While using the term *God*, I am speaking to those among us who subscribe to any and all religions, as well as to those who consider themselves agnostic or atheist. In fact, my religiously affiliated clients often tell me that the more they experience their Child, the more deeply they understand and experience their own beliefs, and all my clients find themselves experiencing spirituality on a level they never expected. Inner Alignment Training invites you into a deeper, more direct experience of your relationship with Source—the energy that unites us all.

The Infinite Child is also a state of being that links us all in meaningful and magical ways. As you come to know your Child more deeply, you will have personal and concrete experiences of your oneness with everyone else. It is through your connection with your own Infinite Child—and thus with all the Children—that you are able to upgrade your significant relationships.

So, where did your Infinite Child go? The answer is—*nowhere.* Your Infinite Child never left. He or she is still here, living inside you, waiting to be welcomed into your life. But you are no longer consciously aware of your Child's presence, and you no longer experience that Child with the same immediacy you once did.

Think of that lost Child as the version of *you* who has been buried beneath automatic ways of coping with challenges and traumas, which you acquired while growing up. Your Infinite Child has become a remnant of the past, abandoned and forgotten, leaving you disconnected from this truest aspect of who you are, and living instead as your Little Adult.

Because you have become so disconnected from your Infinite Child—your source—you lack the power to truly resolve your relationship problems and create even more valuable life experiences. Even if you do seem to resolve those issues or create positive experiences, deep down, you still do not feel satisfied or fulfilled.

The point of I AM Training is to help you discover your Child, first by experiencing him or her as separate from the coping strategies of your Little Adult. Once separate, you will be able to connect with your Child and receive support from your most powerful self—the part that can heal your heart, create miracles, and manifest the reality you *choose* to live in.

Creating a bond with your Child calls for developing your True Adult in alignment with your Child. That alignment will bring your Infinite Child back into your life for a blissful, joyful reunion. Once the bond between your Child and True Adult is established, your Infinite Child becomes like a dear, long lost friend, someone you knew at one time who is deeply familiar to you, someone whom perhaps you have even sensed just below your consciousness. I AM Training provides a pathway for your Child to come through and be revealed to you. The Child is a mystery that unfolds, a light coming out of the darkness to meet you as you learn how to open the space to receive that light.

Core Wounds:

Legacy of Disconnection

None of us escapes the inevitable wounding of life. At some point in your childhood, your Infinite Child lost a level of connection to the Big People, resulting in what I refer to as a *core wound*.

A core wound is the painful emotion you feel when you experience a disconnection from those all-powerful people who are supposed to love and protect you. The part of you who experiences this pain of rejection and the feeling of helplessness is your Hurt Child. Today, anytime you find yourself reacting to someone or some circumstance or feeling a negative emotion, the experience is reminding you of a time in childhood when you felt cut off—*invalidated*—by a Big Person.

The pain of core wounds varies in severity, but all core wounds, if they are not healed, remain with you. Held by your Hurt Child, they impact every aspect of your life. Remember, the Child in you is timeless, and so your experience is not restricted to the linear time frame in which the traumatic events may have occurred. An example of core wounding was given in the story of my client Samantha, whose mother traumatized her by severely punishing her as a child. As an adult, Samantha still suffered from her early childhood trauma, which had formed a deep and lasting core wound that left her feeling vulnerable and unsafe in the world. Like all of us, Samantha had experienced her core wound as a constant, unchangeable undercurrent to her life.

However, you don't have to have been severely abused or mistreated, like Samantha, in order to have a core wound from childhood that impacts your life today. The painful experience of any disconnection was enough to create a fissure within yourself. Because parents, teachers, religious figures, or other authorities were not capable of fully understanding you and meeting your needs during your childhood, they could never properly welcome you to the planet as the Infinite Child you were. That lack of understanding often occurred as disapproval and displeasure, responses that happened over and over again, widening the fissure and deepening your core wound.

There were times in your childhood when the Big People were able to welcome and understand your Hurt Child's pain. At those times, your feelings were received and validated, and the pain or upset you felt was fully resolved. You were restored to yourself, safe again and free to feel the union with your infinite self.

However, each time a Big Person didn't meet your need to be validated, your painful upset turned into negative thoughts and feelings about yourself. The message conveyed to you through the displeasure and disapproval of the Big People was that you should become someone *other* than who you were in order to please them. This requirement felt threatening, because you depended on the Big People for all of your needs, and you needed to feel a positive connection with them. You learned to fear their disapproval, as though your very existence was at stake.

Over time, all of your attempts to make things right with the Big People only reinforced your belief that being yourself did not work. If being yourself didn't work, then who you were, you concluded, must be unacceptable. Children do not distinguish their *behavior* from *themselves*. Consequently, when the Big People react negatively, even when their reaction isn't personal, a child still believes *I am not what they want, so who I am is not okay.*

Such beliefs underlie the primary core wound for all human beings, which is *I am unacceptable as I truly am.* Following this belief is a secondary belief, which is *I can never be good enough to please the Big People.* Later in life, that belief becomes *Who I am will never be good enough, no matter what I do.* While this is never the truth, we all live with the effects of these core wounds as beliefs, leading to trust and intimacy issues, and low self-esteem.

As dire as this all sounds, your early wounding wasn't the fault of the Big People. You may be blaming the Big People, especially your parents, but the reality is that, having forgotten their own Child within, they were unaware of just how much you needed to feel connected to them. They only knew how to teach you in the ways their parents had taught them, which was to impose their limited view on you. They saw their role as needing to control you and keep you in line in order to "shape" you to fit into life and its demands. Their expectation was for you to do as you were told, but what you needed was to feel the truth of your connection with them before you could fulfill their wishes.

Emotional wounding is an inevitable part of the human experience, and it is necessary for true evolution and growth. As you heal your wounds, the experiences that caused them turn out to be great gifts, laying out a path to self-discovery and life purpose. It is the uncovering of those very personal core wounds and the healing process you undergo in addressing them that leads you to who you are and why you are here.

I AM Training makes the healing of all wounds, including early core wounds, possible. When you are aligned with your Child of the Infinite, the source of all the answers to your conflicts in life, you can receive valuable guidance and information about your wounds. Your Infinite Child is more knowledgeable about you than any expert, including therapists, life coaches, and healers. With I AM Training, you have access to every experience, thought, feeling, and interpretation your Child has ever had—the full footage of your life's movie made visible by the higher intelligence of your Infinite Child. Now you can heal your Hurt Child, who is still carrying the weight of your past, and, in the process, free the full expression of your Infinite Child.

But first, let's meet your Little Adult.

Meet Your Little Adult

Out of your Hurt Child's core wounds, a new persona evolved to protect you and ensure that you would fit, *somehow*, into the Big People's world. An extension of your Hurt Child, your Coping Child, or Little Adult arose to cope and strategize for your Child's survival. You became a Little Adult in the face of the Big People's inability to grasp your true nature as an Infinite Child.

Furthermore, in your Little Adult's efforts to survive, you lost contact with your Infinite Child. Given the trauma your Child experienced when basic emotional needs for safety and understanding were not met, your Little Adult felt your Child was best kept out of harm by being kept out of sight. Your Little Adult then replaced your Child, becoming adept at coping with problems and managing life, or so it appeared.

As a Hurt Child forced to cope, your Little Adult likely did what most Little Adults do, which is to blame others—or even themselves—for their suffering, always trying to fix one or the other.

Little Adults believe that they can only struggle against others or be victims of others' struggles against them. There are no other choices—they are perpetually trapped in me-versus-them ways of relating, hopelessly entangled in either playing the blame game or feeling like a victim of life.

Here's another way to think of it. Little Adults are children running from their pain because they don't have what they need in order to *heal*. Therefore, because they either direct their focus outside of themselves or become lost in their inner turmoil, they cannot truly succeed at making things right for their Child. In I AM Training, the Big Person who wasn't there is replaced by a True Adult—*you*—who now has the capacity to address your Hurt Child's pain.

I emphasize that your Little Adult is not actually an adult. The word *little* refers to a child attempting to do a Big Person's job—like a stand-in who lacks the required abilities and skills of a True Adult. A strong sense of survival compels the Little Adult to put together an identity that feels safe and workable. Again, a Little Adult is really a Hurt Child, functioning in the best way he or she can.

Of course, regardless of how good things may appear on the surface, Little Adults often feel, deep down, like powerless failures—there's always an undercurrent feeling that pulls and nags, forming an inner, unconscious monologue: *Something's wrong… with me… with other people… with life.*

The following story illustrates how a Little Adult is born when the Infinite Child is traumatized by the inevitable disconnection that occurs in childhood. We see how the Hurt Child attempts to manage the pain by shifting into coping mode, becoming a Little Adult.

Birth of a Little Adult

Like all children, little Nicole loves to explore, finding the world to be an exciting, intriguing place. Even though she is still crawling, she seizes any opportunity for an adventure, especially when Mommy and Daddy aren't watching her closely.

During one such opportunity, Nicole makes her way into the living room and spies something that captures her attention. Bright colors are shifting around the room, emanating from an object sitting on a low table a short distance from her. She crawls as fast as she can to get to the mysterious object and then pulls herself up on the couch beside it. Breaking into a big grin, her little fingers touch the object. She moves her fingers down the sides and inside its grooves, feeling its smoothness with delight. As the sun hits the object through the window, a rainbow of color reflects off the walls around her.

Excited, she grasps the object and brings it to her mouth to explore it more fully. Suddenly and without warning, it slips through her hands, hitting the floor with a loud crash. Shocked and frightened, she bursts into tears. Her magical object has vanished into countless little pieces all over the floor. Surely the Big

People will soon come to comfort her. She hears footsteps. *Oh good, help is on the way!* She's already feeling some relief as they enter the room.

But instead of the soothing voices she expects, a shrill sound pierces the air, jolting and disorienting the young child.

"Oh no! My Waterford crystal vase!" her mother yells. "No, no, no! We told you not to touch Mommy and Daddy's things!"

Now even more traumatized by such harsh tones, little Nicole is bewildered that somehow she has caused the Big People to become angry.

Don't they see I'm scared, and I need them to comfort me? I wasn't trying to hurt anything—why are they so mad at me when I'm just being me? Little Nicole is devastated.

This young child has just had her first experience of being made wrong and shamed—her reality rejected. In the face of this frightening and deeply disturbing circumstance, she suppresses her natural, spontaneous expression. If she is unacceptable to the Big People—the gods—then it can't be safe to be herself anymore. This is an example of core wounding. She then needs protection from any further wounding by her parents, and since there's no other adult to turn to, she turns to her own version of an adult, her Little Adult.

Three days later, little Nicole makes her way, once again unnoticed, into the living room. On the same low table, she spies something new and again very attractive. Naturally living in the moment, she is filled with excitement. She can't crawl fast enough to get to this new object, forgetting her previous experience. Only now, a Little Adult is on board, ready to launch into protective mode in order to keep her safe.

The words of her Little Adult sound similar to the Big People's harsh disapproval when they discovered her earlier "mistake." *No! Do not touch Mommy and Daddy's things! Remember what happened last time? Mommy and Daddy yelled, and it was so scary!* Nicole's Little Adult remembers what happened the last time when she picked up an object in the room and will now attempt to protect her from having to go through feeling shamed and rejected again.

But Nicole cannot deny her natural impulse to interact with this new, exciting object. Like a magnet, the object draws her in from across the room. There she goes again, as fast as she can crawl, locked onto her target.

Her Little Adult protests: *Why don't you listen?* She then feels required to be stronger: *You are a bad girl! Don't touch Mommy's things!* Her logic is: *Better I judge you before the Big People do. It will be less painful for you to be judged by me than by them.* (This is the beginning of self-judgment, a tendency to judge ourselves before others do, sometimes even by saying out loud: *What an idiot I am—what was I thinking?*) But Nicole's Little Adult's warnings dissolve into background noise, not yet strong enough to stifle and control the young child's natural enthusiasm.

Mesmerized, and still not heeding the warning, Nicole wraps her tiny fist around the object. It is smooth and solid, and, of course, she immediately brings it to her mouth for a richer experience. But now, remembering what happened before, she grips the newfound treasure tightly as she lowers herself down to the floor. She is determined, no matter what, to hold on to it. But, alas, gravity prevails and she falls down. The impact causes her parents' fragile wooden statue to snap, splintering into several pieces and leaving only the leg of the figure in her hand.

Just then, Nicole's Little Adult pops up. *I told you not to touch that! Now look at what you've done! You should have listened! You're in trouble now!* But it's too late. Nicole is now frightened and confused. She doesn't understand why things are going so wrong when she only wants to have fun and to celebrate life. Somehow it's all her fault. By the time the Big People come into the room, she begins to cry, hoping they will see how much she needs them. Sad eyes convey her now internalized sense of shame: *I know, I know, I shouldn't have touched it! I've already heard it from my own Little Adult!*

But feeling frustrated with their daughter, Nicole's parents can only see another violation of their wishes. They launch into another angry tirade, hoping to correct their disobedient child. "How many times do we have to tell you not to touch our things?" With a slap to her hand, Mommy scolds, "You're a bad girl! Do not touch Mommy and Daddy's things!"

Our curious young child is again traumatized and deeply hurt. Her loving bond with the most important people in her world has been violated. She has discovered that being herself—the spontaneous expression of her Infinite Child—not only gets her yelled at by angry, distorted faces peering down at her, but also brings her physical pain. She concludes, once again, that being herself is not what the Big People want, and she will be rejected and unloved if she continues to freely follow her inspirations.

The next time temptation occurs, Nicole will have learned her lesson: It's better to listen to the voice of her Little Adult who knows better than she how to cope with the Big People. At least then, she'll be able to give the Big People what they want—a "good girl." Then and only then will the threat they pose to her existence be eliminated once and for all, or so she thinks. Over time, her parents' good-girl requirements prevail, and Nicole's Infinite Child is overtaken by the protective, suppressive coping strategies of a Little Adult.

▲

The story of Nicole and the vase demonstrates how development of the Little Adult begins with our earliest experiences, including those that occurred when we were still preverbal. In Nicole's case, her Little Adult took on the role of the good girl focused on pleasing her parents. But not all children go along with the good-girl or good-boy method of survival that Nicole did. Some give up trying to please the Big People when they find it doesn't work anyway, and instead take on a rebellious role. They then act out as the "bad child" that the Big People seem to expect them to be.

Until the Big People have references for positive, loving methods of conscious parenting, it's nearly impossible to avoid recreating one's painful childhood experiences in the next generation. The kinds of negative responses that lead to the development of such coping strategies—good/bad child—range from mild negativity to severe abuse. But children suffer from what feels like rejection from the Big People, even when the negativity is mild. The point is that any form of criticizing, judging, or shaming—in short, making a child wrong—is traumatizing to that child. Yelling, scolding, threatening, punishing, ignoring—all common Big People responses—are violating. Such responses inject negativity and judgment into the wide-open heart and mind of a child, causing core wounding. Such treatment conveys to children that they, rather than their behavior, are wrong or defective.

You may recall some of your own experiences of receiving a negative response from the Big People when you were a young child. Perhaps when you were expressing yourself exuberantly, their words felt crushing to you: "Stop screaming at the dinner table! What's the matter with you? You should be ashamed of yourself!"

You might recall feeling shocked, disoriented, and thrown into a state of disbelief and confusion. You wondered, *What are they talking about? Are they really talking to me? Why are they so angry?* Harsh expressions such as *You're a bad boy!* or *You're a spoiled little brat!* seemed to come out of nowhere, contradicting your own experience of reality and threatening your sense of who you were.

The following is another seemingly innocuous example of a Big Person's disconnection from the child, making the point that a child can receive a harsh message from an important Big Person in his or her life, even when the Big Person's actual act is not abusive.

Imagine a young child, clutching a drawing and approaching his mother with excitement. The mother says, "Shush! I'm on the phone! Just wait a minute." The child tries to wait patiently, watching his mom do dishes while juggling the phone. Finally, when it seems as though his mother has forgotten about him, he whispers, "Mommy… Mommy…" Then, a little louder, "Mommy… Mom…" He gently tugs on her apron, "Mom…"

"Not now!" snaps the mother, before apologizing into the phone, "I'm sorry, my son's not being respectful while his mother's on the phone."

Hanging his head, the young boy turns and slowly walks away, crumpling his drawing of his mommy and himself holding hands, surrounded by hearts.

In light of such events, whether minor or more severe, I have modified the term *Post Traumatic Stress Disorder* (PTSD) to reflect the so-often-minimized impact that childhood trauma from the Big People's responses can have. My own term, *Post Traumatic Childhood Moment* (PTCM), refers to the trauma of the past—times when we didn't feel seen, heard, or connected with by a True Adult—being re-experienced in current life. No one gets through childhood without enduring at least one or two significant traumatic events, and most of us have a list of them. This underscores that, whether we're conscious of it or not, we are all contending with PTCM eruptions every day.

Our current lives are indelibly shaped by those painful moments we experienced in childhood. The results of such moments have had a lasting impact on our nervous systems. Rather than revert to a state of calm after a PTCM, many of us experience a constant undercurrent of low-level anxiety. You might feel as though your nervous system remains on a low boil. When a current moment looks, feels, sounds, or in any way seems related to a childhood event, we experience a PTCM, and the low-boil undercurrent erupts into a nervous system spike. We then find ourselves in Little Adult coping mode, having a fight, flight, or freeze reaction.

Little Adult Takes Over

Over time, as you encountered more and more of such hurtful and confusing messages from the Big People, your Little Adult became an increasingly encompassing presence in your life. Any negativity expressed toward your Child or in your Child's environment was immediate grounds for your Little Adult to jump in for a rescue attempt. As a result, the innate spontaneity you knew as a child was further suppressed. In place of free self-expression, your Little Adult took over in a vigilant endeavor to ensure the "right" thing was done to avoid further trauma.

Your Little Adult worked overtime to shield and then hide who you really are—an Infinite Child—out of fear of being misunderstood and powerless to make others understand you. This happened first at home, then at school, and later in the workplace and in every other aspect of your life. Parts of you had to be stifled or tucked away for your safety. Painfully, as a result of your Little Adult's vigilance on your Child's behalf, those stifled parts of you were cut off from your consciousness.

As time went by, more acceptable ways of behaving further replaced your Child's natural expression, leaving you even more lost to yourself. As you grew and interacted with coworkers, bosses, friends, and others, they all appeared to your Little Adult like the people who raised you—the original Big People. Whatever the circumstance, anything perceived as criticism or judgment would have led to a PTCM, causing the present to look and feel like *what already happened.* In those moments, you were *triggered*, or activated, into Little Adult protective mode, reacting automatically to something that wasn't even real.

Sadly, all your Little Adult's attempts to protect your Child have had no real power to be successful. No matter how seemingly successful those attempts might have been on the outside, your Child's feelings have remained unaddressed. You may have even disconnected from them altogether.

In spite of your Little Adult's inability to truly protect your Child, however, he or she was indeed successful in getting you to this point in your life. It was your Little Adult who persisted in moving you through all your difficult moments of disconnection and wounding. Even while feeling inadequate, without the wherewithal of a True Adult, your Little Adult didn't give up.

When confronted with obstacles, your Little Adult tried even harder to meet the demands of the moment, whether by engaging in an attempt to make things right or by retreating and even isolating from others. In any case, the reality that your Little Adult found a way through all the daily challenges of life took courage that is, frankly, heroic. Such courage deserves to be acknowledged. Still, none of a Little Adult's efforts will ever work, because in addition to pushing aside the Child's feelings, all these efforts are those of a child trying to do an adult's job.

Today, the same Little Adult coping methods that have kept your Child safe for so many years are keeping you trapped in your life. You may have noticed all along, deep inside, an unidentifiable feeling that *something is very wrong here.* You may have felt a desire to walk away from your current life and start anew, to be whoever you want to be rather than who you were programmed to be. Such inner turmoil is your Child's way of communicating to you that the way you've been living is not fully the truth of who you are.

As you develop inner alignment, you learn that you are not the Little Adult you have come to identify yourself as, but rather a developing True Adult, welcoming your Infinite Child who has been waiting to be expressed in your life. By using the tools for I AM Training, you learn to separate yourself from that created persona or false front—the "you" who never fully felt like *you,* but who took over your life. You learn to distinguish the behaviors and coping strategies that belong to your Little Adult, and no longer confuse them with yourself. You then have an opening to begin engaging as the previously absent True Adult and to become ever more present in your Child's life.

Spotlight on Little Adult Triggers

It's not always easy to recognize when your Little Adult is triggered, taking you in the wrong direction and derailing you from the life you want to be living. The following summary will assist you in identifying some of the more obvious signs of Little Adult activation in yourself and in others.

SIGNS OF LITTLE ADULT ACTIVATION

Anxiety or Insecurity: These reactions arise when a Child's needs are not addressed by the comforting presence of a True Adult. Lacking that presence, a Little Adult takes over, anxious and fearful that things won't work out in a positive way.

Compulsions: These are reactive feelings of anxiety which manifest as *musts* rather than choices to say or do something in an attempt to quell anxiety in the absence of a True Adult. The expression of these feelings is what we call compulsive behavior.

For example, one might feel compelled—often unconsciously—to talk, move, or eat in an unnaturally quick manner. Or perhaps one feels an intense impulse—an anxious need—to make a case for his or her point of view when in conflict with someone. Rather than moved by the flow of guidance from one's Child of the Infinite, one who is expressing a compulsion doesn't move in harmony with others, or do what's in his or her best interest—he or she is out of relationship within, and with others.

Compulsions can also manifest as addictive behaviors—gambling, shopping, alcohol and drug abuse, engaging in non-intimate sex, excessively watching TV; even reading books can become a compulsion. It's all about the motivation behind the behavior rather than the behavior itself.

Aggressive Communication: This includes reacting to others by speaking rapidly, loudly, or excessively, as well as talking over or interrupting them. These communication styles are demonstrated when a Little Adult avoids the anxiety or other uncomfortable feelings of a PTCM, and tries to control the conversation to prevent feeling thrown off balance.

Judgment or Criticism: A Little Adult feels the need to create a sense of superiority out of fear of not being good enough. This includes comparing oneself—as better or worse—to others.

Tunnel Vision: A Little Adult insists that the only valid viewpoint is his or her own. A Little Adult tries to avoid being exposed as wrong or incompetent or as not knowing what he or she is talking about. Little Adults hold fast to their point of view because being open to another person's point of view feels too risky to their tenuous sense of self. This is an attempt to remain in control and appear confident when they are not.

Defensiveness: A Little Adult lives in a "me-against-them" world, feeling potentially cornered, or backed up against the wall. Little Adults experiencing a PTCM believe they are being attacked, dominated, made wrong, judged or criticized, and may perhaps feel powerless to stand up for themselves. Such a perceived threat triggers a Little Adult into protective mode.

Your developing awareness of these Little Adult reactions is a crucial part of your I AM Training, increasing your objective clarity when your Little Adult is about to take charge of your life. Once you are able to identify the signs of Little Adult activation in yourself, especially at the moment when it's happening, you are on your way to becoming a True Adult and creating the inner alignment that will have you living the truth of who you are.

LITTLE ADULT REACTIONS AT A GLANCE

You know your Little Adult is triggered when you are:

▷   Reacting automatically to people or situations

▷   Rigid and closed off; resistant to change

▷   Aggressive or defensive

▷   Biased or opinionated

▷   Invalidating of others

▷   Judgmental or critical of others or self

▷ Controlling, dominating, or needing to be right

▷ Blaming or shaming of self or others

▷ Anxious and nervous about outcomes

▷ Feeling self-pity and victimization

▷ Fearful

Your Turn:

Expression and Observation: Child's Journal and True Adult Log

Throughout your training, I will be offering you opportunities to personalize your experience. I recommend you do all the activities that are provided for you. However, if you skip one or more of these activities, please know that what is most important is that you continue reading. You can always go back to do the activities which are listed in the Appendix for easy reference.

As part of learning how to develop a relationship with your Child, you will need to acquire two empowering notebooks: the *Child's Journal* and the *True Adult Log*. Writing in these notebooks has numerous benefits, as you will discover throughout your training. For example, it gives you an opportunity to express yourself safely and without judgment and it provides your Little Adult a space to relax. It will also help you develop your ability to remain calm and centered in the face of other people's reactivity.

You will be invited to write in your empowerment notebooks regularly, as directed in specific activities provided at the end of each chapter. You can also write in them whenever you are spontaneously moved to do so.

Selecting your empowerment notebooks is an opportunity to get to know your Child and begin forming a bond while also developing your True Adult.

47

► **Take your Child shopping.** Go to a store that sells a large selection of notebooks.

▷ *Choose your Child's Journal first.* As you survey the display of notebooks, pick one that you are drawn to on a feeling level, not one that appeals to your practical or intellectual side. For example, if your Child picks a *cartoon character* or an action hero notebook, don't resist that impulse. Go with it. Often my clients tell me how surprised they are when their Child is drawn to a "childish" notebook or one that was not an expected choice, and how they were initially tempted to reject it. One client, a big, burly martial artist, brought in his Child's Journal to show me: "Are you ready, Ron?" Then he smiled as he pulled out his Spiderman notebook, covered in superhero stickers. The point is not to squash your Child's spontaneous desire.

▷ *After your Child has chosen his or her journal, select a True Adult Log.* Pick the one that you, your Child's observer, are most drawn to. Let your choice inspire the True Adult you are on your way to becoming.

► **Label your notebooks.** On the cover of your Child's Journal, write *My Journal* or *(Your Name's) Journal*, using the name your Child would like to be called. On the cover of your True Adult Log, write *True Adult Log*. This labeling adds to the power of your experience of both the Journal and the Log by creating a personal connection to each of them.

► **Write in your notebooks.** Now that you have acquired your notebooks, you can begin to use them in the following ways:

▷ In your *Child's Journal*, write as your Child, expressing whatever he or she wants to express. This may mean venting raw feelings (Hurt Child) and reactive thoughts, including judgments (Little

Adult/Child in coping mode), as they surface, without restraint or judgment. Your Infinite Child may also be expressed in your Child's Journal as inspirations, clear guidance, or creative and artistic ideas.

▷ In your *True Adult Log*, record any observations you have of your Hurt Child's feelings and Little Adult's reactions in your daily life. That will help you become more objective and less reactive and will speed up the development of your relationship with your Child. You can also record any insights you will gain when you do the activities in future chapters. You may even find that your Child of the Infinite brings you breakthrough information that inspires you; write that in your Log as well. Writing in your True Adult Log builds your True Adult skill as an observer.

▷ You can also write in your notebooks if your Child brings up memories or if you have a Little Adult reaction in response to something you read at any point during your I AM training. Use your True Adult Log to record anything you notice about your Child's expression, including insights that are noteworthy to you. Watch for any concern or fear that you won't benefit from this training or any of the specific activities. For example, "Nothing ever really works for me." Or, "It's just going to be a waste of my time." Little Adults routinely try to predict how life will happen, attempting to protect the Child from disappointment or self-judgment. Anytime you have a negative assumption or belief, a wound program is running you. If that happens, it's valuable to write it in your True Adult Log.

Here are some writing activities you can do in your notebooks to further support the expression of your Child and the development of your True Adult:

Activity #1. Child's Journal:

Getting a Glimpse of Your Child

The following activity involves writing with both your dominant and your nondominant hands. It was inspired by the art therapist and author Lucia Capacchione, who used nondominant handwriting as a method for inner dialoguing. Your nondominant hand will be used by your Child, while your dominant hand will express your response as a True Adult. Here are the steps to initiate connection with your Child. You will need a pen and a pencil or two different colored pens.

1. Write an invitation to your Child. First, imagine you are talking to a young (physical) child who is hurt and alone, and is perhaps hiding under the bed, in the closet, or behind a chair. How would you speak to him or her? You'd probably speak softly and with patience, understanding that it might take a moment for the child to feel safe enough to come out. It is the same when writing to your Child.

Begin by writing the name you were called as a child or a nickname you like. You may use your own inviting words or the following to get you started: *Hello, (your name). I'm here now. I'm wondering if there's anything you want to share with me.*

2. Respond to the invitation as your Child. Using your nondominant hand, take a different writing instrument and place it on the page, starting a new paragraph. Be receptive to any internal communication that you might see, hear, or feel. Then, with your nondominant hand, write the words that come to you until your hand stops and you feel complete. If nothing happens, that, too, is okay. Let go of any expectations or judgments about the outcome. However the communication comes through, embrace the experience. You are discovering your Child.

3. Respond to your Child's communication. Use the same writing instrument you began with and write a response to your Child. You can acknowledge, in your own words, what a big step it was for your Child to courageously and vulnerably connect and share with you. Even writing the words *Thank you* can be valuable. You might be tempted to ask your Child a question, but it's best not to, because asking a question imposes an expectation on your Child to answer and limits his or her spontaneous expression.

Helpful Tips for Connecting With Your Child

▶ **If nothing happens during your Child's turn**—you've been waiting for a few moments but the pencil is not moving—that too is a form of communication from your Child. It may simply be that writing, in that moment, is not comfortable for your Child. Maybe your Child is telling you that he or she is not ready to communicate with you and it's going to take more time to build the relationship. Any attempt to communicate with your Child, regardless of the response, will always be worthwhile, because it lets your Child know that you care and are interested. This in itself is a fundamental step forward in developing a healing relationship with your Child.

▶ **You may get a response from your *Hurt Child*,** who is angry and feels abandoned after years of not having had communication with you. Your invitation may have evoked buried feelings from painful events that occurred in the past. The expression of those feelings is actually a good sign. Such feelings must be acknowledged as part of the productive communication that leads to much-needed healing. Joy may also surface, as your Child lets in a connection with you that he or she has longed for.

▶ **Welcome any expression**—positive, negative, or silent—from your Child. Every relationship is personal and develops uniquely. For some, this exercise can be a profound opening to a new and spectacular world. Some might even feel taken into some of their

Child's dark past, where no True Adult was ever before available to be present. Whatever your experience, whether exhilarating, overwhelming, or in between, it is just that—an experience. The activities throughout the book will assist you to develop and strengthen the inner structures you need to maintain your solid and safe True Adult presence in the face of all of your Child's feelings.

Activity #2. True Adult Log:
Becoming an Objective Observer

This activity provides an opportunity to observe and record your negative reactions to people or circumstances. As you record your reactions, you begin to develop the ability to be separate from them. Such objectivity frees you from the dominating grip of Little Adult negativity, and it is a required step in developing as a True Adult.

Write as if you are an objective reporter, using the third person (he, she, or they) or your name to describe an upsetting incident and your reaction to it. Here is an example that my client Lucy wrote:

Today, John got mad at Lucy because she had run up some credit card debt without letting him know about it. I notice that Lucy gets angry and frustrated whenever John brings up her credit card debt. I also notice she gets defensive when John becomes annoyed or angry with her. She storms off, yelling at him that he isn't her father.

My clients are often surprised at how much better they feel after doing this activity. This can be your experience as you, too, upgrade your structures on your way to developing your inner relationship.

▲

What's Next...

Your Child is about to receive what up until now he or she has only hoped for—the chance to be fully accepted and validated by a loving, interested adult: *you* as a *True Adult*. In chapter 4, you will see how a True Adult emerges when you learn to listen in a new way that welcomes your Child and creates a solid foundation on which to build *your ultimate relationship*.

CHAPTER 4

TRUE ADULT:
THE SOLUTION

Unlike the Child, who is present in an individual from before birth, the other structure in the Inner Alignment Relationship Model, the True Adult, is a perspective that must be developed. None of us are born as True Adults, but we can learn to cultivate the qualities and develop the muscles that make it possible for a True Adult to emerge in our lives and relationships.

True Adult qualities include the objectivity to become aware of your Child and the receptivity to connect with your Child. It is by cultivating these skills of True Adult objectivity and receptivity that you create a new relationship that properly welcomes your Child of the Infinite into your life. This leads to the healing necessary for inner alignment, which in turn continues to advance your development as a True Adult. Then, the beauty of who you truly are is authentically expressed in the world, and you continually evolve into more and more of that beauty and truth. It is a magnificent, synergistic relationship, beyond brilliant in its cosmic design.

In the last chapter, you began your journey of inner alignment by doing some activities that helped you receive your Child's presence and begin to observe your Little Adult's triggered reactions. This was a crucial step in beginning to develop yourself as a True Adult. In this chapter, you will further explore the receptive aspect of being a True Adult for your Child. You will also learn a listening skill that makes inner alignment with your Child possible and empowers you as a True Adult in all your relationships.

Discover Your True Adult

A True Adult stands apart from a Little Adult, who is in truth still a child. Little Adults operate on automatic pilot, responding to people and circumstances based on the programs learned from past experiences. True Adults are not run by early programming; they are clear that all such protective programs are never the truth.

Unlike a Little Adult, who is cut off and alone, a True Adult is receptive to the Child in all its separate aspects: Infinite Child, Hurt Child, and Little Adult/ Coping Child, but is not burdened by the Coping Child's noisy thoughts and protective strategies. Separate and independent of your Little Adult's programming, you as a True Adult are free to see a bigger picture of reality.

As you train in Inner Alignment, your Little Adult's perspective is increasingly replaced by that of a True Adult. As a True Adult, you become an objective observer of all that goes on in the world of your Child. Rather than being entangled in your problems, you become a compassionate witness to those problems. Taking things less personally, you no longer need to defend yourself like an embattled soldier, dealing with enemies and obstacles at every turn. With I AM Training, conflicts are less common. When they do arise, you as a True Adult have the guidance and wisdom of your Infinite Child to resolve them.

Anyone can develop into a True Adult, but doing so may seem like a daunting task, especially when you are looking through the eyes of a Little Adult: *A nice idea, yes, but not something I'd ever try. . .I'd probably do it wrong and then be disappointed, judging myself as somehow not okay.* Or maybe it's more like, *I don't need this. I'm actually doing pretty well.* If you have thoughts at all like these, you're not alone. It's natural for such thoughts to occur.

At the same time, the True Adult perspective I'm describing is not something totally foreign to your life. Recall some instances when you were able to be objective and nonjudgmental, remaining nonreactive. However, having such a nonjudgmental perspective is not something you have been able to consistently depend on… yet.

How do you know when a True Adult, and not a Little Adult, is the one in charge? The Little Adult is reactive and automatic in thinking and behavior. As a True Adult, you are comfortable, present, and free from dramatic reactions to people or events. True Adults feel unburdened, even when dealing with difficult situations or some of the deepest wounding experiences their Hurt Child brings to them from the past.

Once you are able to give your Child the experience of being fully heard and deeply validated by an authentic adult—a True Adult—the wounds of your past are truly healed. Like weeds pulled up by their roots, those wounds are gone, never to surface again. As you develop yourself as a True Adult, you experience the truth that nothing your Child expresses is "personal." You no longer get caught up in the dramas of your Child's feelings. Such objectivity is comforting for your Child, who has longed to be received by a neutral, nonjudgmental Big Person.

It takes practice to become a True Adult, much as it does to build muscles at the gym, or to develop cooking skills. Without at least some solidity as a True Adult, you aren't able to receive your Child's expression, and a Little Adult takes over. But when you are strong and solid in your perspective as a True Adult, a Little Adult is no longer needed to protect your Child. Little Adult triggering experiences occur less and less frequently, eventually fading into the background. A Little Adult is no longer required in the presence of a powerful and loving True Adult.

A New Way to Listen

You can develop your True Adult muscles by practicing a skill I call *transformational listening*. This begins with reflective listening, which is the act of listening to and then repeating the words another person has spoken. But transformational listening is more than listening and repeating; it involves extending your receptivity and empathy to create not just understanding, but a deeper experience of the other person's world. This leads to a stronger connection that opens up a new, more powerful space for growth.

In transformational listening, you receive another person's experience on an emotional and energetic level. You *get* what they're experiencing in your own body without judgment or evaluation. This is true empathy. (I often use the word "get" to refer to this receptive process that includes both understanding and empathy.) Transformational listening allows the speaker to feel fully heard, and the listener to feel deeply connected to the speaker's world.

Practicing transformational listening deepens all of your relationships, creating more intimacy and trust, especially when there is a complaint or upset coming your way. This listening skill also deepens your relationship with yourself—your Child—especially when used in a Child–Adult Conversation, the cornerstone practice of I AM Training that you will learn about in the next chapter. For now, I'm going to focus on showing you how to use transformational listening with others, so you can get a clear picture of it and start using it in your personal relationships.

To see how transformational listening works with others, imagine a young child who returns home with a bag full of Halloween candy. Naturally, the child wants to tear through the bag, tasting as many of the enticing choices as possible. But when the Big People take the bag away after only a few pieces, the child cries out. *I want my candy! It's mine!*

Imagine that the Big People, instead of disregarding the child's cries for more, spoke these words: *Oh, honey, of course you want more candy. You've been excited all night, looking forward to trying everything!* Such a response, which is rare, validates the child's feelings without giving permission. Once children have been allowed to express themselves and feel truly understood and validated, they will be more able to hear the Big People's message that too much candy would probably result in a tummy ache.

Unfortunately, the response we usually get when sharing our pain is nothing like the model above. Friends, family members, and romantic partners, when responding to an issue you've shared with them, may all have the best intentions, but they can't resist trying to help fix your painful situation. They want to tell you how to avoid it the next time—just as their Little Adult would tell their own inner Child. They automatically offer their opinions and suggestions, including advice such as *Listen, if I was in your situation, this is what I would do…*

But when you're upset, you don't want advice—you just need someone to listen to your painful feelings without opinions, judgments, or attempts to fix anything. When another can't hear you, or denies your feelings, your Child screams inwardly, *Please, just hear me! I don't need your advice. Tell me it's okay to feel what I'm feeling. Don't tell me to "just get over it."* Advice or other input is often welcomed only after the Child feels heard and validated.

Young children grieving some loss—whether of the Halloween candy, the cancelled trip to the circus, the bike that wasn't delivered on time, or the puppy that was promised but never arrived, are often given the message that their feelings are a burden to the Big People in their lives. They might hear such invalidating responses as, "Knock it off; that's just how it is." "There's nothing we can do about it. Grow up." "I'll give you something to cry about." If every child's pure expression—including complaints and demands—received the empathy and validation of transformational listening, then we would all experience a quantum leap in the emotional health of our society.

True Adults use transformational listening to build relationships instead of inadvertently cutting them off. A True Adult never blames anyone for anything, knowing that whenever there is conflict, each individual in that conflict makes perfect sense, and that we are all just doing the best we can. If something is challenging, uncomfortable, or does not work out well, a True Adult accepts the situation as a lesson and seeks to learn from the experience. The result is a strengthening of the inner alignment between Child and True Adult, creating a sense of confidence, clarity, and compassion within oneself that naturally comes through to others.

Your Turn:

Listening Transformationally

Following are the basic steps for transformational listening that you can practice when someone in your life is upset and comes to you for support. Later, you'll learn how to use this new listening skill when receiving your own Child to develop and strengthen your inner alignment.

STEPS FOR TRANSFORMATIONAL LISTENING

Step 1: Listen and Reflect

Listen to the words said by the other person, and then reflect their words back to them by repeating what they said to the best of your recollection. By repeating another person's words, they know that you are listening to them and that they matter. In addition, you are making sure that you accurately heard what they said. You can ask if there is anything you missed, giving them the assurance that you sincerely care about what they are telling you. **Example:** Speaker: *I'm so angry at John, I never want to speak to him again.* Listener: *You're so angry at John; you never want to speak to him again.*

Tip: You may be concerned that repeating another's words takes too much time. What you discover is that you must slow down in order to speed up. Taking time now will save you time attempting to clear up misunderstandings later. Also, when the speaker feels seen and heard, your time together will tend to be more focused and productive. So, it's actually much faster—and feels so much better—to *slow down* in order to *speed up.*

Step 2: Inquire and Clarify

Ask a question if you aren't sure about the speaker's meaning. The speaker's words are one thing, but their meaning may be another.

Example: Listener: *Are you saying that you resent John for blaming you?* Or, *I'm hearing you say that you feel resentful toward John for blaming you. Is that what you're saying?* By responding in this way, you avoid making assumptions which might lead you down the wrong track, and leave the speaker feeling misunderstood.

Tip: You may be hesitant to suggest a possible meaning out of fear that you might be judged if you are wrong. Making assumptions rather than checking them out with the speaker will likely lead to misunderstandings. Inquiring also invites the speaker to gain more clarity about what they're sharing. This alone is deeply valuable. As people become clearer about what they mean, they will be more available to receive your interest, care, and input. The conversation then becomes a powerful relationship building and learning experience.

Step 3: Acknowledge and Validate — Sense-Making Commentary

When you get how the speaker makes sense (whether you agree or disagree with them), express it. This lets the speaker know you accept their feelings and reactions as legitimate, given their circumstance. I call this validating response *sense-making commentary.* Accuracy is not the issue — their being heard is. When you let the speaker know that they make sense, you validate them, because in their world, they do, indeed, make sense. *Example:* Listener: *It makes sense that you'd be angry and resent John for blaming you,* **because** *you believe you did nothing wrong.* (If you don't yet get how the speaker makes sense — you don't yet feel connected to their world — skip this step and continue to reflect back, inquire, and clarify as needed).

Tip: Never express agreement or disagreement with the speaker, even if you believe that what was said was inaccurate or "wrong." By acknowledging and validating the speaker, you are not agreeing or disagreeing with what they have said. Rather, you are confirming that what the speaker said makes sense from their perspective. (People are more available to new perspectives after they feel that their own perspectives have been truly understood and validated.)

In the next chapter, when you learn to use transformational listening to align with your own Child, you will see how the feelings of each person's Child are always 100% valid, given their perspective.

As you practice these transformational listening steps with another person, you are developing a vital aspect of yourself—a True Adult. By building the muscle of receptivity to others, you create an environment in which your own Child feels safer to share with you.

▲

What's Next...

In *Part II: Developing Your Ultimate Relationship*, you will be learning about the key practices and tools of I AM Training. In chapter 5, I'm going to introduce you to the Child–Adult Conversation and show you how I coach my client in having a real-time Conversation with his Child. In chapter 6, I will introduce you to the *Inner Alignment Chart*, a tool to support you in having your own Child–Adult Conversations.

Part II

DEVELOPING *YOUR ULTIMATE RELATIONSHIP*:

Inner Alignment Method Training (I AM Training)

CHAPTER 5

A SACRED CONNECTION: THE CONVERSATION

When your Child is finally acknowledged and validated by a True Adult's transformational listening, you experience complete and unconditional acceptance. You then hear with new ears, see with new eyes, and receive life in a magical, expansive way. All your relationships and daily experiences move you more deeply, creating a greater sense of fulfillment in your life. This self-acceptance and personal expansion becomes part of your ongoing development as a True Adult when you practice the tools of I AM Training.

A new tool you will learn about in this chapter—one that is the cornerstone activity in developing your ultimate relationship—is the *Child–Adult Conversation*. This is an actual dialogue that is spoken out loud between you as a True Adult and you as a Child. In the Conversation, you change physical positions by switching back and forth between two seats. Each time you change seats, your perspective also changes as you speak as either your Child or as the True Adult you are becoming.

Yes, you are going to learn to talk—and listen—to yourself. By having a Child–Adult Conversation, you get to know yourself as both Child and Adult. The Conversation balances, expands, and integrates both right and left sides of the brain while aligning the inner structures of who you are. The result is a *gestalt,* an organized whole that is greater than the sum of its parts—Your Ultimate Relationship.

Let's see what a Child–Adult Conversation looks like when I'm coaching a client in a therapy session. You'll see a demonstration of transformational listening as I receive what my client Joe has to say. You will also see Joe, himself, use transformational listening to receive his own Child. A profound healing connection is the result. (For clarity, when I use the term *Child* in my sessions, I'm using it to cover all three aspects of the Child. This is because in those instances, the particular aspect doesn't need distinguishing; what matters is that a True Adult is present and available to align with the Child.)

Joe:

Never the Right Stuff

Joe arrives on time for his first session. After a brief handshake, he pulls back abruptly, clearly indicating that he's anxious. Joe takes a seat and begins to speak in a tight, shaky voice.

"I'm here because I'm a total loser with women." He pauses, looking down. I listen, giving him my fullest attention but showing no agreement or disagreement. Joe avoids making eye contact.

"Last night it happened again," Joe continues. "I went out to a bar, and while I'm sitting there, an attractive woman walks in alone. She sits at the opposite side of the bar next to an empty barstool, and I want to join her. My heart is pounding and I start to sweat. I tell myself to calm down, and I rehearse what I want to say in my head: *Hi, my name is Joe.... May I buy you a drink?* Finally, I stand up and almost knock my drink off the bar. I straighten up and walk toward her. I keep thinking of my line, *Hi, my name is Joe...*

"I arrive where she's sitting, and she turns to look at me. She smiles. I say, 'Hi...' and then I freeze. Nothing comes out of my mouth.... I can hardly breathe. She gives me another smile, but I just stand there, like an idiot. I'm mortified...

and then I just bolt... as fast as I can! I'm so stupid... such a loser," Joe proclaims, turning toward me.

He pauses for a moment, obviously distraught over the recollection of the painful scene. He continues, his voice increasing in intensity. "I don't even remember driving home. The next thing I know, I'm sitting on my living room couch, crying. I keep thinking, *What's wrong with me? Why can't I just be normal and say hello to a woman?*

"Then I see your business card my friend gave me, that I've been looking at for months. I picked up the phone and, well, here I am."

As Joe speaks, I feel his frustration and despair about being trapped in a repetitive situation and seeing no way out. Compassionately and without any personal reaction, I reflect back to him those feelings that I sense are coming from his Hurt Child. "Joe, I hear how frustrated and sad you feel about not being able to connect with the woman in the bar. How humiliating it must have been to see an attractive woman, approach her, and then just freeze up! That must have been very painful, especially when it has happened so many times before."

Joe sighs, and I pause for a moment. I continue, "It must have taken a lot of courage to just go for it and walk up to her, making you feel all the more defeated when you froze and ran out of the bar." I pause again, noticing that Joe is quietly taking in my words. I wait until it feels right to continue, connecting more deeply with my sense of his Child's devastating experience.

"And then to end up at home, sitting on your couch, feeling so hopeless and alone and, somehow... not normal. How could you *not* feel hopeless and alone after trying for so long, unsuccessfully, to connect with women?" I pause again. "It makes sense to me, Joe, that you would finally call me for an appointment. You want to put an end to this continuously painful cycle."

Joe is appearing more relaxed, his earlier anxiety now clearly diminishing. His Hurt Child has just been heard and fully received, possibly as never before, and the experience has left him speechless. We sit in silence, energetically basking in the space generated by our interaction.

I share with Joe about the Inner Alignment Method and Relationship Model, and then begin to introduce him to transformational listening and the Child–Adult Conversation. "I'd like to show you how you can take a big step toward freeing yourself, Joe." He nods, and I continue. "What I'm about to ask you to do may seem awkward at first, but if you follow my instructions, you will have a powerful experience with what I call a Child–Adult Conversation." Joe nods again.

"The chair you're sitting in now is your *Child's Seat*. I'm going to ask you to sit there whenever you are expressing your immediate, raw (or any) emotions, such as the frustration and humiliation you've just described. You will also express from that seat any reactive thoughts that come up, like the judgments you have about yourself.

"Now, I'm going to ask you to choose a different chair. This will be your *True Adult Seat*. It is from there that you will always respond to your Child."

Joe looks around the room at the different seating options and I give him some direction: "You might have a feeling, intuition, or impulse about where to sit as a True Adult. If so, take the hint: It's your Child's communication about his choice for where he'd like you to sit. If nothing comes up, just choose any seat. It's fine either way."

Joe stands up, looks around, and moves onto the couch.

Once he is seated in his True Adult Seat, I explain to him further about Inner Alignment. "When you were a child, you experienced emotions that no adult was fully present to address in the way you needed. Now, your inner Child from the past, who still needs that connection, gets to have an adult—you— who is present and available to hear him express his feelings. Only when your Child's feelings and thoughts are heard, connected with and reflected, can you emerge as a True Adult, properly respond, and heal. From there, the present and future are freed from the past and open for you to create your life as you choose it to be."

Joe nods. Speaking from his True Adult Seat, he says, "Ron, I know what you mean about the connection to my past. This thing with women—the way I feel, it's so... old. It reminds me of being a kid and living with my parents."

"I'm not surprised, Joe. Your observation is significant. So, in a moment, I'll have you move into your Child's Seat and let your Child speak about what happened back then. As a True Adult, you'll be calling your Child by the name he was called as a child or by any name that feels right to you."

Joe quickly says, "Joey. He's Joey." He begins to move, then hesitates. "Okay, Ron, but this is kind of weird... this idea of talking to myself."

"I know, Joe. That's how most people feel in the beginning. You will see how natural it becomes as you do it. It's a very special experience to have. I encourage you to just jump in.

"As Joey, you only need to express your feelings and thoughts about how the bar experience reminds you of childhood, or anything else you want to talk about. Then, when you move back and respond as a True Adult, I'll coach you in what I call *transformational listening*."

In his Child's Seat, Joe takes a deep breath and, speaking as Joey, begins. "I've felt this way before—humiliated, angry, and then sad." He is silent, appearing to be lost in the feelings that are coming up for him.

After a few moments, I signal him to change back to his True Adult Seat.

Once seated, Joe turns to me and says, "Ron, as Joey was describing those feelings from his childhood, he was flooded with painful memories of when I—I mean, *he*—tried to please his mother, and she would never say anything back to him."

"Yes, those feelings are coming from your Child, Joe. And the way you just told me about your Child's experience is exactly the way we do it. In your True Adult Seat, when you're talking to me, you speak about your Child as *he* or *Joey*, so you maintain a state of objectivity—separateness—from your Child. And, Joey gets to hear and experience a True Adult speaking with another adult on his behalf. Now, turn and look at that empty seat where Joey was just sitting. Repeat back to him what he said about the memory of his painful experience with his mother."

Joe turns to face the empty chair and begins to address his Child. "Joey, you often felt humiliated, sad, and angry when your mother didn't respond to you. She'd just keep standing there, looking down and scowling at you. It seemed like forever. Then, she would turn away and go back to whatever she'd been doing."

Joe chokes up as he continues speaking to his Child. "It made you feel like something was wrong with you, like you were just not right and never would be. And worse, you're just now realizing that your dad always went along with her, never stepping in to tell her what a good kid you were." Joe stops talking.

After a moment, I prompt him to switch seats. "Whenever you have an empty or blank feeling, that's the time to switch seats."

Joe nods in understanding, and switches.

From Joey's seat, he cries out, "That's just crazy! I was a really good kid—I only wanted to please Mom and Dad. I did whatever they asked! I was always respectful, not only of adults, but of everyone.... But they just didn't get it. What more did they want from me?" His voice is filled with raw emotion, the experience of his past not just a memory, but a living experience of the impact he's been carrying and living all these years.

"When you are ready," I say gently, "I'd like to speak with your True Adult." I gesture for him to move to his True Adult Seat and then wait until he is settled there before continuing.

"Now, when you're ready Joe, reflect back what Joey just said. If you have some thoughts about how he makes sense, tell him that. Be specific about the feelings he expressed. For example, rather than saying 'It makes sense you would feel *that way* because…' you would say, 'It makes sense you would feel *angry* because…'"

Joe faces his Child's Seat and begins. "Joey, you knew you were a good kid." His voice is low and hesitant, so I gently suggest some words to say: "You wanted nothing more than to please your parents, your teachers, and everyone you interacted with."

Joe repeats my words with an emphatic tone and then adds his own, "You were nice to absolutely everyone. It makes sense that you wondered, What more did they want from you before they'd say something positive? It's like you were never the right stuff!"

Joe sighs and looks down as he shakes his head, having no further words for his Child. "What do I do now?" he asks. "I don't know what to say."

I reply, "When you don't know what to say, switch seats again so Joey can respond to you, his developing True Adult, who is listening and responding to him after all these years."

Joe switches, taking his Child's Seat. I notice that as Joey he is slouching and appearing defeated. He speaks as his Child, "Well, I was a good student but not a great student. I wasn't very good at sports. I never had any girlfriends…"

After a pause, Joe gets up from his Child's Seat, without my prompting, and sits in his True Adult Seat. He speaks directly to his Child.

"Joey, it makes perfect sense you wouldn't feel very good about yourself. You are so used to your parents not seeing anything positive in you… you think you've got to be really great at something to feel good about yourself. 'Good' was not enough! How were you supposed to have any confidence? No wonder you've been terrified of women. It's amazing you've had the courage to actually walk up to any woman at all."

In the pause that follows, Joe moves to his Child's Seat and speaks: "You're right; I am courageous, and even though no one else might ever see it, it's true.

It feels so good that you understand me—I just can't believe how good it feels. I want to talk with you more often like this—like, all the time!"

Joe switches seats again. As a True Adult, he says, "Wow—I can really feel you, Joey!"

Joe then turns to me, "I don't know that Joey's ever felt quite this good before. He's waited a lot of years for this. What a great feeling, not only for him... I'm feeling pretty good, myself."

"I know," I reply. "It's amazing what a profound difference you can make as a True Adult, simply by listening to your Child. It means everything to a Child to be shown interest, compassion, and respect. And, it's got to feel good for you, as a developing True Adult, to know how to be there for Joey."

Joe nods. "It's pretty strange, but I think I'm getting it. I can feel it deep inside; something has changed in me." He pauses. "Thank you, Ron, for teaching me how to be the adult Joey's been missing. I can feel how he needs me, and now I can be here for him. He'll always have me..." Joe's voice trails off. Then he says, "I love that little guy. He really is a great guy."

"What you have just experienced, Joe," I comment, "is the beginning of a relationship with yourself. This relationship will grow deeper and more solid as you practice listening and responding to your Child in this way. Your Child can then express his feelings and give you the information you need to heal those painful wounds from long ago. The transformational listening skill you have just practiced is the pathway to that deep healing."

"It seems so real," Joe replies, "like it's all happening right now, when it is really about something that happened a long time ago."

"That's right," I respond. "When Joey was young, like all young children, he needed the Big People to see and hear him with respect, interest, and compassion. He still needs that acknowledgment, and until it happens, his past will always influence his present and future. It's like the movie, *Back to the Future*.

When they changed the past, the present and the future changed, too. You are freeing Joey from all the negativity he experienced when his parents didn't truly connect with him in the way he needed.

"By having a Child–Adult Conversation, as you just did, you will continue to cleanse your Child's past, redefining who you are. Your Child can finally relax with the comfort of you as a True Adult by his side. Then, with your ability to be separate and thus nonreactive, you will be free to see how to most effectively meet your Child's needs. You will find yourself living in a world of clarity, empowerment, and joy. You can have interactions and relationships that are free from what happened in the past. Only then does the past become history.

"You will find that the more time you spend relating to your Child in this way, the more Joey will experience being worthy of respect from others in the same way he experiences it from you, his True Adult. That will be a dramatic shift for him from seeing and experiencing others as though they were his parents and being afraid of them. That fear is the source of your lack of confidence with women, Joe. As you, as a True Adult, hear and respect your Child, that will all change."

Our session now over, a more self-assured Joe leaves my office. As a result of having been truly heard, likely for the first time, Joe's Child was able to share his deeper feelings and thoughts. He was no longer alone with the painful impact of the original hurtful experiences with his mother. But the real magic began when Joe became a True Adult for his own Child, because only Joe can fully comprehend the depth and intricacies of his Child's early wounding experiences.

Joe continued working with me, developing a deeper relationship with his Child over time, first with my coaching and then on his own. By practicing True Adult building activities and having further Conversations with his Child, Joe grew increasingly as a True Adult. He began dating and eventually found "the one," marrying within a few years of starting his process of I AM Training. His wife also came in to see me, resulting in the two of them becoming a powerful healing team. They continue to see me on occasion to fine-tune and upgrade their skills.

As Joe discovered, having a profound connection with your Child allows you to go to depths that the helpful words of another—even a coach/therapist such as myself—could never take you. Because you have access, 24 hours a day, to every thought, feeling, and experience your Child has ever had, you are in the position to be the most effective coach/therapist—True Adult—for your Child. For this reason, I have developed supportive practices and tools to enable you to establish yourself as a True Adult and have Child–Adult Conversations on your own. The steps below will help you get started. In the next chapter, I will offer you another valuable tool to support your process.

The Child–Adult Conversation

When I introduce my clients to the Child–Adult Conversation for the first time, I don't explain the specific steps, but rather guide them to jump right in, as I did in my interaction with Joe. However, I've laid out clear steps so that you can do it on your own without my physical presence. Eventually, you will be able to have your own Conversations, learning to do so through progressive levels of skill that I will teach you in part III.

For now, simply read through these steps to familiarize yourself with the process. Later, when I take you into training sessions with my clients, you will be able to follow their Child–Adult Conversations, preparing you for your own.

STEPS FOR A CHILD–ADULT CONVERSATION

Step 1: Choose a location

Find a place where you can be assured privacy. Arrange two separate chairs facing each other, one for your Child and the other for you as a True Adult. During the Conversation, you will be moving back and forth between the two chairs.

Step 2: Prepare to receive your Child— *in your True Adult Seat*

In the True Adult Seat, you want to be as empty and open as possible— an objective witness—in order to receive your Child. To empty yourself, notice any thoughts or feelings that come up and identify them as belonging to your Child. From there, imagine lovingly and respectfully giving them back to their source—your Child. This is one practice that will assist you in developing a skill necessary to make the greatest difference for your Child: to be separate—not caught up in reaction. Allow yourself a moment to experience at least some level of separateness, then switch seats.

Step 3: Express any feelings and thoughts you have— *in your Child's Seat*

As your Child, express your feelings and thoughts about an upsetting incident or interaction. It might be an incident with a friend, your romantic partner, a family member, or someone at work. This can be a current or past incident, or even one from your childhood.

Continue until you feel there is nothing more to say, and you experience a sense of being complete or blank. That is your cue to switch seats. Stand up and return to your True Adult Seat.

Step 4: Reflect back your Child's words— *in your True Adult Seat*

Look over at the chair you just left, which is now empty. Imagine your Child still sitting there, feeling all the hurt, anger, humiliation, shame, confusion, or whatever he or she has just expressed. Now begin to speak to that Child. Use the three steps for transformational listening as described in chapter 4 on page 74 and 75. Pause for a moment, then stand up and move to the other seat.

Step 5: Express feelings and thoughts—*in your Child's Seat*

Now back in your Child's Seat, express any feelings and thoughts you are having. Then continue the Conversation by repeating these most recent steps—5 and 6—switching back and forth until you feel complete. Always give your Child the opportunity to have the last word, regardless of whether anything is said. Then, move into your True Adult Seat.

Step 6: Complete the Conversation—*in your True Adult Seat*

As a True Adult, sit silently with your Child, allowing yourself to feel the difference that your presence is making for this most important person. Your Conversation is now complete.

Why Have a Child–Adult Conversation?

Essentially, the Conversation connects you to your Child, ultimately allowing you to experience your Infinite Child, the source of your greatest wisdom and guidance. At the same time, it reverses the early programming that disconnected you and threw you off course in the first place.

From an early age, most of us didn't have a positive reference for being fully seen and heard by parents or other Big People. As a young child expressing yourself freely, you were often met with a negative reaction, and you learned to stifle or shut down your spontaneous responses. Consequently, you stopped fully seeing and hearing yourself, preventing you from knowing *who you truly are*—your Infinite Child.

Because of these early experiences of rejection, you may feel a degree of reluctance or discomfort at even the thought of having a conversation with your Child. This is common and understandable. But just know that every step—even the seemingly small ones—that you take in connecting with your Child restores what is your birthright: to be spontaneously and freely yourself.

In a Child–Adult Conversation, you and your Child create this new, miraculous experience together. As a True Adult, you discover perspectives that enable you to speak to your Child with respect and compassion. The words you speak as a True Adult might feel inauthentic in the beginning. This is common, especially when the Child is reluctant to come out. Your continued response can create the safety needed for your Child's feelings to come forth. You may then be surprised to find yourself feeling empathy for that Child in the chair across from you. With experience, the Conversations you have will feel more authentic.

The following is an opportunity for you to open the door to connect with your Child, and for your Child to connect with you. You are about to enter into a written Conversation by writing back and forth with your Child in your Child's Journal. You might find that you have a profound experience of a new and beautiful world. On rare occasions, however, such an opportunity can open the door for the Child to express more than one might be expecting—or even want. While I have found this more challenging experience to occur rarely, I have offered some guidance for such circumstances in the Appendix on page 321.

Your Turn:

Writing a Child–Adult Conversation

In Part III, you'll be learning how to have your own Child-Adult Conversations. For now, I want to invite you to taste that experience by writing a Conversation with your Child in your Child's Journal.

In chapter 3, you participated in a journal activity using your nondominant hand to express your Child in writing. In the following activity, you will give your Child the same opportunity; only now, you as a True Adult will be responding to your Child using transformational listening. Switching back and forth between dominant and nondominant hands will not be necessary. However, feel free to do so if that feels right to you.

In this activity, you as a True Adult will be entering your Child's Journal, which is your Child's world. This will be a nice opportunity for your Child to experience the presence of a True Adult where one had been missing. As you take another step into this new experience, choose a relationship issue that is not a particularly difficult one for your Child. If you were about to learn how to surf, it would be best to begin with small waves; similarly, choose a less challenging issue for this activity. The issue might even be the one that your Child already wrote about in the nondominant hand activity. As a True Adult, you will be adding transformational listening to your written response so that your Child gets to have another level of conversation about the chosen issue with a Big Person.

As you did before, have your Child use a pencil, while you, as a True Adult use a pen, or use different ink colors to distinguish the separate expressions. Make separate paragraphs for each of you, or skip a few lines between your responses. You might want to begin each section with the heading *Child* or *True Adult*. You can certainly be creative in your personal method of switching between Child and True Adult.

WRITING YOUR CHILD–ADULT CONVERSATION

1: Invite your Child to open the Child's Journal

Let him or her bring to mind an upsetting incident from the recent past.

2: Invite your Child to express whatever is there to be expressed

This might include complaining, blaming, or ranting and raving. Writing as your Child, let out whatever has been held in—for example, anger about how a person may have treated you, or something that was said to you. Fully welcome any of your Hurt Child's feelings as well as your Little Adult's reactive thoughts, including judgments of the other person or even of yourself. Write until your Child completely exhausts his or her feelings and thoughts about the conflict. Your writing might run a paragraph, 5 pages, or 20 pages. Continue until you come to a natural stop.

3: Give yourself a moment to stand apart from your Child's feelings and thoughts

Imagine, as a parent—or teacher, coach, or therapist—that you have just heard what a person you care about (your Child) has expressed to you.

The idea here is for you to develop your ability to become an objective witness who can see the bigger picture.

4: Respond as a True Adult to your Child

In writing, reflect back your Child's feelings and your Little Adult's reactive thoughts. Simply repeat exactly what your Child has written to you, using the same words your Child used ("You're feeling angry . . ." or "You're thinking that . . ."), as described in steps 1 and 2 for transformational listening on page 74. (Later, in chapter 7, you will have a chance to practice step 3, sense-making commentary. For now, simply reflect the feelings and thoughts your Child has expressed.)

5: Switch back to your Child and repeat steps 2–4

6: Continue to switch back and forth between Child and True Adult

Write until you feel complete, allowing your Child to have the last word.

7: Sit silently for a moment as a True Adult

Be present to the experience your Child has just had.

The connection between you as an emerging True Adult and your Child deepens through communication, as does any relationship. In part III, you will learn to have a Child–Adult Conversation as I take you through three levels of skill building, each one adding to your ability to connect more deeply with your Child.

If feelings come up during this or any other activity, invite your Child to write about them in his or her Journal. This is helpful in giving your Child the experience that his or her feelings matter. I recommend that you use your True Adult Log at least once a day to strengthen and develop yourself as a True Adult. Even if you only write one sentence, you will be making a significant difference in developing a strong True Adult and enhancing your quality of life.

Helpful Tips:

Refining Your Listening

You may want to refine your transformational listening skills by practicing the following suggestions. They will be familiar to you from having seen some of them demonstrated in Joe's session.

▶ **Address your Child by name.** To maintain objectivity, refer to your Child using your name or a name that intuitively feels good. It could be a name that expresses endearment or one your Child was called at an earlier stage in life. Several of my clients refer affectionately to their Child as *Little One*, or *My Little One*. Also, use the pronoun *you* rather than *I* to maintain your objectivity and separateness. By referring to your Child as someone separate from you, you create an objective distance, allowing your Child to feel heard and understood by someone else—the best possible someone else, *you!*

▶ **Don't feel you have to write down every word your Child has expressed.** It may be too long and tedious to do so, unless it feels important for you. Your authentic feelings of care and interest are ultimately what matter to your Child. A True Adult's desire to make a difference, and effort to do so—regardless of how well it's done—are most healing for the Child. This is the foundation that will make it safe for your Child to help you get what he or she needs you to get.

▶ **Avoid using the words *I understand*.** A common experience that many people had while growing up occurred whenever the Big People said that they understood. The Child would then finally relax and feel better. But the very next comments the Big People made were proof that they had not actually understood in the first place. Consequently, your Child might feel set up when you write that you understand. Furthermore, "I understand" makes it more about the adult than the child. The focus becomes about *your understanding* rather than about *your receiving* what has been shared. Instead, I recommend writing, *I hear that you feel..., I get that you feel..., Of course you would feel..., It's easy to see how you would feel...,* or *How could you not feel...?*

▶ **Don't be stopped if your Child resists being seen, heard, and responded to by a True Adult.** Resistance to this new level of intimacy can take the form of being disinterested, tired, bored, or generally aversive—all of which are Little Adult strategies used in relationships with others, as well. Because your Little Adult is used to being the one in charge, suddenly having someone else present and responsive, as in this activity, can feel uncomfortable—even confusing—causing you to want to stop. Remember, your Child has spent years hoping for a Big Person to be present and available, only to be repeatedly disappointed.

If this has been your experience, my recommendation is simply to jump in and do the activity, regardless of any reluctance you might feel. While it may take time to feel that you are doing anything other than just going through the motions, your effort is most valued by your Child, and is actually healing in itself. Just notice those feelings with compassion and respect as you step in as a True Adult and respond to this most important person in your life.

▲

What's Next...

By now, you are getting a taste of the power of I AM Training and how it develops *your ultimate relationship*—the one you have with yourself that makes it possible to have better relationships with everyone else in your life.

The way out of the Little Adult trap, in which you react in a futile attempt to fix and change yourself and other people, is to go further along the path of *healthy separateness*. We will explore this process more deeply in the next chapter. With the tools I will give you, you will be able to draw boundaries and make distinctions that allow you as a True Adult to emerge naturally and dependably, creating a new place from which you can live an increasingly more joyous, powerful, and rewarding life.

CHAPTER 6

HEALTHY SEPARATENESS: THE CHART

In this chapter, you will take an essential step in developing your ultimate relationship by learning to establish what I call *healthy separateness*. Healthy separateness is a condition in which the inner boundaries between your Child and True Adult are clear and distinct. Healthy separateness also includes recognizing the difference between two aspects of your Child—your Hurt Child and your Little Adult.

Boundaries are healthy and important to have in all relationships, not only in your inner relationship. As children evolve and grow, they naturally draw new boundaries between themselves and their parents, or the Big People who are responsible for them. A 2-year-old screaming *No!,* an adolescent rebelling, a young adult moving out of the house—we all know that separating from our significant Big People and becoming distinct individuals is a developmental requirement tied directly to our happiness and well-being. In a love relationship, boundaries allow two people to maintain their individuality so that they can come together as whole beings, better able to contribute to, and benefit from, each other. As you develop your healthy separateness within, you'll find that you have a greater and more natural ability to do the same with others.

In your inner relationship, such a state of healthy separateness is required for your ongoing alignment and empowerment. Using the tools and practices of Inner Alignment Training, you start to learn by distinguishing your Hurt Child from your Little Adult, so that you no longer experience them as the same identity. Rather, you distinguish them as feelings versus reactive thoughts. As you become a witness to both, you naturally emerge with more objectivity as a separate True Adult. Then, as you are available to address your Hurt Child's feelings through Conversations, a bond develops and trust grows. You find yourself receiving wisdom and guidance from your Infinite Child as you gain a magical new perspective on who you are and how life works.

In this chapter, you will learn to use a new tool, the *Inner Alignment Chart*, to accomplish this state of healthy separateness, supporting you in emerging as an objective, solid True Adult. You will see how the chart works to help establish healthy separateness for my client Sherry, who learns to use the chart for issues in her relationships. I will also show you how to use your chart for support and guidance when having a Child–Adult Conversation.

Hurt Child–Little Adult Merger

You have learned how your Little Adult took control and, over time, suppressed the spontaneous expression of your Child. This was done to shield your Child from the pain of rejection, judgment, and other kinds of disconnection by the Big People—first, your parents or other caregivers, then your teachers, and later your bosses or other authority figures. Your Child even feared rejection from friends, colleagues, and significant others. Over time, you ceased to recognize your Child, who was largely eclipsed by your overprotective, sometimes overbearing, Little Adult. During that eclipse, your Hurt Child (feelings from past wounding) merged with your Little Adult (reactive thoughts and actions) to form the person you experience yourself to be today.

A first step toward healthy separateness is to distinguish the reactive thoughts and actions of your Little Adult from the natural feelings of your Hurt Child. By doing so, you're able to unmerge the two. Your Hurt Child's feelings are real, sourced by past wounds that are still festering inside of you today. But the reactive thoughts and actions that follow them are not real. They are always an attempt to cope with and fix whatever is perceived as threatening. Only when those reactions are clearly recognized by you as a True Adult can those wounds be healed, allowing the pain to finally go away.

Once your feelings and thoughts are recognized and distinguished as those of both a Hurt Child and a Coping Child/Little Adult, you as a True Adult can step in and address your Child's experience through a Child–Adult Conversation. Before such recognition, when all thoughts and actions are believed to be the truth, there is not a separate True Adult available who is strong enough to enable a Conversation.

For example, if you are feeling anxious and fearful about speaking in front of a group, it's a sign that your Hurt Child needs the comfort of a True Adult to receive those feelings. But in the absence of a True Adult connection, your Little Adult goes into reaction, with such thoughts as, *I'm going to screw up; they're going to hate me and throw me off the stage!* Such thoughts are the reaction of a child (Little Adult) attempting to cope with life's circumstances. These thoughts are never based in truth, but without the presence of a True Adult, can become a self-fulfilling prophecy.

In chapter 3, when you did the non-dominant hand activity and recorded your Little Adult's reactions to daily situations, and in chapter 5, when you wrote out your Child–Adult Conversation, you were already establishing healthy separateness. Now, you will see how I assist my client Sherry to develop healthy separateness as she engages in a Conversation with her Child. Later you'll see how Sherry uses an Inner Alignment Chart to facilitate her separateness when she is on her own, without me.

Sherry:

Invisible and Powerless

Sherry comes to see me because she is feeling frustrated and powerless in many areas of her life, and is beginning to feel desperate. After taking a seat on the couch, she begins.

"Ron, I'm 38, and I've never been married." She pauses, swallowing hard, and then continues. "I always seem to be pushed aside, whether that means being ignored when I try to say something, or someone else getting credit for my accomplishments at work. It seems that other people always get what I want—and I'm always left out. It's just becoming too painful for me."

I listen with compassion as Sherry describes her feelings of powerlessness, which are common for so many people, even when they're not cognitively aware of it. She continues: "The other night, I'm at a party, talking with this interesting guy I just met. The next thing I know, my friend Donna struts over—with her great body, great clothes, great hair—and the guy immediately shifts his attention off me and right onto her. I'm left standing there holding my drink, watching them talk and flirt—like I'm some kind of ugly stepsister."

Sherry is quiet for a moment as she recalls the humiliating experience, then continues. "I felt so... *invisible*... *worthless*... like I just didn't matter at all." Choking back tears, she stammers, "I... I'm still angry. I resent Tony, the guy, for being so rude and insensitive, and I resent Donna for stealing him away from me. I decided to have nothing more to do with either of them. Not that I expect to ever see him again, anyway."

Tears fill Sherry's eyes and I hand her a tissue. Having listened to her Child's expression, I reflect back what she has shared with me.

"Sherry, of course you would feel angry and humiliated after Donna broke into your conversation with Tony. And, it's easy to see how you'd feel resentful toward both of them. It makes sense that you'd judge yourself as unattractive, as though you were an ugly stepsister. How painful that whole encounter must have been for you."

Sherry continues her story. "I couldn't believe it was actually happening again. Even getting myself to talk to this guy was a big deal. But I went for it anyway, and it was going okay, I thought. Until…" Sherry pauses, taking a deep breath and letting out a strong sigh, "Donna barges in and takes over, and I just disappear into thin air."

I respond. "Yes, I get that it was a big deal for you to connect with Tony and not have your fears stop you. That was no small accomplishment. It was going well, until you were interrupted by someone you thought of as a friend. It's easy to see how you would feel invisible, as if you'd ceased to exist for either of them."

Sherry responds, sounding sad and defeated, "I really thought he was about to ask me out when Donna interrupted us. But he's probably seeing her by now. Why would he want anything to do with me at this point?" She looks to me for an answer.

Instead of answering, I continue to reflect her feelings and thoughts. "Sherry, I can feel how hard this has been for you. You were right there with Tony, and it seemed to be going well. Now you're thinking the moment was lost, that he's probably seeing Donna now. It makes sense to me that you would be feeling hopeless, like, *What's the point?*"

"That's exactly it, Ron. *Hopeless*." Sherry is silent for a moment and then says, "I just don't know what to do anymore."

After explaining to Sherry how I AM Training works, I invite her to enter into a Conversation with her Child. "Sherry, let's have you connect with your Child, the one who has just expressed those feelings about the incident with

Tony and Donna. To begin, where would your Child want you, her developing True Adult, to sit to have a Conversation with her?"

Sherry points to the chair diagonal to where she'd been sitting. She gets up from the couch and takes the chair that will become her True Adult Seat.

I begin to orient her to her first Child–Adult Conversation and include an explanation of *healthy separateness.* "Whenever you are upset or in pain, regardless of the circumstances, your Child is showing you an early trauma from her past. Back then, when she needed an adult to be there for her, there was no one. As a result, your Child went into coping mode as a Little Adult. Now you are going to learn how to become separate as a True Adult. Such a state of separateness is healthy and necessary for your Little Adult to be relieved of her impossible job."

Sherry nods, and I continue. "I'm about to show you how your Child can have an adult, a *True* Adult, present and available whenever she needs one. As you sit here in the True Adult Seat, be open and available to your Child, who may bring up a memory that sheds light on your current upset. If she doesn't, that's okay too. Begin by responding to her like I did about what happened with Tony and Donna."

Sherry closes her eyes and is silent for a few moments. Suddenly, her eyes widen. "Oh wow, I can't believe it! Ron, this thing with Donna and Tony—it reminds me of when I was 14 years old and at my friend's birthday party!"

"Good! Your Child has brought you a memory already. Now stand up and move to your Child's Seat, so she can speak."

Back on the couch, Sherry's Child describes the event that happened when she was 14. "I'm talking to Chris, the cutest guy in 8th grade—at least, *I* thought he was! My friend Ann comes over wearing her older sister's sexy dress, and right away Chris starts talking to her. They both ignore me. I feel humiliated and look down at my dress, thinking it's childish. I'm furious with my mother for not letting me wear the dress I wanted to wear."

Sherry stops and takes a deep breath. "I've had these same feelings so many times since then—humiliated, rejected, angry, and then sad—in similar circumstances. But it never occurred to me that they were actually related. It's fascinating…"

I interject, "Sherry, when you're ready, I'd like to speak with your True Adult."

Before Sherry gets up from the couch, she responds. "Ron, it's such a relief that you are going to talk to my True Adult, because *I* don't have a clue."

Sherry takes the True Adult Seat and speaks: "Ron, I could feel the pressure my Child was under, being the one who had to figure everything out for herself. Growing up, my Child was always under pressure, and I guess that's never really changed."

Sherry is silent. Suddenly, she looks as though a light has been turned on inside her. "Oh, I get it! Whenever my Child is trying to figure things out to make life work, she's being a Little Adult, a Child in coping mode—just like you said. The pressure is because there's no *real* adult present to handle things. When my Little Adult does try to figure it all out—like she learned to do in childhood—it doesn't usually go so well. Even if things do work out, it feels like so much stress, work, and effort." Sherry is glowing with her new insight.

"What you just did, Sherry, is distinguish yourself as separate from your Coping Child, your Little Adult. That's the beginning of establishing healthy separateness and clear inner boundaries."

Sherry looks at me with a puzzled expression.

I continue, "Did you notice how natural it was for your Child to bring you valuable information when she had a different seat—her own?"

"Yes, I did, and it was shocking how easy it was. As soon as I sat down, memories started coming to me. I really did feel different in that other seat."

"That's because when you shift positions, you allow your Child to move into her own space—not just physically but also *energetically*. Then you can receive information about childhood events that are repeating in your life—like the incident with Donna and Tony." Later, when you are back in your True Adult Seat, you are better able to separate and then discover yourself as a True Adult.

"This is very exciting!" Sherry pauses, clearly thinking about what I have just said. "I can see how my experience at the party of being pushed aside by Donna and ignored by Tony was something very old, from my past. But Ron, how can something that happened back when I was 14 get healed by having a Conversation with myself now?"

"Great question, Sherry. Even your experience at age 14 has roots in your earlier childhood, when you went through something painful and didn't have a True Adult to see it, hear it, and connect with you about it. As you continue to engage in Child–Adult Conversations, memories of those buried childhood experiences will come to the surface. In a Child–Adult Conversation, your Child's feelings—the humiliation, anger, and sadness—will finally be heard by you as a safe and loving True Adult."

"But Ron, that sounds hard to do, even scary. Why would I want to bring all that back?"

I'm aware that Sherry is now responding fearfully, as her Child goes into coping mode, but I continue speaking to her True Adult, strengthening her separateness.

"That's a great question. I'm glad you asked. For a Child without a True Adult present, it would be scary to bring all that back. It would be retraumatizing to feel all those horrible feelings and to, once again, not have a safe Big Person there. However, for your Child to be able to see you as a safe True Adult, take you by the hand, show you what happened, and be truly understood by you, is actually a gratifying and healing experience. That's what we all crave deep down inside."

"I must admit, as you were talking, Ron, I could feel my Child experiencing each thing you said. Then, the visual, of my Child taking me by the hand—it's already feeling so comforting! You do have me intrigued."

"Well then, here's the benefit of, as you said, 'bringing all that back.' Without realizing it, you are already living your painful past, as though you were still that powerless Child without a Big Person to step in for you in the way you needed. Now, there's someone who can do something to turn your pain and unhappiness into joy. That someone is you as a True Adult."

Sherry jumps in, "Ron! I think I'm starting to understand how it all works! A True Adult knows that those painful memories are always the past being recreated in the present, making them seem like the truth. That's what happened with Tony and Donna!"

"You're right, Sherry. The current upsetting experiences are always what *already happened*—old programs replaying themselves as similar experiences in the present. This is the plight of your Little Adult: living as though the past is a blueprint for life."

Sherry looks as though the picture is becoming clearer, so I continue. "When those old, painful feelings recreate themselves in your current life, you as a True Adult can experience your power to step in and be there for your Child in the way the Big People were not, by having a Child–Adult Conversation. This is how you free your Child from living as though the powerless, painful past is the truth.

"The ability to maintain healthy separateness from your Hurt Child and Little Adult will take some practice to develop, but soon it will be second nature. At the end of our session, I'm going to show you a tool that will support you in that process. But for now, I invite you to turn toward your Child's Seat and simply be with her. You might even get a nonverbal sense of what it is like for her to experience your presence as a True Adult."

Sherry is silent, eyes closed. Her body language conveys an intent focus on the seat she has just left. She nods slowly for a few moments, as if receiving a message from her Child, and then stops. Taking a deep breath, she turns to me and says, "That was very powerful! I *felt* her, little Sherry, like she was real. There was a real person there—*me*! I'm actually learning how to have a relationship with myself . . . with my Child. Does everybody experience what I'm describing to you, Ron?"

"Yes," I reply, "but the amount of practice it takes for each person to develop a relationship with their Child varies. Each person's inner relationship develops uniquely. You and little Sherry will become more familiar with each other as you take time connecting with her in Child–Adult Conversations."

As our session nears its end, I introduce Sherry to the Inner Alignment Chart and show her how to use it to support herself in developing healthy separateness. I explain that by using a Chart, she can have Child–Adult Conversations on her own, outside of our sessions and without my coaching.

The Inner Alignment Chart

The Inner Alignment Chart is a tool I developed to help you establish a state of healthy separateness between your inner structures so they can align in a powerful new way. As you saw in Sherry's session, once you separate from your Child as a True Adult, a relationship is possible, and is then realized and developed through Child–Adult Conversations.

The Inner Alignment Chart helps you to distinguish your Hurt Child's feelings from your Little Adult's coping methods—reactive thoughts and actions. So often people are unaware of what they feel and of what is actually behind those feelings because their Little Adult, triggered into protection, obscures the Hurt Child. At the same time, Little Adults automatically react to and take personally what others say and do and what happens in life. It's quite a quagmire for our Little Adult, who doesn't know how to create healing or safety for the Child, and can't help but take everything personally.

Only when the Child's feelings and the Little Adult's reactions are distinct, and no longer merged as one experience, can you emerge as a True Adult, properly address your Child's feelings, and heal. Conversely, if your deeper feelings—and their origins—remain obscured by your Little Adult's reactive thoughts and actions, they will remain inaccessible, impeding and perhaps even precluding healing.

The Inner Alignment Chart creates an opportunity for you to step in as a safe Big Person who can begin to sort out what's been going on for your "little one." By writing down a triggering incident, you can explore and chart what you notice— Little Adult's reactive thoughts and actions, as well as your Hurt Child's possibly more obscured feelings. As you practice observing both your Hurt Child and Little Adult by using the Chart, you continue to separate and emerge as a True Adult.

Let's follow Sherry as she shares the Charts she filled in about the issues that came up in between our training sessions. At the end of this chapter, you will have an opportunity to fill in your own Chart for an issue of concern to you.

Sherry's Second Session:

Developing True Adult Objectivity

When Sherry returns for a second session, she shows me two Charts she did regarding incidents that occurred during a visit with her family. As you follow along with her process, think about your own life and how you might use a Chart to help you establish healthy separateness after an upsetting event occurs. Then, when it's your turn to do your own Chart for an incident in your life, you'll be more familiar with the process.

In her session, Sherry begins by sharing about the first of two incidents:

"The incident happens at a family dinner. We're all sitting around the table, and I'm sharing about my job. But just as I'm about to tell everyone about my upcoming promotion, my sister and her new husband start whispering to each other and giggling. Then they rudely laugh out loud at their secret joke. I look at my parents who smile and nod for me to continue. I feel a strong surge of anger and want to leave the table. But I stay and stumble on, barely finishing, unable to tell them how I really feel."

Sherry tells me how later that evening she took time to herself and filled in a chart about the upsetting incident. This is what she wrote in her chart:

Sherry's Inner Alignment Chart (#1)		
Incident – Family dinner, Thanksgiving; I'm sharing about my job. My sister and her husband are interrupting my story by whispering and laughing.		
Hurt Child's *Feelings*	**Little Adult's Reactive** *Thoughts* **(usually judgments of self or others)**	**Little Adult's** *Actions* **Imagined and/or Actual**
I feel Angry	How dare my sister be so rude?	**Imagined:** Tell them they're both acting like jerks.
I feel Hurt	They're acting like jerks.	Storm out and not talk to them for the rest of the night.
I feel Irrelevant	Obviously I'm not worth listening to.	
I feel Invisible		**Actual:** I ignored them and continued talking.

Sherry then shares a second incident that had occurred that same evening.

"I was helping my mother clean up in the kitchen, and I mentioned to her how angry I'd felt at my sister and her husband for their rude interruption at the dinner table. My mother replied, 'Oh sweetheart, they're newlyweds, and that's how new couples sometimes act. Just let it go and enjoy the rest of the evening.' My mother was attempting to be helpful, but her response only made me feel worse."

As a result of her mother's well-intentioned remarks, Sherry felt no opening to further express her Hurt Child's feelings. Her Little Adult was afraid that any continued sharing would upset her mother, leading to disapproval and judgment. Remember, Little Adults are always protecting their Child from the Big People's judgments or negativity, often by substituting their own Little Adult's judgments to shut the Child down before the Big People do.

Sherry wrote out a second Chart for the incident that happened in the kitchen, again using the four steps to clearly distinguish her Child's feelings, reactive thoughts, and actions.

Sherry's Inner Alignment Chart (#2)

Incident – After Thanksgiving dinner, I'm sharing with my mother my upset about being rudely interrupted. My mother responds to me, saying, "Just let it go."

Hurt Child's *Feelings*	Little Adult's Reactive *Thoughts* (usually judgments of self or others)	Little Adult's *Actions* Imagined and/or Actual
I feel Dismissed	She doesn't care about my feelings.	**Imagined:** Tell my mom that I hate how she always sides with my sister and just doesn't get it.
I feel Angry	I don't really matter to my family.	
I feel Misunderstood		
I feel Sad	I shouldn't be so sensitive.	I'll never share my feelings with my mom again.
I feel Alienated	I always make such a big deal about things.	**Actual:** I just walked away to not let it get to me.

When Sherry studied the two Charts she had written, she was able to illuminate her wound of feeling pushed aside and overlooked and the way it was still impacting her life. In both events, Sherry's Little Adult suppressed her Hurt Child's feelings in an attempt to protect her Child. She may have felt better on the surface by ignoring her feelings, but Sherry's Child remained unacknowledged and uncared for. With such self-denial, her Little Adult gained a firm, protective foothold that led Sherry to just walk away, hoping everyone would think she was fine with what had happened. However, if she'd already developed her True Adult, Sherry would have been clear that her sister and brother-in-law's behaviors were only about them, and not personal toward her.

As a True Adult, she would perhaps have continued sharing if it didn't matter to her whether her sister and brother-in-law heard her. If it did matter to her, she might have comfortably said something like, "Hey, you guys, I know you're having fun. But I'd love for you to hear what I'm sharing because the two of you are important to me and I want you to know what's been happening in my life."

This same pattern of denying her Child's feelings had surfaced in the incidents with Donna and Tony at the party, with her sister and husband at the dinner table, and with her mother in the kitchen. Sherry was able to see how, in each of these events, her Little Adult had basically stuffed down her Child's feelings; she had reacted from fear and judgment, rather than from authentic alignment with her Child.

Over time, Sherry became more objective about her feelings, thoughts, and actions by filling out an Inner Alignment Chart whenever a painful incident occurred. Her new objectivity led to more Child–Adult Conversations and deeper healing of the core wounds that had caused her to feel and react the way she did. Soon, Sherry was able to express herself more authentically in alignment with her Child and emerge in all of her relationships as a True Adult, no longer under the domination of an overprotective Little Adult.

Your Turn:

A Chart for Your Issue

I invite you to fill in your own Inner Alignment Chart for an issue or incident that is upsetting or painful in your life. You can duplicate the template presented below, or download a template from my website (InnerAlignment-Method.com).

My Inner Alignment Chart		
Incident –		
Hurt Child's Feelings	**Little Adult's Reactive *Thoughts* (usually judgments of self or others)**	**Little Adult's *Actions* Imagined and/or Actual**

Some of my clients create a separate notebook for writing out Charts. Others put the Charts they've printed from my website in a loose-leaf binder. Regardless of your personal preference, it's valuable to have a method of organizing your Charts so that you can easily follow your patterns of reactivity, as well as track your progress in developing healthy separateness.

Follow these steps:

FILLING IN YOUR *INNER ALIGNMENT CHART*

Step 1: The Incident

Briefly, in 1 to 3 sentences, describe an upsetting interaction you had with someone. This can be an argument with a partner or close friend, remarks at a family dinner or other social gathering, a situation at work— any interaction in which things didn't go the way you would have wanted them to go and you were left with negative feelings. Write in the present tense (to create a more immediate experience) about what someone said or did. For example, *I am at my high school reunion when an old friend insults me.*

Step 2: Hurt Child's *Feelings*

Write down your Hurt Child's spontaneous and immediate feelings about the interaction. For example:

I feel Shocked.
I feel Hurt.
I feel Angry.
I feel Sad.

Step 3: Little Adult's Reactive *Thoughts*

Write down your Little Adult's reaction to the incident, such as, *What the heck just happened*? Include any possible judgments of self and others. For example, *I'm so stupid for even talking to Jane.* Or, *She is so rude.*

Step 4: Little Adult's *Actions* Imagined and/or Actual

Write down what your Little Adult did—and also imagined doing—in an attempt to cope with the upsetting incident and feel better. Did you react to that remark or situation with a sarcastic comment or tone? Did you imagine punching that person in the nose? Did you choose to ignore how your Child felt, suppressing your feelings? For example, I wanted to pull her hair out, or find some way to make her look bad in front of everyone (imagined). Or: When I saw Jane later in the evening, I avoided her while acting like what she said had no effect on me (actual).

Helpful Tips—Using the Inner Alignment Chart

Here are some additional tips for filling in and using your Chart:

▷ You can use this method with any issue, not just issues that involve other people; however, for purposes of getting started, it's simpler if you choose an issue that involves another person.

▷ It's best to use present tense in order to create a more immediate experience. You will be writing in short, simple phrases about your experience. As a True Adult, you are being trained to be objective, clear, and concise—*Just the facts, Ma'am*. Little Adults are too reactive to be concise, so even by describing the incident briefly (as you saw Sherry do) you are developing your True Adult muscles of separateness.

▷ Feel free to start with thoughts first, and then feelings, based on what you're more aware of as you go. Write in the order that best suits you each time.

▷ Take your time as you fill in the information. Enjoy the process of observing your Child in this new way. It can be an illuminating experience, or it may even be uncomfortable or confusing. Your Child and Little Adult may not be accustomed to so much visibility. Just know that it's all part of the process and that you have the greatest potential for growth when you step outside of your comfort zone.

▷ After you've completed your Chart, continue to notice when upsetting situations arise in your day-to-day life. Write those down in your True Adult Log. Then, you can create a Chart for each of these situations. After you've charted at least four or five upsetting interactions, you will more easily notice and identify your Little Adult's strategies on a day-to-day basis.

As you continue to use the Inner Alignment Chart, your ability to instantaneously separate from your Little Adult, in any reactive situation, will increase.

Your Little Adult will relax when you, as a True Adult, are able to step in and provide what your Child really needs.

Over time, you'll learn to do the Chart mentally without needing to fill in the form. However, with experience, you may still find that physically filling in the Chart brings additional benefits. I recommend that you collect your Charts and review them periodically to identify the patterns of your Little Adult's reactions and behavior. Reviewing your Charts will also help you notice how your Little Adult's reactions diminish and eventually disappear when True Adult objectivity replaces the anguished, merged experience of Hurt Child and Little Adult.

In chapter 12, I will show you how to extend your Chart to include a True Adult's perspective on the upsetting incident, along with new options that become apparent for the most effective action in your situation.

By using an Inner Alignment Chart, you are taking a big step toward establishing healthy separateness between your True Adult and Child, as well as between your Hurt Child and Little Adult. Then, and only then, can you develop the ultimate relationship with yourself that is the source of all your creativity, self-expression, and joy.

▲

What's Next…

You now have a toolbox of I AM Training practices to develop and strengthen your relationship with yourself: the two empowerment notebooks (Child's Journal and True Adult Log), the Child–Adult Conversation, and the Inner Alignment Chart. The more you use these tools, the more you will be able to receive your Child and bring about resolution, peace, and a higher quality of relationship with everyone, whether they are romantic partners, close family members, coworkers, or new people you encounter in your everyday life.

In part III, I'll show you, in more in-depth sessions with my clients, how the Inner Alignment Chart and the Child–Adult Conversation work together to help heal past wounds and navigate the rough waters of life. By participating in the provided activities, you will attain three increasing levels of skill as you have Conversations with your Child. Such skill development will make possible a direct and intimate relationship with yourself for ongoing healing, growth, and power in your life.

Part III

DEEPENING *YOUR ULTIMATE RELATIONSHIP:*

Inner Alignment in Love, at Work, and at Home

AN ORIENTATION TO THE MORE COMPREHENSIVE CLIENT SESSIONS

I n part III, you will see how I AM Training works in extended sessions with my clients, giving you a sense of the depth of transformation that is possible when you develop a relationship with yourself.

You will join me as I train my clients to use the tools of Inner Alignment to heal their wounds and thus have more successful and fulfilling relationships. You will see how establishing Child–Adult connection leads to new possibilities for an empowered life with a long-term committed partner, with coworkers, superiors, and subordinates, and in families. While the specific issues covered in the following chapters may not be applicable to you, the process used is always relevant and valuable as a model for whatever you may be dealing with in your own life.

I want to share a few concepts that will orient you to the I AM Training sessions that follow in the next six chapters, and will help you to further your own personal process as you sit in on the sessions.

All clients and sessions are composites. The dialogues between my clients and me are representative, not actual. For the sake of clarity and efficiency, I have portrayed the clients expressing themselves more clearly—and understanding the process sooner—than is the average. I do this for demonstration purposes only, not to offer false representation that I AM Training is easy or fast, although it is for some. Each person learns at a unique rate of progress, as I've seen in my many years of guiding clients. Furthermore, we can't compare our process with another's, because each person's process unfolds in a multidimensional rather than a linear way. It's through regular practice that I AM Training becomes most engaging and life-changing.

Sessions are experiential. Because developing Inner Alignment is an extremely experiential process, it is best learned when you can witness the actual movement that occurs, and receive an authentic experience. By following the sessions, some of which are lengthy, you learn through immersion without needing to have a cognitive understanding of what's going on. Further, you have an opportunity to consider your own issues while observing my clients' processes.

Each session builds progressively. The sessions you'll be observing progressively demonstrate the deepening relationship that is possible through live Child–Adult Conversations. At the end of each chapter, I will provide you with activities that will enable you to use the tools of the Inner Alignment Chart and the Child–Adult Conversation to develop a relationship with your own Child. These activities take you through three levels of skill building, preparing you to have a Child–Adult Conversation on your own. They will strengthen you as a True Adult, empowering you to begin the lifelong process of growth and evolution that is possible with I AM Training.

Sessions use special terminology. When speaking to my clients, I use the term *Child* to refer to all aspects of the Child: Infinite Child, Hurt Child, and Coping Child or Little Adult. Occasionally, I use the more specific term, but only when necessary. I have chosen the more general term, Child, in most cases where the client's process doesn't require specificity.

Listen to the Child. As you read the sessions, do your best to listen, without effort or analysis, for how each client's Child makes sense. This will train you to listen in a new way to your own inner Child, as well as to your own physical children and the Children within us all. Learning to listen to the Child is the major theme of this book. In the sessions that follow, you will see how I train people to do that in their everyday life situations.

Your Child may communicate with you while you are reading. Children are beautifully raw and authentic. Therefore, while reading the words my clients express, your own Child may bring up material from your life, perhaps even material that seems unrelated to the issue at hand. Your job as a True Adult is simply to notice your Child without judgment, expectation, or agenda.

Keep your Child's Journal available while you read the sessions in case he or she wants to express something through writing. Or, take out your True Adult Log and record any insights your Infinite Child brings to you or observations you're having about your Child's experience. For example, Christy becomes a bit anxious when she meets new women. Or, Jeremy pulls his shoulders back and puffs out his chest when he sees other guys approaching.

Even if you are not moved to write in either of the two notebooks, know that simply noticing memories or insights that your Child brings to you has great value. Your receptivity lets your Child know that a Big Person (a True Adult) is finally available and interested, encouraging further communication.

CHAPTER 7

ROMANTIC RELATIONSHIPS: INNER ALIGNMENT IN LOVE

All romantic partnerships, whether a marriage, a long-term relationship, or even a new relationship, have their challenges. In the beginning stages, the challenge is to go from the bliss of falling in love to discovering a deeper level of intimacy: *in-to-me-see*. As the relationship progresses and more intimacy becomes possible, *staying* in love and keeping the magic alive become the challenge, as well as continuing to build on what you have. Whether you are in a beginning or a longer-term relationship, sustaining intimacy requires fulfilling a commitment, not only to the other person but also to yourself, on a day-to-day basis. Although it is challenging, you have an additional option: to live in a state of empowerment, exhilaration, and expansion.

Maybe you aren't in a romantic partnership, but you'd like to be. Have you been avoiding relationships because patterns from the past keep resurfacing, and you don't know how to deal with them? Perhaps you've become resigned; you no longer hold any hope of finding a life partner. With the tools of Inner Alignment, relationship challenges—which include not having one—occur not as problems, but as opportunities for growth and movement toward the possibility of deeper commitment, love, and fulfillment. Relationship, or the absence thereof, becomes an adventure, rather than the torturous or numbing experience so many people find themselves trapped in. This is because the healing of wounds becomes the vehicle for you as a True Adult to free your Little Adult and create a profound relationship with your Child.

In this chapter, my client Jennifer grapples with a common relationship issue, jealousy, as well as with a deeper issue, fear of abandonment. She learns how to connect with and empower her Child using the bridge of her receptivity as a True Adult. In her second session, in chapter 8, you will see how a trusting bond between Child and Adult develops, resulting in a surprising revelation and a new future for Jennifer.

The Never-Ending Honeymoon?

When you meet someone new and fall in love, it's glorious. You feel joyful, excited, and exhilarated about having this new person in your life. Your world is blissful, and your partner can do no wrong. Gradually, as you grow closer, each person feels safer to open up and express more and more of their uniqueness. Soon, there are two very different people in the relationship, paving the way for disillusionment and distrust. Conflicts arise, feelings get suppressed, and misunderstandings lead to your first argument, and then to your second. For most couples, it's an enormous challenge to deal with ongoing conflicts without killing the magic.

When conflicts don't get resolved, you eventually tell yourself that the relationship isn't working, that you're bored with it, or that your partner isn't the same person you fell in love with. But the fact is that no matter who your partner is, the same issues are going to come up in your relationships over and over again. Why? Because they are *your* issues, the ones that stem from your earliest wounds and traumas, when there was no True Adult available to receive your expression of pain. When you as a True Adult are not yet available to your Child, it's easy to expect that your romantic partner will "be there" for you unconditionally, filling in for the missing True Adult.

When a Little Adult is in charge of your relationship, you can't help but reinforce both your own as well as your partner's reactive judgments and defensiveness. Even minor conflicts tend to escalate into mushroom cloud proportions, threatening to destroy, or at least temporarily derail, your relationship. The fallout from such conflicts can go on for years, poisoning your relationship with resentment and creating serious obstacles to intimacy.

Or, you find yourself merely surviving, missing the intimacy and fulfillment you had hoped for. This is called *settling*, and it often looks and feels like being trapped. Settling is the best that most people believe they can hope for, given the dominance of Little Adults in most relationships.

Until you become a True Adult available for your Child, receiving his or her pain while healing the underlying wounds, you'll continue to run in circles with no chance of lasting intimacy. Those childhood wounds will still be triggered even when you as a True Adult are present. However, your Child will be able to share with you whatever you need to know to be able to heal the past. Painful conflicts are then easily diminished. When they do occur, those conflicts become opportunities for *upgrades* for each of you as individuals, as well as for the two of you as a couple.

I AM Training—the work of healing your old wounds—is similar to developing new muscles at the gym. You need to show up and be willing to do some weight lifting. There are plenty of weight-lifting opportunities in a relationship—more than in any other area of life. Long-term, committed partners tend to activate each other's deepest wounds. Without True Adult skills, they have no way of resolving what's happening *right now*, let alone what happened long ago.

A richly intimate, committed partnership for life is possible; the honeymoon doesn't ever have to end. As you are learning, your relationship with yourself is fundamental to your relationship with your partner, because it is in your relationship with yourself that you do the deepest healing work for creating a profound relationship with your partner.

Let's look in on a session with Jennifer to see how she works with her relationship issues of jealousy and fear of abandonment. She learns about maintaining clear boundaries—*healthy separateness*—to gain her Child's trust so that powerful healing can occur. Once trust is established, Jennifer can engage in a Child–Adult Conversation to uncover the mystery of past events that are currently plaguing her relationship.

In Session With Jennifer:

Jealousy and Abandonment

Jennifer comes to see me for help in her relationship with her long-term, committed partner, Brian.

"Brian and I have been together for six years," she begins, her voice betraying the emotion she's trying to hold back. "But things haven't been going so well lately." She stops for a moment as a tear rolls down her cheek. I hand her a box of tissues and remain silent, continuing to bring her my full attention.

"I know he loves me, but whenever we go out socially, women hang all over him—he's so good-looking. I'm jealous when I see him laughing and flirting with other women, and I want to scream at him to stop. Why does he have to talk to other women when he's got me—aren't I enough?"

While I don't respond to Jennifer's rhetorical question, I continue to empathize with her painful self-reflection as she continues.

"So then I spend the evening comparing myself to every woman he talks to. *Am I as pretty as she is? Is she more interesting than I am?* It gets so bad that I start questioning whether Brian loves me at all.

"Sometimes I get so angry, I want to get back at him by flirting with every guy I talk to. But then I think, *What if he sees me and doesn't care?* That would really throw me off the cliff! This is how it goes, every time we go out.

"When we get home, I try to explain to him how jealous I feel. But he doesn't want to listen; he says, 'Jennifer, you know I love you and only you.

When I talk to other women at a party, I'm just having fun.' Then he kisses me, walks away, and turns on the television to watch sports. I'm left standing alone in the kitchen—where we usually have this conversation—while he heads for the couch with snacks and a beer.

"I feel bad for bringing up the jealousy thing, and I beat myself up for even having such feelings. All I really want is for him to listen to me. I go sit next to him on the couch and ask him to turn off the TV so we can talk. He mutes the TV but continues to stare at it.

"Finally, he tells me he's tired of talking about it. 'We live together; doesn't that tell you that I love you? I'm tired of you bugging me with your jealousy! And I'm tired of you not trusting me.'

"I say, 'But I just want you to listen to my feelings.... If you really loved me, you'd listen!' His response is, 'Look, this conversation is over! You're like this every time we go out. I just want to watch TV and go to bed.'

"At that point, Ron, I lose it and start yelling, 'You care more about your f-ing football game than me!' Then he shuts off the TV, gets up, and stalks off into the den, slamming and locking the door.

"I'm left feeling alone and desperate. I call through the door, 'Honey, I'm sorry! I don't want to argue, I love you.... Please don't do this to me!' I desperately need to feel like he still loves me. But he only yells back, 'Jennifer, get over it! I need some space right now!'

"I go back to the couch, sit down, and just cry. I feel so cut off from the man I love, as if I mean nothing to him. It's unbearable, Ron!" Jennifer pauses, visibly hurting as she recalls these painful events. "The next thing I know, I'm angry at myself for being so weak. I know I'm only pushing him further and further away by causing these scenes, but I can't seem to stop myself. I hate myself for being so pitiful, for telling him I love him and feeling so desperate to connect with him—especially after he's just slammed the door in my face!"

Making It Personal

Stop and think for a moment: Have you ever had a fight with your significant other that left you feeling the way Jennifer felt? You want desperately to connect and to know that you matter to your partner, but everything you do only drives a deeper wedge between the two of you. You feel stuck and alone with your feelings, blaming yourself, your partner, or both, and not knowing what to do.

Or maybe you've been in Brian's position, frustrated by your significant other's jealousy or complaint. In a fit of anger and blame, you slam the door, literally or figuratively, taking some space to regain your equilibrium. Like your partner, you feel unheard, cut off, and misunderstood—basically that what you have to say doesn't matter and that you're powerless to make things right.

In most relationships, partners point to the other—or even blame themselves—as the cause of the conflict. However, with I AM Training, you learn to look to your inner relationship for the source of your feelings.

As you read along, keep your Child's Journal and True Adult Log close and open, available for you to write down your Child's experiences and True Adult observations.

Jennifer sits silently, staring at the floor.

I wait, having listened carefully to her Child's expression of feelings, as well as her Little Adult's expression of judgment and both imagined and/or actual actions. Now, in a soft voice, I speak, reflecting back with empathy all that Jennifer has shared with me, a natural response to my connection into her Child's experience.

Jennifer sighs, raises her eyes from the floor and looks at me. "Ron, I actually feel like you heard me, and that feels pretty foreign, to be honest. Thank you so much. It's like… my feelings are okay, and even what I think is okay. I'm already feeling better!"

But this is only the beginning for Jennifer. As I did with my clients Joe and Sherry, I now invite Jennifer to do what I have just done, which is to be the True

Adult for her Child. This will be the birth of her *ultimate relationship*, which will deepen as she learns to relate to her Child's world and discovers what it means to be a True Adult.

Jennifer's First Conversation With Her Child

I invite Jennifer to move out of the chair she's been sitting in and to take mine, the seat of the True Adult. "Now it's your turn to be a True Adult for your Child," I tell her. "By reflecting back to your Child the feelings and thoughts she has expressed, as I just did, you'll discover for yourself what it means to be a True Adult."

"But, Ron, you're the therapist.... How am I supposed to do what *you* just did?"

"You may be surprised, Jennifer, to discover that you have many of the same abilities that I do. In addition, you have the added benefit of knowing every detail of your Child's entire history, something that no one else will ever have. Given that we're not taught how to actually dialogue with ourselves, it may feel awkward at first. And, just as in any new relationship, it may take some time together before you feel a connection. But once you experience that connection between you and your Child, you'll find that she guides you to what she needs to hear you say. It will just feel right to say certain words. It's a very special, life-changing experience. Are you ready to step in?"

Jennifer nods, and I continue. "To begin, give yourself a little time to settle into your True Adult Seat, imagining that your Child is across from you. You can visualize your Child as you at a younger age, if that helps. If visualizing is difficult for you, just see if you can get an energetic sense of yourself sitting over there. Or, you can simply respond in the direction of the chair your Child was in.

"Now, recall what your Child just shared with me about Brian. Begin your sentences with *I hear that you're feeling...* and name the feeling. Or, *It's easy to see how you would feel…* and name the feeling. Repeat the words your Child used back to her and include as much detail as you can remember.

"If you can't remember anything your Child said, simply relax in your seat and experience sitting across from your Child. If you have a sense of what is going on with your Child, tell her what you do notice. For example, you could say: *I get that you're having a tough time right now.* Once you've shown your interest and care—in any way you are able—switch seats and respond from your Child's Seat so that your Child has an opportunity to speak and be heard.

"As you feel and understand what your Child is going through, reflect back frequently, using what I call *sense-making words*. For example, say to your Child: *It makes sense that you would feel insecure, because you see Brian with all those other women.* By speaking in this way, you are not agreeing or disagreeing with your Child, but rather letting her know that a True Adult is present and that she is being fully received by that True Adult—you."

Jennifer smiles and nods. "I get it. So now I'm going to be the therapist, the True Adult, for myself… right?"

"Yes, you're getting the idea. Now, one more thing before you begin. I recommend you address your Child by a nickname that she might like to be called, such as *Jenny.* Also, always use the personal pronoun *you,* as in *I get that you feel . . .* and name the feeling. By using this kind of objective language, you create an experience of healthy separateness between you as a True Adult and your Child sitting across from you. Establishing such separateness prevents you from losing your True Adult perspective, which would leave your Child feeling alone again."

Jennifer looks across at her Child's Seat and begins: "Little Jenny, I see how painful, frustrating, and confusing it has been for you, not knowing how to work out your jealousy with Brian. You try, but when Brian won't listen to you, you feel like you're making things worse. You get angry at yourself and then you judge yourself—and Brian—which only leaves you feeling even more helpless, overwhelmed, and frightened. No wonder you are exhausted and don't know where to turn!"

Jennifer looks at me, and I prompt her to switch seats. She then gets up and sits down in her Child's Seat. After a short silence, Jenny speaks. "Yes, that's exactly it. Finally, someone gets how hard this is for me."

She switches chairs again. Now, as a True Adult, she reflects these feelings back to her Child. "Yes, Jenny. It's been very hard for you not to have anyone to tell this to without feeling even more rejected and shut down."

Switching chairs, her Child responds. "Yes, and it does feel good to finally be able to say everything, and not be rejected... not be shut down."

After switching chairs, Jennifer speaks as a True Adult to her Child: "It's so new for you to be able to say whatever you need to say, and then to be truly heard without feeling judged or blown off."

Jennifer pauses and then looks over to me. "Ron, I don't know what to say now. I feel like we're done."

I respond: "This is a great beginning. Often when you have that feeling that you're done, it's time to switch seats. This is true in either seat, Child or Adult."

Jennifer moves into her Child's Seat and speaks. "Well, I do feel better, but I still don't know what to do about Brian. I'm afraid I'll push him again, try and get him to listen to me, and just blow it. I'm scared I won't have you there to support me—like Ron just was." Jennifer's Child stops and looks down at the carpet.

I sit in silence. After a few moments, I sense that Jennifer's Child needs a True Adult to step in. Speaking slowly and softly, I say, "When you're ready, I'd like to speak with your True Adult." After a moment, Jennifer switches seats, and I give her some valuable coaching to address her Child's fears.

"Your Child has just experienced you as a True Adult, present and available for her, here in my office. It makes sense that she would worry about being at home with Brian without you, as a True Adult, by her side. She has no reference for you as a True Adult with Brian. It's all very new for her."

117

I go on. "Your Child needs you to continue reflecting back her fear, so she can experience you receiving her further. Never directly answer a question coming from your Child, because remember, *it's never about what it seems to be about.* That's why you want to address the underlying problem, which is her need to be seen and heard by a True Adult. Just by having you respond as a True Adult, your Child will feel supported, and you will be furthering your ability to discover new, True Adult perspectives."

I pause and check in with her. "Are you ready?"

"Yes. I'm starting to understand. But before I talk with my Child, I want to say something to you. Even though it was hard not to say *I* and instead, to use my name, *Jenny*—as if I were talking to someone else—it felt so right! I had an experience of myself as *someone different* from my Child. This must be what you call *healthy separateness.*"

Jennifer straightens in her chair and begins again, as a True Adult, to address her Child. "Well, Jenny, it makes sense you would be afraid of how things might go at home with Brian. You've never had a True Adult with you before, so it makes sense that you wouldn't trust that having me with you would make any difference."

Jennifer changes seats and her Child responds: "I'm just so scared. I don't want to push Brian away again. I'm afraid he'll respond like before and tell me he can't do this anymore, can't go through another argument with me."

Jennifer switches again and speaks as a True Adult: "Of course, you don't know how *not* to get into the same argument; that's how it's always been. And you're afraid if you do, you'll push Brian away even more."

Jennifer is silent. Then she looks at me and says, "Ron, I don't know what else to say. I'm really afraid I won't be able to prevent another scene with Brian."

I reply: "Jennifer, you just did a great job responding to your Child's fear. By staying separate, as a True Adult, and choosing not to fall back into her fear, you are building True Adult muscles. As you and your Child continue to have conversations together, she will experience the healing that occurs naturally as the result of the relationship being developed between you. Simultaneously, she will be healing the wounds that relate to her issues with Brian.

"Meanwhile, your Child has a True Adult present and available for her, to receive whatever she is feeling. Your Child is on her way to discovering that she matters. She is being seen and heard, and isn't alone anymore. Further, having a True Adult show up allows your Little Adult to relax and let go of her need to be in control."

Jennifer nods and lets me know she is following me. "I don't know what to say now."

"That's perfect, Jennifer. You don't have to know what to say. Again, just open yourself to receive, silently, what your Child has shared with you and get a sense of how she's feeling. If you don't know the difference between what she's feeling and what you're feeling, just assume that what you're feeling is actually her; she's always sending her feelings and thoughts to you. It might be, at this point, that no further words are necessary. Just be with your Child and whatever feelings and thoughts are present. When you feel complete together, let me know."

Jennifer stares intently at the chair where her Child is sitting. She begins to slowly and rhythmically nod her head. She takes a deep breath, sighs, and smiles.

"Ron, I feel a remarkable sense of calm ... as if I just took care of myself, *by myself*, for the first time! It's like ... and this sounds crazy, but I was *there* for myself. My Child doesn't feel so alone, like she's so used to feeling. She feels heard and truly understood for the first time by the most important person in her life—*me*, as her True Adult!"

I nod, appreciating how quickly Jennifer has jumped into establishing True Adult presence and availability for her Child. "Congratulations! I can hear you are already beginning feeling the power of this relationship."

Before we end our session, I teach Jennifer how to fill in an Inner Alignment Chart. I explain how using a Chart to record upsetting events will support her in further separating from her Hurt Child and Little Adult, and emerging as a True Adult. I recommend that she fill in a Chart for any upsetting events she might experience before our next session, to use as a springboard for her next Child–Adult Conversation.

Your Turn:

Building True Adult Muscles

You are ready to begin training in healthy separateness to strengthen your True Adult muscles and prepare to have a Child–Adult Conversation on your own.

There are two parts to this activity: Part A gives you steps for creating your own Inner Alignment Chart for an issue regarding a love relationship. Part B gives you an opportunity to dialogue with your Child in a journal writing activity, practicing the transformational listening skills you learned in chapter 4.

A. *Chart Your Romantic Relationship Issue*

In chapter 6, you created your own Inner Alignment Chart and started to clearly distinguish your inner structures. Now, use a new copy of the Chart to look at a personal issue related to love relationships, such as jealousy, financial matters, or intimacy. In the next chapter, you will be using this new Chart as a guide for engaging in the first level of a Child–Adult Conversation.

Remember, the purpose of writing the Chart is to increase your awareness of your Hurt Child's feelings and your Little Adult's reactive thoughts and actions. This recognition helps you establish the experience of *healthy separateness*, strengthening yourself as a True Adult and deepening your ultimate relationship.

Download an Inner Alignment Chart template from my website (Inner-AlignmentMethod.com) and fill it in according to the following steps. For your convenience, I'm providing a review of the steps that were introduced in chapter 6. More detailed direction is available in chapter 6 on page 122.

MY INNER ALIGNMENT CHART

Step 1: The Incident

Briefly describe an upsetting interaction you had in your committed relationship or with your spouse. If you're single, use an upsetting interaction you had with someone close to you, perhaps a friend or family member. This can be an argument or any interaction in which things didn't go the way you would have wanted them to go and you were left with negative feelings. Keep it brief, 1 to 3 sentences.

Step 2: Hurt Child's *Feelings*

These include feelings about the interaction such as:

I feel angry.
I feel sad.

Step 3: Little Adult's Reactive *Thoughts*

These include judgments of yourself, of your partner, or both.

She's such a nag.
I'm so weak.

Step 4: Little Adult's *Actions* Imagined and/or Actual

Describe what your Little Adult imagined doing—either at the time of the incident, or later, upon reflection—and then ultimately did to cope with the upsetting situation.

I'm going to ignore her for a while.
From now on I'll just say, "Yes, Honey" to everything.

B. *Journal Activity: Write a Conversation using Sense-Making Commentary*

In chapter 5, you had a chance to write out a Child–Adult Conversation in your Child's Journal, using transformational listening to reflect back your Child's expression. Now, write another Conversation using the material from the Chart you just completed in part A for your love relationship issue. This time you will be adding a new component to your True Adult responses, that of *sense-making commentary*. This is the third step of transformational listening from chapter 4, which is reviewed below. When you, as a True Adult, respond to your Child by using sense-making commentary, your Child will feel more deeply heard and understood, further solidifying your mutual connection.

Below are directions for how to use sense-making commentary when responding to your Child.

HOW TO USE SENSE-MAKING COMMENTARY

1: Use sense-making commentary whenever you know what's behind your Child's experience

Don't worry about being right or wrong—your Child's response to what you say or write will let you know. If you don't know how your Child makes sense, stick with the simple reflection of your Child's words.

2: In reflecting back, use words that indicate *how* your Child makes sense

By using sense-making commentary, you are adding concrete validation to the simple reflection of your Child's words.

Here is an example: It *makes sense* that you would feel insecure, *because* Brian paid more attention to other women than to you. Here are a few variations:

It *makes sense* that you feel _____ because _____.

It's *easy to see* how you would feel____ because____.

Of course you would feel _____ because _____.

How could you not feel _____ because _____?

3: Remember the "because" part of the response

By adding a cause, when you know or sense one, you are assuring your Child that you're not just repeating the words he or she has said. Rather, you're assisting your Child to explore more deeply what the current incident has stirred up. This way, it can be cleared and healed.

4: Avoid saying "I understand"

Your Child makes sense regardless of whether or not you understand how. If you say, *I understand that you feel____*, the dialogue focuses on the experience of you, the speaker. If you say, *It makes sense that you feel____*, the dialogue remains focused on the Child. Avoid using *I understand*, except at those rare times when such wording might specifically feel good and right to your Child.

An example of a written Child–Adult Conversation using sense-making commentary is presented in the following journal entry, which Jennifer wrote when she was struggling with her jealousy and abandonment issues. You can see how she uses transformational listening to reflect back her Child's feelings, thoughts, and actions, adding sense-making commentary to make her Child feel even more heard and "gotten."

123

Jennifer's Child's Journal

Child: I feel so angry at Brian for telling me to just get over my jealousy. I feel so hurt when he says, "It's not an issue—I'm faithful!" And when I ask him to just listen to my feelings, he gets angry, goes into the den, and slams the door. Then I get angry at myself for being jealous. I know he's faithful. I feel like an idiot for being jealous whenever he talks to another woman at a party. I don't want to share about my jealousy with him anymore because he might shut me out again. I'm afraid I'll lose him if I keep talking about it. But why can't he just listen for once? Maybe I'll start flirting with a guy at the next party and see how he feels!

True Adult: Little Jenny, *it makes sense that you would feel* hurt and angry about how Brian is with women. *It must be* so hard to have Brian blow you off by just telling you that he is faithful. *Of course* you would be angry that he doesn't listen to you so you can feel heard and understood. And *it makes sense* that you would then judge yourself for being jealous, *because* you know that Brian is faithful. *It's easy to see* how you'd be afraid that if you can't talk to him, there would be no way to work out your feelings. And Jenny, *it makes sense* that if you don't know what else to do to feel better, you would think about flirting with another guy out of desperation, so Brian would see how it feels.

▲

What's Next...

In the next chapter, Jennifer returns for her second I AM Training session, and discovers how the trust that has developed in her newfound connection with her Child can help to heal hidden wounds from her past that have been painfully impacting her life.

CHAPTER 8

ROMANTIC RELATIONSHIPS: EXPONENTIAL HEALING

By now, you're seeing just how much the quality of your relationship with your spouse or long-term committed partner depends on the quality of the relationship you have with yourself. As you establish connection and build trust within yourself—between your Child and you as a developing True Adult—it becomes easier and more natural to sustain an intimate and trusting relationship with another person.

As you continue to use the Inner Alignment Chart to separate from your Hurt Child and Little Adult, drawing healthy inner boundaries, you simultaneously strengthen your True Adult muscles. Then, as a True Adult, you can connect with your Child for deeper healing of the issues that have kept you from having happy, gratifying relationships with others. In this chapter, you will receive training for your first spoken Child–Adult Conversation, supported in your back-and-forth dialogue by the words you wrote in your Chart for a love relationship issue.

A deeper level of healing is available for Jennifer when she returns for a follow-up session, and has her second Child–Adult Conversation on the jealousy and abandonment issues in her relationship with Brian. The revelation that Jennifer's Child brings to her frees Jennifer from the buried emotional pain that has been blocking intimacy in her relationship. You will see how she "time travels" with her Child, back to the original childhood incident—this time as the True Adult her Child has always needed, and has been waiting for all these years.

Exponential Healing

The conflicts you experience in your relationships today all stem from old wounding experiences that you've been carrying around with you since childhood. Now every argument you have with your partner triggers those old unresolved wounds, regardless of the subject matter of the argument. Anything that looks, feels, or sounds—even vaguely—like what happened long ago reminds your Child of an earlier trauma, and causes you to react in the present as you had to in the past.

The wounds of your childhood get reopened with each love relationship you have, making remarks and events seem so highly personal. Your Child is not bound by linear time, which is why your unhealed past is able to filter through to your present existence. But the fact is this: When you're having a negative emotional reaction to someone or something, it's *never* about what it seems to be about. It's always about something deeper, something buried in the past that is now beyond your conscious awareness.

Have you ever had an argument with a partner and gotten so heated up in the battle that you forgot what the argument was about in the first place? You forgot because the issue you were fighting over wasn't what the argument was actually about. While a fight about something as insignificant as who last cleaned up the kitchen may start and end with a litany of past kitchen offenses, it is still not about that. Rather, it's about your early wounding experiences as a Child, when you didn't feel seen, heard, or connected with by a True Adult, and thus felt powerless to make things right.

When you align with your Child, you are able to transcend time and revisit those events from your past that created the traumas that are still being activated in the present—that are still "alive." Then, every wound becomes an opportunity for you to take a quantum leap into profound healing. Such time travel takes you as a True Adult back into history, when a True Adult was needed but was absent. I call this process *exponential healing*, an accelerated healing of past wounds that transcends time and is permanent, resulting in *true* change.

Exponential healing is possible through Child–Adult Conversations that put your Little Adult comfortably to bed, freeing your Child to experience a different future, one that is free from the past. Your Child takes you back to the exact time and place where there was no True Adult to receive his or her expression of pain. This time, with you as a True Adult there to receive your Child, your internal wiring is updated, distinguishing who you have learned to be—a Little Adult—from who you actually are at your core—a Child of the Infinite. As a result of this time travel and the rewriting of your past, your present and future are instantly transformed.

Through such exponential healing, the baggage from your past magically disappears, as though the pain of historical events had occurred in someone else's life. You remember the events, but they no longer have power over you. You are free from the endless painful cycles of negativity that had been filling your space and sapping your energy. Increasingly, you feel a sense of being reborn, energized, inspired and ready to create your life. This is what maturing and evolving actually mean, and they are only possible to the extent that you have freed your Child from the past.

Let's go now into Jennifer's second session. You'll see how the core wounds beneath her jealousy and abandonment issues in her relationship with Brian are revealed through her Child–Adult Conversation, leading to the exponential healing of those wounds.

Jennifer's Second Session:

Healing the Past

When Jennifer returns a week after her first session, she is eager to learn more about how to deepen her relationship with her Child. She brings with her a few completed Charts about incidents that occurred during the week. As a result, she has expanded her ability to recognize that difficult feelings are always part of her Child's healing process, rather than the truth. After a brief greeting, we get started on Jennifer's next level of training.

"Jennifer, I want you to begin by asking your Child where she wants to sit and where she wants you, her True Adult to sit."

Jennifer's Child selects two different seats, and I guide her to begin in the True Adult Seat. As she settles in, I remind her of the need to become separate before starting to connect with her Child. This will help her, as a True Adult, to avoid getting pulled into and merging with her Hurt Child's feelings or her Little Adult's thoughts.

I begin. "Being separate in a Child–Adult Conversation means you maintain your objectivity. Imagine that you arrive for your session and begin talking anxiously about a stressful situation. I listen but lose my objectivity and react as though your feelings are my own feelings. I then become as visibly anxious as you are. How would you feel at that point?"

Jennifer responds, "It would be awful! I'd think there's no hope for me and my situation… that it's even worse than I thought it was."

"Exactly. As your therapist, you expect me not to get caught up in your emotions but to remain separate as a True Adult, knowing that nothing is wrong and that healing is on the way."

Jennifer nods in agreement, expressing her understanding.

I elaborate: "Now, consider that it's the same when your Child is upset or experiencing difficult feelings. As a True Adult, you want to be as objective as a therapist must be, essentially becoming a therapist for your Child, just as I am a therapist for you. You can listen with compassion and feel what your Child is feeling, yet you are fully able to distinguish that her feelings are not yours.

"To assist you in doing this, imagine there is an empty basket on your lap. Now visualize putting any burdensome feelings or thoughts you have into the basket. These feelings might include apprehension about how your Child is going to 'perform,' or judgments you have about this process. Then hand the basket over to the source of these feelings and thoughts, your Child sitting in the other seat. By giving back what belongs to your Child, you maintain a clear and empty space, freeing you to respond to whatever your Child brings up in our session with empathy, respect, and love."

Jennifer nods again, and I continue. "This will all become clearer as you continue to have Conversations with your Child and deepen your new relationship. The Inner Alignment Chart, your Child's Journal, and your True Adult Log are all powerful tools for developing your ability to remain separate. As you use them, you naturally define your inner boundaries to emerge as an increasingly solid, separate True Adult for your Child."

"Great, Ron. I'm ready to try it," Jennifer says eagerly. "I wrote out a Chart for a few incidents, and it was very helpful. Then something happened last night that I didn't get a chance to write a Chart for, and I'd like to tell you about it."

I invite Jennifer to move into her Child's Seat so she can share. "Okay, so last night, Brian and I went to a concert, and afterward we went out with a few friends to get something to eat. Everything was going great. I felt good with Brian and enjoyed talking with our friends. Then the waitress arrives, and I'm surprised to see it's Katie, an old friend from high school. I introduce her around the table, ending with, 'Katie, this is my boyfriend, Brian.' Katie smiles at Brian, who smiles back at her. Then, eyes still locked on Brian, she says, 'Jennifer, you struck gold!' Brian says something stupid about gold, and everyone laughs.

"Everyone except, of course, me. I'm seething. And then, to make matters worse, Katie puts her hand on Brian's shoulder and asks, 'What are you guys going to start out with?' As she takes our orders, Katie keeps eyeing Brian. And maybe he thinks I don't see, but I catch him smiling back at her a couple of times. Then, after Katie finally leaves, Brian turns to me and whispers in my ear how much he loves me. He kisses me on the cheek and says, 'Sweetheart, you've got some great friends.'"

Jennifer pauses, takes a deep breath, and continues. "The jealousy just roared through me—again! I didn't kiss Brian back but instead started talking with my friends. While we all chatted away, I felt like slapping Brian and running out of the restaurant. I felt so angry at him and at Katie, whom I hadn't seen for years. Then I started judging myself again for feeling so upset, but I vowed that I wouldn't bring my jealousy up to Brian when we got home."

Jennifer now sits, arms crossed, in silence. After a few moments, I say to her, "When you're ready, I'd like to speak with your True Adult."

She stands up, walks over to her True Adult Seat, and sits down. As a True Adult, Jennifer looks over at me and acknowledges, "I'm still feeling my Child's feelings pretty strongly. Maybe I should take a moment to get separate."

I smile and nod, appreciating her recognition. "Jennifer, I'm so impressed with your self-awareness. It takes separateness to realize that you need to become more separate. You may want to try the basket visualization again and give your Child's feelings back to her. Let me know when you've done that, and I'll offer you some guidance for responding to your Child."

Jennifer begins to focus on becoming separate from her Child. After several moments, she looks with intensity in the direction of her Child and nods her head slowly. She then turns to me. "Okay. I'm ready. I may not be totally separate, but that seems pretty impossible, right?"

"Yes. Any degree of separateness you are able to establish, even a little, is an accomplishment to build upon. Having the Conversation with your Child, as you are about to do, will further strengthen your separateness, making it possible to have a deeper, healing interaction with your Child."

Receiving Her Child's Memories

I begin to coach Jennifer. "As best you can remember, reflect back your Hurt Child's feelings and Little Adult's thoughts that were just shared, including her judgments of Brian, Katie, and even herself. As you are doing this, be available to receive any memories associated with that experience that might come up."

Jennifer looks at me with concern. "But Ron, what if I don't remember anything?"

"It makes sense that you're concerned about not remembering anything from your childhood," I say, "because back then no one was available to receive your Child's feelings and help her explore her painful emotional experiences. As a result, the memories of those experiences have been kept behind a closed door, suppressed and inaccessible. It might take time for your Child to feel safe enough to bring them to you."

Jennifer nods in agreement and begins. "Little Jenny, I hear how jealous, angry, and humiliated you felt when Katie flirted with Brian and put her hand on his shoulder." Jennifer sighs audibly, then continues. "When you heard Katie tell you that you struck gold while staring at Brian, you were already starting to worry. Then, when you thought Brian was flirting back in front of everyone, you just imploded with jealousy."

Jennifer stops, and a few moments of silence pass. I have the sense she is receiving a memory from her Child, and coach her further. "Trust that when a memory comes to you, it is coming from your Child, moment by moment, rather than something that you are thinking of or making up. Then, speak the memory to your Child as it comes to you. As you continue trusting what your Child brings to you, you'll discover more and more details of the past event."

Suddenly, Jennifer leans forward and begins speaking to her Child, her voice shaking with emotion. "And, Jenny, it makes sense... it all makes sense... especially because when you were 11 years old and you had that special night with your dad.... It was right after the divorce, and you were so excited to be with him, just the two of you, for a special night out."

Jennifer pauses, receiving more of the memory her Child is giving her. Her Child is now feeling safe, having felt heard by her True Adult's sense-making commentary. She continues, "Little Jenny, you so loved being with him, just the two of you. It meant so much to you. And then, just as you were starting to feel close to your dad again, that woman he knew from work comes over and starts talking for what seemed like forever. Not just chatting, but smiling and laughing. And your dad focuses all his attention on her! Even though his arm is around you, he's only talking to her.

"Jenny, it makes perfect sense that you would feel so annoyed with your dad, and sad too, even as he tried to reassure you by putting his arm around you. Of course you would be angry with him for ignoring you on your special night out. You thought, *How could you do this to me when we get so little time together, just the two of us?*

"And yes . . ." Jennifer stops speaking, breathing deeper and faster as she stares straight ahead. My sense is that her Child is bringing more of the memory to her.

After a short silence, she resumes speaking. "Jenny, how could you not be angry when you whispered in your dad's ear that this is your special night together and he just kisses you and tells you that he loves you—and then goes back to talking and laughing with that woman?"

Jennifer is now present to her Child reliving the memory as if it were happening now—which, for her Child, it is. She remains separate as a True Adult, time traveling with her Child, back to that moment when she was an 11-year-old, struggling for her dad's attention.

She continues to reflect back the painful experience her Child is bringing to her. "It makes sense, Jenny, that you would feel so angry and sad. And it makes sense that you'd judge your dad for ignoring you and judge that woman for intruding on your special time. How could you not feel unimportant, and even worse... invisible?"

At this point, Jennifer stops. She takes a few deep breaths, covers her face with her hands, and starts to cry. I sit in silence, feeling deep compassion for her Hurt Child who is revealing this devastating piece of history. I'm also aware that Jennifer might understandably lose her separateness from her Child's feelings, now that she is more fully connected with her Child in this painful memory.

After a few moments, Jennifer stands up without a word and moves from her True Adult Seat into her Child's Seat. She dabs her eyes with a tissue and begins to speak. "I can't believe Dad would treat me like that. I know he loves me, but it's like I don't matter. As soon as anyone else is around, I become invisible. I hate that. He says I'm special, but that's only when no one else is around—particularly a pretty woman." Jennifer's Child pauses and looks down, then up at the empty chair across from her. She stands up and moves out of her Child's Seat and into her True Adult Seat.

"How painful for you, Jenny. You always felt special to your dad. It makes sense that you wouldn't feel very special when he ignores you for a woman he barely knows. Ever since your parents divorced, you've felt insecure in your relationship with your dad. I know you know he loves you, but it makes perfect sense that you don't feel very secure when he treats you like that."

Jennifer stands up and switches seats again.

"Exactly!" Jennifer's Child exclaims loudly, responding to her True Adult. "I wish it could be the way it was before he and Mom divorced. I was always my daddy's special girl..." Jennifer puts her head into her hands and breaks into deep sobs. I remain silent, present to her Child's suffering and honoring the sacred connection she is having with her True Adult.

After a few minutes, Jennifer stops crying, switches once again to her True Adult Seat and begins speaking to her Child. "Jenny, I can feel how much sadness you've held inside all these years since your parents got divorced." She pauses, then continues. "I can feel your pain. I get that you no longer feel like your daddy's special girl. All these years, you've felt abandoned, as if someone close to you had died. You've been carrying this all by yourself for years, never feeling safe enough to talk with anyone about it."

Jennifer moves and speaks from her Child's Seat: "Yes, and it feels so good to talk with you about it now. No one else could ever understand how it's been for me like you can. It happened so many times—at the zoo, out to lunch, or at some event. Women coming over to him and taking him away from me. And he always kept his arm around me—always! But still, I always felt left out... humiliated... angry... and alone!"

Jennifer switches and speaks again from her True Adult Seat: "I hear, Jenny, how this same scene happened so often for you, a woman taking your dad away from you. Even though he'd try to reassure you, you always felt humiliated, angry, alone... and sad."

She switches seats. "Now I'm remembering more," her Child says, letting out a deep sigh. "I was afraid that if I tried to get Daddy's attention back, he'd get angry with me and push me away. I was afraid if I made a scene, I'd lose his love."

Switching seats, True Adult Jennifer pauses for a moment, then leans forward. Her face lights up with a flash of insight. She looks at me and suddenly cries out, "Ron, it's exactly the same with Brian! My Child is afraid she'll lose his love if she demands too much, just like she was afraid to lose her dad's love! In fact, in all her other relationships, too, it was always the same way." Jennifer leans back in the chair.

I respond to her, "I can only imagine, Jennifer, what a relief it must be to discover what has been behind your relationship struggles with men. Now it would be great to express what you understand directly to your Child."

Jennifer turns and faces her Child. With newfound confidence and True Adult separateness, she says, "What a relief it must be for you, Jenny, to finally be able to express your deeply buried feelings about those painful times with your dad."

Jennifer's Child: "Yes! What was I supposed to do? I couldn't talk with anyone about it. And I was ashamed that I wasn't enough to hold my dad's attention. All this time since, I just kept pretending it would be different with the right man. But I was afraid, deep down, that it was just me—and that it would never be different."

Adult: "Of course you would think it must be your fault. What else were you supposed to think? Who could ever love and value you if, as it seemed, your own dad didn't?"

Child: "That's it! If my own father isn't interested in me when another female comes into the picture, why would any man be?" Jennifer's Child is silent, before exploding with frustration. "I hate this! I don't want to talk about it anymore."

Jennifer turns to me and says, "Ron, I guess we're done. My Child doesn't want to talk anymore."

Sensing from my own Child that Jenny is not finished yet, I reply softly. "I'd like you to switch seats, so I can speak with your True Adult."

Once she has switched, I continue. "My sense, Jennifer, is that your Child feels trapped and powerless, not actually finished. She is saying she doesn't want to talk anymore, because the programming that comes out of such wounding experiences always feels like the unchangeable truth. So naturally, your Child would feel hopeless, and that there's no point in speaking any more about it.

"Additionally, your Child isn't used to having an Adult there for her, as you are now. She needs you to connect with her further, rather than step away."

Jennifer takes my coaching and continues, addressing her Child. "Jenny, it makes so much sense that you wouldn't want to talk about this anymore. You always felt so helpless with your dad, like that's just how it is, as if it's etched in stone. No wonder you would go from being angry to feeling bad about yourself, and then give up in defeat. And it makes so much sense that you would repeat this pattern in all your relationships with men. Every time a seemingly similar incident happens, it throws you right back into that same cycle. It's been endless ever since those experiences with your dad."

Child: "That is so true! Ever since my dad treated me that way, I've felt that who I am isn't enough. All I could do was pretend to myself that I was enough. With Brian, I tell myself that *I* am his girlfriend, not those other women, just like I would tell myself when I was with my dad... that *I'm* his daughter. His arm is around *me*. *I'm* his special girl. But then it would wear off when he still seemed to be more interested in them. Just like Brian is with other women."

Adult: "What else were you supposed to think when your dad was choosing to focus on other women while he was with you? And since the divorce, he already wasn't spending much time with you. You already felt like you weren't his special girl anymore. You just tried to hold on to believing that you were special in those moments when you were with him. Then other women would show up and you'd snap back into that horrible feeling of losing him, just like your mom felt when your dad left her."

Jennifer pauses in her Conversation and addresses me: "Ron, this is astounding! I'm discovering so many new things I didn't know before. This memory just keeps on coming, and it's all making so much sense to me."

"You're discovering, Jennifer, that when you're open to your Child, she can take you where she needs you to go to heal her early wounds. Then, by reflecting back what you get from her, and expressing how she makes sense, you create the safety for her to share herself more fully." Jennifer beams with this acknowledgment of her new ability to effectively connect with her Child.

"Now, let's shift back to your Conversation with your Child."

Jennifer nods and, with some prompting, continues where she left off. "Jenny, how were you supposed to know that your father's behavior was not about you? Or that your mother's pain over losing her husband was not somehow

your fault? You were a young, vulnerable child with so many questions... so confused... and you had no one to talk to about any of it."

Child: "I was sort of in shock. I didn't know what was happening or what
to do. I just wanted to be with my daddy."

Jenny begins to sob and I continue opening my heart to the world of this
Child who until now has had no Big Person making it safe for her to express and
sort out her feelings. She was left on her own to maneuver around her feelings in
order for life to go on—the job of a Child in coping mode, the job of a Little Adult.
I am moved deeply by witnessing Jennifer as a developing True Adult who is
learning to step in on behalf of her much deserving Child.

After several emotional moments, Jenny lifts her head up and looks directly
at the seat of her True Adult across from her. She then stands up and moves
into it. As a True Adult, Jennifer focuses intently toward her Child for several
moments before she speaks.

"Wow, Jenny. That was like opening a full closet and letting all the clutter
spill out so you can sort through it. And I get that you needed me to be here with
you, so it wouldn't feel so scary and impossible—like how it's always felt for you
in the past."

Child: "Yes, I couldn't do this by myself! What were they thinking? That's
the problem.... Mom and Dad were so lost in their own stuff, they simply didn't
think about me at all. They couldn't even get through their own mess. They were
like me, an overwhelmed child, not knowing what to do with their own feelings,
let alone consider what I was going through. No wonder I didn't even try to talk
with them about any of it. It didn't even cross my mind."

Adult: "You're realizing that the way your parents were with you had nothing to do with you. In fact, it was all about what they were going through. They
were each a Child in coping mode. You felt you were totally on your own, just
like how you've felt with Brian and in your previous relationships. You needed
me to be here with you to finally be able to sort this all out."

Child: "That's so right! You're the only one who can really help me make sense of this. I would never be able to work it out with Brian without you helping me. Maybe I'll be different with him now that I've been able to speak with you."

Adult: "Little Jenny, you're realizing that having this Conversation with me can change how you are with Brian. And that may change how he is with you when other women come along. I hear you telling me right now that you don't know if that's how it works. But you do feel like something has changed inside of you, allowing you to be different."

Child: "Yeah. I don't even feel the need to think about Brian right now. I just feel so appreciative that I have you here with me, not focused on someone else instead of me. I can feel how much whatever I need to say matters to you. You really listen to me!"

Adult: "Jenny, I get how critical it has always been for you to feel truly seen and heard… and by me, the most important person, who will always be with you. No one else can get you like I can."

Child: "That is *so* right—it's shocking and wonderful! I want to have more of these Conversations with you."

Jennifer switches seats and then, as a True Adult, turns toward me. "Ron, I'm not sure what to say now."

I respond, "My sense is for you to now be silent with your Child and with what's been said between you."

Jennifer faces her Child intently for several moments, then slowly begins to nod her head. She turns to me. I see that she's ready for me to speak to her.

"Your Child felt safe enough to bring you more and more memories— *buried treasure* from the past—because she trusted that you, as a True Adult, would be there for her. She showed you how she was afraid to lose her dad's love. This revelation allowed you to see the connection between her relationship with her dad and her relationship with Brian, as well as with all her previous partners." I pause, noticing tears welling up in Jennifer's eyes.

Jennifer speaks to me quietly. "Yes, Jenny was afraid to lose her dad's love. And now she's worried that the same thing will happen with Brian."

I respond: "And because there was no adult to help her heal that early wound, it has resurfaced over and over again, causing problems in all her relationships with men."

Still in her True Adult Seat, Jennifer shakes her head. "I'm feeling the same way with Brian as I did with my dad… jealous of other women, angry, judging him for not loving me enough… and then getting that reassuring kiss and words of love from him that I never trust! Now with Brian, just like with my… I mean *her* dad… she, my Child, is feeling ignored, unloved, unheard—and yes, like she's *invisible!*"

I interject with further coaching. "Now share that powerful insight with your Child directly."

Jennifer's eyes close, and she is still as she experiences the intensity of her insight. After a moment, she turns to speak to her Child.

"Jenny, I can feel how critical it is for us to talk together like this. It's making a whole lot of sense to me why you've gotten so upset with Brian. Of course you would feel angry, jealous, and sad when he is enjoying the company of other women and not focusing on you. It feels exactly the same as it did with your dad. And even more, it's upsetting when he tells you he loves you and that you shouldn't be bothered by what he does." She pauses and then goes on. "Jenny, how could you not be *very* bothered by what Brian does when you feel exactly the way you felt with your dad?"

Jennifer begins to cry—a slow, soft sobbing. After a little while, she looks up, wiping away tears as she switches into her Child's Seat and says, "It helps so much to have you here to talk with me…. I never felt that anyone cared enough to listen, so I've never told anyone about this."

Jennifer's Child pauses for a moment and seems to shift with her new experience of having someone else by her side. She speaks again to her True Adult.

"I'd like you to talk with Brian about all of this, because maybe it will turn out differently than if I try to talk with him," Jenny says, a note of relief in her voice.

Her True Adult responds, "It makes sense, Jenny, that you'd want me to talk with Brian about this. It's not fair for a child to carry that burden, especially when talking has never worked with Brian or your dad. You need an adult's voice to speak on your behalf—mine, the voice of your True Adult."

Sensing that both her Child and True Adult have finished their Conversation, I speak. "It's always best to give your Child the last opportunity to speak, even if she says nothing. Then, receive your Child and what she has shared with you in silence, like you did before."

Jennifer switches seats. Now, as Jenny, she sits straight up in her chair—silent, powerful, and content.

Then, after moving back into her True Adult Seat, Jennifer exudes elation and confidence as she gazes deeply at her Child's Seat for a minute or two. She slowly nods to her Child, turns to me, and smiles. I smile back, affirming the profound difference that Jennifer has so bravely made in her Child's life. Her session is now over.

Jennifer's Ongoing Transformation

Jennifer leaves my office with a new sense of her Child's presence in her life. As a True Adult, she's learned to recognize that her jealous feelings toward Brian belong to her Child. Her Child had been trapped in the past, repeating the trauma with her dad over and over again, until her True Adult was finally present to receive her painful memories. The connection Jennifer's Child now experiences with her True Adult has begun the deep healing of her relationship issues. This is the magic of *exponential healing.*

Over the next several months, Jennifer continued to work with me once a week to practice having Conversations with her Child. She also made remarkable progress using I AM Training on her own. Little by little, she was able to piece together so much history that had long since been buried. The more this history surfaced, the more Jennifer was able to listen to and receive her Child's expression of painful feelings. Her Child felt unburdened, light, and free, finally supported by the transformational listening of a True Adult.

Jennifer was pleasantly surprised to find that, as a result of her new relationship with her Child, her relationship with Brian continued to improve. During follow-up sessions, Jennifer shared her progress with me.

"I've been able to talk with Brian about my Child's past experiences," she told me. "Instead of feeling angry with Brian, as I did when I used to share my feelings with him, I now feel separate as I tell him how little Jenny is feeling. It's like I'm an adult speaking with Brian about a child... someone we both love and care about. He tells me he doesn't feel me pushing him away or becoming cold and distant anymore. Instead, he feels respected and valued when I share my Child's vulnerable feelings with him.

"Then we get to share with each other. We've been exploring his feelings and history as well. It's like we're wise and devoted parents, exploring what's going on with our children. We're learning what it means to actually get to the bottom of a problem and clear it up for real."

By using the tools of I AM Training, Jennifer and Brian have learned to explore difficult emotions as they come up, knowing those feelings are never about what they seem to be about. Rather, they are always about wounds from each of their individual histories. They still have upsets and struggles in their relationship, but such conflicts are now understood and worked with as opportunities for healing. As a result, Jennifer and Brian's relationship has deepened, becoming more profound and joyous for both of them.

Your Turn:

Having a Child–Adult Conversation—Level 1

In this activity, you begin to build the skills needed to have a spoken Child–Adult Conversation. For this first level of skill building, you will read out loud from the Inner Alignment Chart you filled in for a love relationship issue in chapter 7. In the upcoming chapters, you will develop your skills further by adding a physical back-and-forth movement to match your dialogue (level 2). You'll also add the True Adult response of sense-making commentary (level 3) to connect more deeply with your Child.

On level 1, begin by reading your Chart all the way through as your Child, and then read it again as a True Adult. These two positions, Child and Adult, will become the two voices in a Child–Adult Conversation. By speaking in and listening to both voices, you begin, as a True Adult, to have a Conversation with your Child. It may be interesting to note that some people find that their spoken voice is different in each seat, while others find their voice remains the same. Any way your voice is expressed is the right way for you.

Think of using your Chart as "training wheels" for learning to have a spoken Child–Adult Conversation. You've seen my clients have Conversations with my assistance, but when you attempt to have your own Conversations, it can feel awkward. Your Inner Alignment Chart will make it easier by guiding each side of the conversation, using the words you have written on the Chart as a script. At some point, you will develop enough skill to have spontaneous Conversations without needing the Chart for support.

Here are the directions for having a first-level Child–Adult Conversation:

LEVEL 1: READING YOUR CHART AS CHILD AND AS TRUE ADULT

1: Set up two chairs

They should face each other and be clearly distinguished as the Child's Seat and the True Adult Seat. (Labeling each designated chair with a 3-by-5-inch card can be helpful in the beginning.)

2: Begin in the Child's Seat and read the Chart out loud all the way through

Read each item within each section, using the pronoun *I*.

3: Switch to the True Adult Seat and read the Chart out loud again

This time, use the pronoun *you* to reflect back your Child's words.

4: Switch back to the Child's Seat when you are finished

Sit silently for a moment and experience any feelings and thoughts that are present for you in your Child's Seat.

5: Switch to the True Adult Seat when you are ready

Now that you have read your Chart in both voices, sit for a moment and silently receive any feelings or thoughts coming from your Child.

When you are finished, take the opportunity to express any feelings that may have come up during the activity by writing in your Child's Journal. These feelings can be negative, positive, or both. Also, write your observations and insights about your Child's experience in your True Adult Log. Writing in your empowerment notebooks is always valuable, *even if you only write one or two sentences.* For your Child, there is an experience of mattering to someone who is paying attention. For you as a True Adult, separateness and solidity build with each log entry.

▲

What's Next...

In this chapter, you saw how a Child–Adult Conversation can help resolve issues in a love relationship by allowing you, almost literally, to travel back in time and revisit the origins of wounds that are causing your current upsets and conflicts. In the next chapter, you will see how the Child–Adult Conversation illuminates issues that arise in the relationships you have with the people in your workplace.

CHAPTER 9

WORKPLACE RELATIONSHIPS: INNER ALIGNMENT AT WORK

Whatever your occupation is—whether you work in a big corporation or a small business, whether you are an entrepreneur or a practicing professional—you have probably experienced a good deal of Little Adult activity in the workplace.

Little Adults—Children in coping mode—are everywhere. They can be clerical workers, medical, legal, or other professionals, skilled laborers, public servants, even CEOs—anyone in any position. Some strive to move up and get ahead, others hang back and underachieve, but all are engaged in protecting their Child at the cost of any deep satisfaction and fulfillment in their jobs.

When you are in Little Adult mode at work, as in any other situation, you are always simply doing the best you can to make your life work. In those moments, your efforts are based on what you learned in childhood about how to win approval from the Big People in order to fit in and survive in the world.

In contrast, True Adults in the workplace are less common, the exception rather than the rule. Whether serving in a leadership position or as a supporting member of a team, a True Adult is recognized not only by the qualities of dedication and responsibility, but also by those of authenticity, receptivity and integrity. Openness and availability are qualities that you develop when you practice I AM Training and strengthen your connection with your Child. As your Little Adult relaxes, safe in the presence of you as a True Adult, you experience True Adult leadership that empowers you to create the greatest possible outcome in any situation.

In these next two chapters, you will see how my client Randall resolves his workplace issues by using the tools you have been working with: the Child's Journal and True Adult Log, the Inner Alignment Chart, and the Child–Adult Conversation. You saw previously how Jennifer was able to become separate from her Child's coping methods and connect with her Child to resolve issues in her love relationship. Randall goes through the same process in his sessions, but he learns to use his new skills when difficult interactions occur at his workplace, helping him to deal with his feelings and reactive thoughts that have led to serious problems for him.

Let's go into a session with Randall to see how he uses one of the tools of I AM Training to work through issues he's having in the workplace. Then, in his second session, you'll see how Randall engages in a Child–Adult Conversation to reveal the roots of his difficulties, leading him to a new experience of himself.

In Session with Randall:
Anxiety, Humiliation, and Isolation

Having been referred by his friend, Randall comes to see me because of job-related anxiety and insomnia. He works at a branch of a large department store where he has recently been promoted to the position of retail sales manager.

As we start the session, Randall sits on the couch across from me. He is professionally dressed and seems relatively confident.

"I've been a manager now for three months, and I feel like I'm stuck between a rock and a hard place," he begins. "I want to do my job and do it well, but the people in my department are gossiping about me behind my back. Not all of them, of course…" Randall pauses, inhales deeply, and then frowns. "Some are nice to me—but really only to my face. Behind my back, they're saying that I don't know what I'm doing… that I'm not as good as our previous manager."

Randall pauses, looks down at his feet, and appears to be holding his breath. He continues. "They tell jokes about me, like I'm the substitute middle school teacher. And they treat me like I am a substitute, not their real boss. It's hard, because I'm managing people who used to be my peers." Randall's voice is strained.

"I've tried talking with my boss about the situation, but he brushes me off. 'They're probably just jealous because you got promoted first,' he says. Then he tells me to stop worrying about it, that it goes with the territory. To top it off, he tells me, 'You'd better get used to it. You need a thick skin if you want to keep this job.' After talking with him, I end up feeling even more pressure and worry than I did before." Randall looks at me, clearly exasperated. "I'm afraid I'll mess up, lose my promotion, maybe even my job," he says, before pausing to take a deep breath.

"To make matters worse, one of the salespeople who wanted my job, a guy named Bill, is trying to turn everyone against me. I catch him whispering with other sales staff that I now supervise. They laugh and then look right at me. It's unnerving.

"Sometimes I want to confront Bill and use my authority to tell him to knock it off. Or call a meeting with my team to talk about what's going on. But I'm afraid those siding with him will pretend that nothing is happening and make me look like a fool. They'd like that, to make me look bad, so my boss would have a good reason to come down on me."

Randall pauses to reflect. "I went to my boss about Bill a second time, but he gave me the same advice as before: 'A good manager puts his feelings aside and gets the job done. He doesn't let other people's pettiness get in the way of his job.'

"I keep thinking about what he said, but it doesn't seem to help. I still go home every night feeling angry and anxious. I'm angry at myself for letting Bill get to me and for not having a thicker skin. I want to write him up and get back at him. Then I worry that if I do something like that, he'll go straight to my boss and make up some story, and my boss will get on my case and replace me with Bill."

Randall shakes his head. "Ron, I don't know what to do with all these feelings. Every night, I worry so much that I don't sleep well. Then I'm tired and stressed out when I go to work. I've even tried to approach Bill to talk with him, but he gave me a look that said *Don't bother me,* and walked away. I'm feeling so angry… so frustrated… and alone."

Having expressed his anxiety about his workplace situation, Randall now sits silently in his chair. I too am silent, allowing myself to feel the emotions Randall has expressed, while at the same time maintaining a sufficient degree of healthy separateness to be effective as a therapist and True Adult.

After a few moments, I speak, reflecting back to Randall the message I have been hearing from his Child. "Randall, I get how difficult and painful it's been for you, being a new manager. Instead of finding your friends and coworkers supportive of your new status, you're feeling unsupported and even threatened by many of your coworkers, and even your boss. It's easy to see how you'd feel angry, anxious, and confused about what to do—all at the same time. You feel like your new job is on the line, unless you pretend that all this upset and negativity doesn't exist. But obviously, that doesn't work. So it makes sense that you'd be up at night, trying to figure out how to deal with such a challenging and threatening circumstance and the turmoil you feel as a result. That's a whole lot to deal with all at once." I pause.

Randall takes a deep breath and exhales slowly. His face relaxes as he starts to speak. "Ron, for the first time since I became a manager, I feel some relief. Just listening to you say it back, really getting me… I don't know why… I just feel more relaxed." He pauses, then declares to himself as much as to me, "Actually, it's like finally someone is hearing me!"

I smile and respond, "Randall, you feel relieved, because your feelings— what I call your Child's feelings—have just been heard without any judgment, advice, or threat. You were able to hear that all of your feelings and thoughts are completely valid and acceptable.

"Your Child is someone you will be getting to know more and more. With I AM Training, I'll be showing you that your spontaneous emotional responses—the anxiety and anger you've been experiencing—are your Hurt Child's responses to what's happening in your life at any given moment."

Randall is catching on. "Okay, Ron, so my Hurt Child is the one who has all these feelings, but what about my thoughts? What about when I beat myself up for letting Bill get to me, or when I think about getting back at him by writing him up? And when I imagine Bill going to my boss and turning him against me—all these anxious thoughts that keep me up at night. How do they figure into your approach?"

"Those thoughts that come up right after your Hurt Child's feelings belong to what I call your Coping Child." I give Randall a basic orientation to the Inner Alignment Relationship Model: Child—Infinite, Hurt, and Coping (Little Adult)—and True Adult. I remain silent, giving him the space to respond.

"Ron, now I realize what I've been doing at work," he replies quickly. "I've been squashing my feelings, judging myself and other people, and then trying to come up with all these strategies. At the same time, I'm trying to maintain my professionalism as a manager. But the more I try to act professionally, like my boss wants me to, the worse things get. I… my Little Adult… just doesn't know what else to do."

Making It Personal

We've all learned, like Randall, to "act professionally" when difficult situations arise at work. As a Little Adult, you want to fit in and meet others' expectations in order to keep your job (or if you're self-employed, to keep customers or clients). Typically, however, acting professionally means *not* expressing your feelings, the emotions that belong to your Child. And while it may not be in your best interest to express such feelings at work, they do need expression. But rather than express your feelings in their raw, reactive form, such as anger, you learn how to clear them out so that you can then express them in a responsible and effective way.

Take a moment and identify a situation in your workplace—past or present— involving another person who has been difficult for you to work with. (If you are self-employed, choose a situation with a customer, client or colleague.) This might be someone who is verbally abusive or hostile in a nonverbal way. Or choose any workplace situation that has left you feeling irritated or anxious.

Stop and ask yourself: *How do I usually deal with this person or situation?*

Do you, like Randall, try to ignore what's going on, suppress your feelings, and then beat yourself up for being so weak? Or do you blame the person or situation, judging others or yourself and using a pejorative label *(I'm/ he's such an idiot!)?* Maybe you try to manage the situation by confronting people in an attacking, manipulating, or strategizing way. In any scenario, whether you are reacting by pushing your feelings down or venting them through confrontation, your Little Adult is doing his or her best to cope.

Keep your Child's Journal and True Adult Log close by as you continue to move through the chapters in case any feelings or thoughts get stirred up for you. It is a valuable opportunity to build your inner relationship by inviting your Child to express in your Child's Journal whatever surfaces, and for you to write any meaningful observations in your True Adult Log.

Randall's next question comes naturally as a result of the insight he's just gained. "So how do I deal with these feelings when I'm working at the store? I mean, those times when I get so upset about Bill? And also at night, when I want to go to sleep and can't because I'm in such turmoil?"

"This is the question, Randall. You need to be able to deal with your emotions when they're happening, both at work and at night when you can't sleep, and I can help you do that. The first step is to fill in an Inner Alignment Chart."

I give Randall a blank Chart and show him how to use it. I explain how, by writing in his Chart, he will be able to distinguish his Hurt Child's emotions from his Little Adult's coping methods—reactive thoughts and actions. This is the beginning of Randall's training in healthy separateness, which he will need in order to connect with his Child and develop his perspective as a True Adult.

Here is how Randall filled in his Chart for his situation at work:

Randall's Inner Alignment Chart

Incident – I attempt to talk with Bill and hash things out. I walk toward him, but he gives me a look that says *Don't bother me*, and walks away.

Hurt Child's Feelings	Little Adult's Reactive Thoughts (usually judgments of self or others)	Little Adult's *Actions* Imagined and/or Actual
I feel Angry		Imagined:
I feel Humiliated	He's such a jerk.	I'll surround myself with my friends on
I feel Frustrated	I'm so mad at myself for even being bothered by this thing.	the team and act with indifference toward Bill and his
I feel Anxious	I can't win here.	friends.
	Bill's a sore loser.	**Actual:**
I feel Tormented	I should be able to handle this.	I'm just going to act like it doesn't
	I need a thicker skin like my brother.	bother me.
		I'll keep trying to be strong and thick-skinned.

After Randall completes his Inner Alignment Chart, I invite him to read it out loud, first as his Child and then as his True Adult. (You had a chance to do the same back-and-forth activity at the end of chapter 8 when you read your Chart out loud.) In doing this activity, Randall's Child experiences being heard, while he simultaneously develops himself as a True Adult. Randall is now ready to strengthen himself further as a True Adult by having a Conversation with his Child that will begin to heal the wounds from his past.

True Adult Training

Randall's development as a True Adult begins when I ask him to recall our earlier interaction.

"When you first told me about your problems at work, do you remember how I responded to you?"

"Yes, you repeated back to me what I'd said to you. You also told me that my feelings were not messed up, that they actually made sense. It was a tremendous relief when you did that."

"I'm so glad. You certainly deserve tremendous relief. As a True Adult, I was listening to you and responding in a way that gives you a reference for how your Child can be accurately heard and understood," I explain. "When you as a True Adult step in, as I did, and reflect back your Child's feelings and thoughts without judgments or opinions, your Child feels validated, supported, and gotten, and relieved because—finally—a True Adult is here!

"Now back to your question, Randall, about dealing with your emotions at work or when you're lying in bed at night, worrying about something that happened during your day." Randall leans forward as I continue. "You already began to do for your Child what I did—see and hear him—just by writing the Chart. Later, you will learn how to interact with your Child, just as I interacted with your Child a little while ago. In other words, I'm going to train you to be a True Adult for your Child, so that your emotions no longer take over your experience, especially when you need to be focused and effective in your life."

Randall's eyes open wide. "Really? Is that what a True Adult is?"

"Yes, and it's a truly profound experience, as you'll see. I'm going to show you how to be a True Adult anytime and anywhere, even at work. The truth is, you can be a better True Adult for your Child than anyone else could ever be because you have access to every thought, feeling, and experience your Child has ever had—the movie of your life.

"As you develop your ability to be a True Adult, you'll gain a sense of calm, inner connection, and emotional well-being. You'll support your Child in authentically expressing himself to others—powerfully and effectively. This is something your Little Adult could succeed at only superficially, at best, because your Child's deeper feelings had been unaddressed all these years."

Randall nods quizzically. "I think I understand Ron, but how can I possibly do this True Adult thing on my own—the way you are doing it with me?"

I explain: "You can, Randall. The key is learning to have a Child–Adult Conversation. You'll have an opportunity to do that in our next session."

Randall's session is a few minutes away from ending, so I begin to wrap it up. "Right now, all this is merely a preview of what's in store for you. As you go through I AM Training and cultivate a relationship with yourself, your inner relationship will become as real to you as the relationships you have with the people in your life. In fact, it will be even more intimate and profound."

Randall breaks into a grin and punches the air with his fist. "Yes!" he exclaims, confirming his understanding.

"To get you ready, I want to show you an activity that will help you to see what is really going on when you are upset by incidents at work."

I give Randall another blank Chart and tell him to fill it in over the coming week when any upsetting situation arises at the store. I instruct him to read his Chart out loud, just as he did in our session, but this time he will be doing it in the moment, in a private place where he can't be overheard. I let him know that when he returns for his second session, I will coach him in a Child–Adult Conversation regarding that issue.

Your Turn:
Building True Adult Muscles

The following activity will continue to strengthen your True Adult muscles and prepare you to have a Conversation with your Child. Again, there are two parts to this activity. Part A gives you the steps to fill in your own Inner Alignment Chart. Part B provides you with an opportunity to dialogue with your Child in writing, practicing the transformational listening skills you learned in chapter 4.

153

A. *Chart for Your Workplace Issue*

In this activity, you will be filling in a Chart for an issue you have with a person or a situation at your workplace. The issue might be a dominating boss, a disrespectful employee, or impatient or irate customers or clients. If you have no workplace issues or don't currently work, use an issue you had in the past. In the next chapter, you will use this Chart to have the second level of a Child–Adult Conversation.

Download an Inner Alignment Chart template from my website (Inner-AlignmentMethod.com) and fill it in according to the following steps. Again, the steps are a review of those that were introduced in chapter 6.

FILLING IN YOUR *INNER ALIGNMENT CHART*

Step 1: The Incident

Briefly describe an upsetting interaction you had with someone in your workplace. This might be an argument or any interaction during which things didn't go the way you would have wanted them to go and you were left with negative feelings. Keep it in present tense, and brief - 1 to 3 sentences.

Step 2: Hurt Child's *Feelings*

This might include feelings about the interaction such as anger, sadness, etc.

Step 3: Little Adult's Reactive *Thoughts*

These include judgments of yourself and of the other person or people.

Step 4: Little Adult's *Actions*, Imagined and/or Actual

Describe what your Little Adult imagined doing—either at the time of the incident, or later, upon reflection—and then ultimately did to cope with the upsetting situation.

B. *Journal Activity: Further Practice in Sense-Making Commentary*

In chapter 7, you had a chance to use your Inner Alignment Chart to write out a Child–Adult Conversation in your Child's Journal. You practiced transformational listening and included sense-making commentary, as described in chapter 4, page 74 and 75, and chapter 7, page 150 and 151. Now, write another Conversation using the material from the Chart you created for your workplace issue.

▲

What's Next…

In the next chapter, Randall returns to my office for his second session. Having completed his Chart assignment for an incident at his store, he is now ready to have a Child–Adult Conversation, leading to the exponential healing of the wounds that are at the root of his workplace issues.

CHAPTER 10

WORKPLACE RELATIONSHIPS: EXPONENTIAL HEALING

R andall's next session is scheduled for the following week, but two days after our first meeting, I receive a voice mail message from him.

"Ron, this is Randall," an excited voice declares. "I did the Chart and then read it out loud in my office with the door closed, just like you said to do. Luckily, no one knocked on the door. What happened was incredible! If you have the time, I'd like another session this week."

Randall's Second Session:

Upset: Your Ticket to Empowerment

Only three days after his first session, Randall is back in my office, sitting across from me. He can't speak fast enough.

"It's the day after our session, and I'm working with one of our new salespeople. Bill walks by me, stops and smiles at the new employee, and says to her, 'After you're done with him, I'll give you some tips that will really help you.' Without even looking at me, he walks away.

"I'm pissed off, but I don't want the new employee to know, so I tell her to take a 15-minute break. I rush to my office, close the door, and pull out my charting notebook to do a Chart. I write it all down so fast, I think the pen's gonna fly right out of my hand!"

He pauses and then races on: "When I finish writing, I read it out loud, first as my Child. Then I read it again, but this time as a True Adult. When I was finished, I just sat there. I felt so good! No memories came up from my childhood, like you said they might, but I got a feeling of relief right away."

"Congratulations, Randall! You created a powerful experience of being there for your Child right when he needed you. The Inner Alignment Chart you filled in helped you to separate your Child's feelings from your Little Adult's reactions. When you read it out loud, your Child had the experience of being seen, heard, and connected with by a True Adult. Just by doing that, you are strengthening yourself as a True Adult and building your relationship with your Child.

"In today's session, I'd like to take you even further, by showing you how to have a Child–Adult Conversation." I invite Randall to choose a seat for his Child and another seat for the True Adult he will become. He signals his choices and then, following my guidance, begins in the True Adult Seat. I explain to him the physical back-and-forth motion of a Conversation, as well as the impact transformational listening can have when he reflects what his Child says back to him.

"You've experienced the positive difference you made for your Child when you connected with him through the Chart. So, you won't be surprised by the difference you'll notice when you connect with your Child through a Chart-guided conversation. Again, be available for him to bring up memories from childhood that will provide you with valuable information about his past."

Randall turns to me inquisitively and asks, "Okay, Ron, but how will I know if I'm doing the True Adult right?"

"Good question," I reply. "First of all, you will be doing the same thing you did when you read your Chart out loud in your office. That was practice for what you are about to do now, which is simply to reflect back exactly what your Child gives to you.

"Say your Child's words back to him without interpretation. This lets him know you heard his feelings and reactive thoughts. You can't do it wrong. As your Child continues to speak with you, he will correct any inaccuracies you might have expressed. The more you practice, the easier it is to connect with your Child as a True Adult. Did you ever play a sport?"

"Well yeah, basketball."

"When you first started playing, were you really good compared to someone who'd been playing for years?"

"Of course not! I had to practice."

"Talking with your Child works the same way. As you experience reflecting back your Child's feelings and thoughts, you begin to feel a connection with him and the conversation starts flowing more naturally. And, regardless of how it goes, you're developing your True Adult and your inner relationship, just by having such a conversation with your Child. So, let's get started and I'll coach you."

Randall leans back and appears relieved. "That's what happened at work. I read the Chart first as my Child and really felt all those bad feelings. But when I read it back as a True Adult, I started to feel calmer—even before I finished reading."

"Randall, that calm feeling was your Child's response to having another person, you as a True Adult, acknowledge his feelings, reactive thoughts, and actions. It's also comforting for your Child when you receive his feelings while remaining clear that those feelings belong to him, and not to you, his True Adult."

"Okay," Randall replies. "So, as a True Adult, I'm picking up on my Child's feelings. That makes sense. I am, you might say, pretty close to little Randy, so it's no surprise I'd feel his feelings. It'll take some getting used to, but I understand that the feelings I have are always my Child's—never mine as a True Adult."

I nod. "Exactly. Just like a therapist, you can have deep compassion for your Child, knowing he is able to sort out and clear his unresolved trauma by sharing it with you. Let's have you begin a Conversation with him. Last time, you used the Chart. This time, you get to *go live*. Instead of reading from your Chart, you engage your Child directly, and he gets to speak spontaneously to you, his True Adult."

Time Travel for Exponential Healing

I begin, "Take a moment and make yourself available for whatever your Child might want to bring to you. Nod when you're ready."

Randall grips his knees and gazes in the direction of his Child's Seat. After a few moments, he nods, and I begin to coach him.

"As a True Adult, Randall, invite your Child to take his seat and say whatever he wants to say. Let him express himself freely, through his words, tone, and volume."

Randall lets out a deep breath and switches seats. In a soft, quivering voice, his Child begins to describe an incident. "Two weeks ago, I was helping Leanne... one of the salespeople I manage. She was dealing with a customer complaint. Leanne is one of Bill's friends, but she was being nice to me, I guess because she needed my help.

"After I handled the complaint, Bill sauntered over, looked at Leanne, and said, 'I could have handled that mess a lot faster. Just come to me next time you need help.' He smiled at Leanne without even looking at me. I felt like slapping the smirk off his face. But I kept my feelings to myself.

"Then, still ignoring me, Bill asked Leanne to go on break with him... and would you believe it? Leanne walked right by me and went off with Bill—without even thanking me!" He pauses and takes a breath.

"I felt so angry, so humiliated! How could he be so disrespectful? How could he think he has the right to give her a break when I'm the manager? And Leanne had no appreciation for my help. She even took a break without checking with me! I wanted to go after Bill and just level the guy, right there in front of Leanne. But instead, I stopped myself and did my best to stuff my feelings.

"Walking around the store right after, I had all kinds of thoughts about getting even. I decided that the next time Leanne asks me for help, I'll just say to her, 'Why don't you go ask Bill?' But then I got mad at myself for letting their disrespect get to me. I'm supposed to be professional—calm and collected. Only I wasn't."

Randall is growing more agitated. I notice he's breathing more rapidly. He continues in a halting voice: "From now on… every time I see Leanne… I'll just ignore her. I'll smile as I go by… as if it doesn't even bother me."

Randall stops. I watch closely, in silence. After a moment, he turns and looks over at me. "Now what?"

I respond, "I'd like to speak with your True Adult." Randall nods. Slowly, I begin to stand. I say, "I'd like you to sit in my seat." Randall hesitates but then moves over into the chair I've just left. I take the chair by his side.

"Now allow yourself to settle into your seat, the seat of the True Adult. As you look over at little Randy, now sitting in the Child's Seat, I invite you to reflect back to him the feelings and thoughts he just expressed. Be open to any memories that might arise. Just be receptive. Trust that if it's right, your Child will guide you to past incidents he wants to talk with you about. Memories don't always come up so early in a Conversation, but sometimes they do."

Randall nods, sits up straight, and looks at the chair in front of him. I assure him that his Child makes perfect sense 100 percent of the time, and suggest that if he understands how little Randy makes sense, to tell him how he does. If he doesn't, Randall can just reflect back the words his Child says.

"The goal here for you, as Randy's True Adult, is to begin to recognize that no matter what Randy is feeling or thinking, he makes sense. As he feels heard, he will remind you of past incidents that he needs to talk with you about."

After a short pause, Randall starts to speak, reflecting back his Child's feelings and reactive thoughts. "You felt so much rage that you wanted to punch Bill." He falters, not sure where to go next.

I acknowledge his reflecting and coach him to take it to the next level. I prompt him, "It makes sense that you'd feel enraged because..."

He takes the coaching and continues. "It makes sense, little Randy, that you'd feel hurt when Leanne walked off with Bill, because she didn't get your permission or even thank you for your help."

His eyes now closed, Randall shifts in his chair and again addresses his Child. "Little Randy, it also makes sense that you'd be planning to ignore Leanne in the future because she was so disrespectful to you. And that if she asks you again for help, you'd tell her to handle it on her own... or find another job... or 'go ask Bill' for help. It makes sense that you'd want to act like it didn't bother you at all because you don't want her or Bill to have the satisfaction of getting to you.

"It makes sense, little Randy, that you walked around the store feeling so much rage and humiliation, thinking of ways to get back at Leanne, and, even more, to get back at Bill, because you felt so powerless and confused about what to do."

A tear rolls down Randall's cheek. I watch silently, feeling deep empathy for his Child's suffering. But I also see a strengthened emotional connection between Randall as a True Adult and his Child.

As I remain present to where Randall's Child will take him next, Randall suddenly slams his fists into his thighs. He opens his eyes, looks straight ahead, and speaks with excitement. "Little Randy, I can see how you would feel all those things because... because..." He falters, clearly continuing to receive a memory from his Child, and then speaks emphatically: "When you were a senior in high school, and you got elected captain of the debate team instead of Jason Smith... he hated you for it!"

Randall is visibly shaken by this sudden connection to his Child's experience, as if he had travelled back in time to the original event. His tone intensifies. "Jason was so pissed off that you got elected and he didn't. That's why he made jokes about you in class and got everyone to laugh at you. He bullied you all year long—in the hallways, in the lunch room... in front of everyone. And, it was even more humiliating when he did it in front of girls!"

Randall continues to receive the memory from his Child. "Yes, little Randy, it makes perfect sense that you felt so humiliated and angry at Jason. He was always ganging up on you with his group of friends, laughing at you and making fun of you. You were angry all the time, and you wanted to punch Jason and knock him out in front of the whole school. Then, everyone would laugh at *him*, especially the girls.

"But you never did that. Instead, you went to your dad and told him what was going on and how angry and humiliated you felt. He just sat there in his armchair and said, 'Randy, you're just too sensitive. I've tried to teach you to toughen up. You can't let things get to you so much.'"

Randall is quiet. Sensing that he is still reliving his Child's painful memory as if it were happening in this moment, I gesture for him to switch to his Child's Seat where his Child can fully express his suppressed pain.

Once seated, Randy speaks, his voice now soft and vulnerable. "After what Dad said, I don't know if I should hate myself for not punching Jason... or for being too sensitive. I'm so confused..."

I wait a moment and then offer gently, "When you're ready, switch so I can speak to your True Adult." Randall draws another slow, deep breath. Then he stands up, takes his True Adult Seat, and addresses his Child directly.

"Little Randy, how could you not be confused? You'd be screwing up no matter what you did. If you hit Jason, you'd feel better. But then you'd get in trouble for losing your cool. Because you didn't stand up to him, you stayed out of trouble, but you were suffering on the inside. I'm realizing that you've always felt trapped in these no-win situations that have just tortured you.

"It never even helped when your friends on the debate team tried to reassure you by telling you, 'Jason's just a jerk... he's just jealous.' And Randy, you've been holding all of that inside you for so many years."

Switching seats now without my prompting, Randall's Child speaks. "See! Even my friends were telling me that I shouldn't be bothered, that Jason was just a jerk. But I *was* bothered…. I *am* bothered! This whole thing just gives me a headache."

Moving back into his True Adult Seat, Randall addresses his Child, becoming more separate as he continues to use sense-making commentary. "It makes sense, Randy, that you would be confused and that this whole thing would give you a headache! You've never had anyone to talk with you about this whole mess until now. And another thing you're bringing to me… your dad said, 'You should be more like your big brother, Jack. No one takes a shot at him, because everyone knows he doesn't get bothered when they do. He's tough and knows how to keep his cool.'"

Randall shakes his head and looks back at the chair where his Child sits. "It makes sense, little Randy, that you would feel like a failure, a loser, a wimp after hearing your dad make those harsh comments. And then he just gets up and leaves the room! You were left sitting there, hating yourself for not being stronger and for disappointing your dad… for not being as good as your brother Jack."

Randall stops speaking, moved by his Child's suffering. He switches back to his Child's Seat and begins to tell his True Adult, "I'm so mad at my dad for not being more understanding of me… not really listening to me. For not supporting me the way I needed to be supported. And even worse, he made me resent my brother, Jack, who I really loved!"

Randall stops, puts his head in his hands, and breaks into sobs. I wait several moments and then hand him the box of tissues. I remain silent, fully present to his experience. He takes a tissue, wipes the tears from his cheek, and holds the tissue to his eyes. After several moments, he switches back to his True Adult Seat.

Leaning forward, Randall looks intently at the seat across from him. "Little Randy, you decided right then and there to never, ever, open up to your dad again." He pauses briefly and then continues, "But that strategy only made you feel better for a few minutes. You walked in a daze, out of the room and up the stairs to your bedroom. Then you shut the door and sat on the bed, feeling so sad and alone."

Randall pauses, then he suddenly exclaims, "Little Randy, it's like... it's like Bill is that jerk Jason, and your boss... he's your dad!"

Randall now leans back in the chair, looks up at the ceiling, and laughs out loud. Turning to me, he says, "Ron, this is unbelievable. This work situation is the same thing as that craziness in high school!"

I reply, "Yes, Randall. You're beginning to see why I say it's never about what it seems to be about. It's always about something in the past. Now tell your Child how he is making sense to you."

Randall turns again toward his Child. "Wow, little Randy. Of course you've been having a horrible time at work with all this abusive crap. You've been feeling just like you did in high school, afraid you'd be screwing up no matter what you did. And you had no one to turn to—no one at all!"

He switches seats, and his Child responds immediately. "Yeah, it's such crap! And I've been taking it my whole life. And to have my dad and my boss dump it back on me like that, without even acknowledging or validating my feelings.... They're the wimps!"

Calmer now, Randall's Child continues, "Yeah... my dad and my boss are definitely not True Adults, that's for sure." He stands up, walks over, and sits down in the True Adult Seat. He addresses his Child.

"Boy, little Randy. I gotta say, I can feel that something just changed for you."

He switches seats and his Child responds, "Yeah, you got *that* right. No disrespect to Dad or even my boss, but you're the only one who's really a True Adult. You have the guts to really hear me. My dad didn't know how to support me so I'd feel confident enough to face those bullies. He and my boss bullied me themselves, just in a different way. No wonder I felt cut off in every direction... that nothing I do would ever be right. I had no one... until now."

True Adult: "It makes sense to me, little Randy, that you are feeling pretty darn good. You know that you deserve, and always have deserved, to be listened to the way I am listening to you right now. You're realizing you're actually strong, not weak. You've been handling bullies for years, coming at you from all sides, with no support or backup. Now that you know I'm here for you, you feel stronger and more prepared to deal with Bill as his boss. You're feeling in charge in a way you've never felt before."

Child: "I do! I almost can't wait to go to work tomorrow. I'm not even worried about Bill. For the first time, I feel like I *am* the boss."

True Adult: "Wow! I'm really blown away. I can feel such a difference in you. It's like you know who you are, for the first time in your life."

Child: "That's right. Having you here with me makes all the difference. I want to have more of these Conversations with you. I feel like I've found my new best friend for life."

Randall switches seats to respond as a True Adult.

I interject. "My sense, Randall, is that now is a good time to complete your Conversation with your Child." He nods with a smile, and I continue. "Feel your separateness, how you are distinct as a True Adult. At the same time, let your Child experience his new bond with you as a True Adult. When you leave this session, he leaves with you, no longer on his own, but now supported by you, a True Adult."

Randall focuses intently on his Child for several minutes, nods slowly, and closes his eyes. After a moment, he looks at me and declares, "That was incredible. Something big changed. He… I… we're not the same person we were just before that Conversation." He chuckles at this odd way of describing his new sense of himself.

"You're right, Randall. Would you like to share more with me about what just happened?"

"It seems so simple… but my Child has needed to be heard without anyone telling him he's wrong, or that he shouldn't feel the way he does. It would have been great if his dad and his boss had been able to listen to him and get him the way I just did. But they didn't, and that's okay, because now my Child has me to do for him what they couldn't do."

"Randall, your True Adult presence in this matter has created the safety and freedom your Child has longed for. I can sense that you're feeling powerfully aligned with your Child and ready to experience the truth of who you are in the world. Go and enjoy!" Our session is over.

Randall's Ongoing Transformation

The next time Randall had an interaction with Bill, it went very differently. When Bill made a snide remark, Randall didn't do his usual suppressing of his feelings while walking around, seething and feeling humiliated. Instead, the following scenario unfolded:

"Listen Bill," Randall said, remaining calm and centered after Bill tried to humiliate him yet again, "I can only imagine how frustrating it must be for you that I got the manager position you wanted. However, given how things turned out and that I was chosen for the position, let's find a way to make it work for both of us."

Following a negative emotional reaction from Bill's Little Adult, Randall used his transformational listening skills to receive and reflect Bill's reaction back to him. Then, after Bill felt heard by Randall as a True Adult and calmed down, Randall sought an equitable solution to their circumstance.

"Since you were also considered for this position, I'd like to give you a leadership role to increase your chance of being promoted, with my endorsement, in the near future. That will strengthen our whole team and make our work environment better for everyone, including our customers. I'd like to meet with you tomorrow right after your lunch break to discuss this."

This new way of relating became possible for Randall because of the dramatic change he had experienced through exponential healing. It wasn't just the words he said that made him more effective with Bill, but rather his unquestionable demeanor as someone in charge that led to a dramatically different result. Furthermore, Bill's Little Adult had the experience of being heard and responded to by a True Adult, which is always what a Little Adult needs in order to stop being reactive. No longer in competition with Randall, Bill was able to relax and become available to a more positive relationship.

Such sudden and rapid change after a deep Child–Adult Conversation is not uncommon. However, it usually takes longer than one or two sessions for a person to develop the safety and relationship within themselves that is necessary to bring about such healing. Still, we never know when that might happen—the process is different for everyone.

Your Turn:

Your Own Conversation—Level 2

In this activity, you will develop your skill at having a spoken Conversation with your Child by using the Inner Alignment Chart you wrote in chapter 9 for a workplace issue. Again, you will be reading out loud from your Chart, but this time, you will have a more direct experience of relationship as you physically switch back and forth between the Child's Seat and the True Adult Seat for each item on the Chart.

As you've seen in the sessions with my clients, this physical back-and-forth movement from seat to seat, as the Child and the Adult each speak, establishes a clear distinction between the one experiencing feelings and thoughts (Child) and the one observing those feelings and thoughts (True Adult). Once Child and Adult are distinct and separate, a deep connection with your Child is possible, and opportunities for exponential healing are more likely to occur. Additionally, the back-and-forth movement gives you a deeper experience of relationship through dialogue—the essence of a Child–Adult Conversation.

LEVEL 2: READING YOUR INNER ALIGNMENT CHART WHILE SWITCHING BACK AND FORTH

1: Set up two chairs

They should face each other and be clearly distinguished as the Child's Seat and the True Adult Seat.

2: Begin in the True Adult Seat

Establish your separateness from your Child by being silent, imagining that all feelings or thoughts are "over there" with your Child.

3: Switch to the Child's Seat and read the incident, as written on your Chart, out loud to your True Adult

Notice how it feels to express yourself to a safe and interested Big Person.

4: Switch to your True Adult Seat and reflect back what was just read by your Child

Repeat the words your Child said, changing pronouns from *I* to *you.*

5: Switch to your Child's Seat and read your first feeling (Hurt Child), using the word *I*

Allow yourself to feel the emotion the word conveys. Experience it as fully as you are able.

6: Switch to your True Adult Seat and reflect back your Child's feeling, using the word *you*

As you feel your Child's experience, keep yourself open but separate, recognizing that the feeling is not yours.

7: Switch to your Child's Seat and read the next feeling, again using *I*

8: Continue switching back and forth for each item

Do the same with the next two Chart sections: reactive thoughts and actions (Coping Child/Little Adult) until all items in the three sections of the Chart have been read by your Child and heard and reflected back by you as a True Adult.

9: When complete, sit in your Child's Seat

Silently acknowledge any feelings or thoughts you might have.

10: Switch one more time to your True Adult Seat when you are ready

Sit silently, being present with your Child and the developing connection between you.

When you are finished, take the opportunity to express any feelings—comfortable or uncomfortable—that may have come up during the activity by writing in your Child's Journal. Also, write your observations and insights about your Child's experience in your True Adult Log.

As you review the steps for reading your Inner Alignment Chart in this manner, you may be asking yourself, *How will I find the time to do this at work?* Sometimes you're going to be too busy to stop and do this activity. However, by simply recognizing in the moment that there is an issue and telling your Child that you will do the Chart activity later, you are letting your Child know that a Big Person is paying attention and becoming more aware of what is going on inside. Such True Adult acknowledgment builds your relationship with your Child. Sometimes, even if you don't plan to do the Chart activity later, just acknowledging your Child's experience can relieve the pressure and transform a negative experience into a positive one.

If you do manage to squeeze the Chart activity in at work, despite your busy day, your emotional space will likely shift even faster for you. Your mind will be clearer, allowing you to function at a higher level throughout the rest of your day. Many of my clients have found that taking a break at the time—or close to the time—of the upsetting incident made the rest of their workday more productive.

As you become more skilled at having Child–Adult Conversations, they will generally require less time, although they will always vary in length. As your Child eventually learns to depend on you, he or she will more readily provide you with information, guidance, and insights regarding your issues. A number of my clients have been astounded to find that all their Child needed was two minutes in order to create a shift from turmoil to comfort and confidence.

Helpful Tips for Having a Conversation
with Your Child

▶ **When at work,** you can do the described activity whenever an upsetting interaction occurs between you and a colleague, superior, employee, customer, or client. I suggest you keep blank copies of the Inner Alignment Chart accessible, or write out the four steps of the Chart on a blank sheet of paper or in a notebook.

▶ **If space is limited,** such as when you're doing this activity in your office, restroom, or car, you may not be able to do the chair switching advised. Instead, simply turn around or cock your head slightly from side to side, or cross your legs back and forth. The key is to physically differentiate between your Child and your True Adult. This will help you to separate—step away—from your Child's feelings and reactive thoughts.

▶ **Write in your Child's Journal** so that your Child can express any feelings that came up during the activity, whether comfortable or uncomfortable. Also, write your observations and insights about your Child's experience in your True Adult Log. Again, writing in your notebooks is always valuable, even if you only write one or two sentences. For your Child, it creates a very real experience of mattering. For you as a True Adult, separateness and solidity are strengthened and will build with each entry.

▶ **It can be helpful to know** that it's natural, when considering having a Child–Adult Conversation, for your Little Adult to become activated, or triggered. You'll know that's happening when uncomfortable feelings such as anxiety, confusion, or fear are stirred up. Your Little Adult might also have thoughts that having a Child–Adult Conversation won't make any difference anyway.

Becoming comfortable with Conversations is like becoming comfortable with anything else in life, such as playing a sport, cooking a meal, or driving a car. You learned to just start doing those things before you were necessarily comfortable with them. It was only through experience that you became comfortable.

It is natural for your Little Adult to want to feel confident and on top of things before even starting. You are learning to free your Little Adult by practicing not already knowing—ultimately the most comfortable and powerful place to stand. This is where you are headed, as a developing True Adult.

▲

What's Next…

As you have seen, powerful healing can occur, even when you are in the early stages of learning how to have a Child–Adult Conversation. Now that you've experienced the power of I AM Training in both romantic and workplace relationships, I invite you to explore a different area that provides yet another opportunity for developing your ultimate relationship: the domain of parenthood and family life.

In the next two chapters, you will sit in on sessions with my clients Jaclyn and Mark as they learn to use Inner Alignment with their children and for deepening their intimacy as a couple.

CHAPTER 11

FAMILY RELATIONSHIPS: INNER ALIGNMENT AT HOME

By now, you've grasped a fundamental principle of I AM Training: No matter what kind of family you grew up in, your primary emotional wounds came from feelings of disconnection that you experienced in your early family environment.

There's just no escaping it. Whether you were raised by two parents, a single parent, grandparents, relatives, or others, and whether the adults in your family were loving, abusive, or somewhere in between, you could not avoid being wounded by the inevitable disconnection of the Big People from your Child.

Those old wounds may no longer seem relevant to you, or they may still be haunting you today. But regardless of how you feel now, that early disconnection your Child experienced had tremendous influence in shaping who you have become. In I AM Training, you learn how to embrace your early wounding experiences and transform them into the discovery of who you really are. As a True Adult aligned with your Infinite Child, your wounds become a vehicle for healing and growth on your path toward becoming your fully mature, evolved self. As a result, your life becomes a meaningful and rewarding adventure.

Perhaps you are a parent yourself now. Or maybe, for any number of reasons, you are not involved in parenting or family life with children. In either case, you will find value in this chapter as you sit in on the training sessions with my clients Mark and Jaclyn. The dynamics you will observe between them as parents and partners, as well as the dynamic each has in their own inner relationship, will shed light on your experience as a Child shaped by your family of origin. Such observation will make you a better parent to your own children, and will enable a more positive impact on any Child with whom you interact.

In this chapter, you will get more practice in becoming separate as a True Adult by observing the feelings and reactive thoughts of your own Hurt Child and Little Adult. This will help you get to the root of your family issues— whether from your childhood or with your own children today—and resolve them. Once you emerge as a True Adult and align with your Child, you are available to be continually guided by your Child of the Infinite to connect to the higher selves of others, especially the young children you may be parenting. Then your family relationships, whatever their configuration, will become more fun-filled and even magical.

Little Adults in the Parenting Role

You've seen how your Little Adult takes over in romantic and workplace relationships, striving to protect your Child from pain and failure. Likewise, your Little Adult will at times take over the job of parenting, attempting to protect your Child from failing at what is likely the most important role in your life. But, as you have seen, your Little Adult's attempts to "do it right" can never truly succeed.

Unless you are aligned inwardly as a True Adult with your Child, your Little Adult is the one parenting your children. This makes everything more complicated and difficult, because your own Child's wounds will dominate and interfere with your ability to wisely parent your physical children. For example, when your children reach any age that was for you a time of early wounding, your own feelings from childhood will be stirred up. Without a True Adult to be there for you, your Little Adult will again react and take over. Parents reacting to their own wounds can never be fully present and available for their own children.

The damage done by Little Adult parenting can be far reaching, leaving open wounds that are repeated, generation after generation. Family feuds are an example of this phenomenon. Even within your own family of origin, you are probably aware of issues that have been handed down, spilling over from your parents into your own family, and eventually from your family to that of your children's families.

Fortunately, for future generations, you can heal your inner Child's wounds from any trauma you or your ancestors experienced, and put a stop to the toxic overflow that causes so much suffering. In so doing, you will be gifting your children with the freedom to fully create their own lives and their own evolutionary adventures.

In my work with clients over many years, I've helped families to develop deep and lasting relationships in which the suffering of the past no longer interferes with the present. No matter what the family dynamic is, Inner Alignment empowers family members to interact not as Little Adults but as True Adults. This can mean interactions between spouses, parents and children, and among all other family members and across generations. Inner Alignment creates the desire for an environment in which everyone's Child within is heard, understood, and respected, whether or not other family members agree with him or her. In addition, it is understood that when we get how others make sense within their perspectives of reality, we are automatically expanded in our own process of enlightenment and maturity. It is within such an atmosphere of mutual facilitation that gratifying family interactions occur.

When you as a parent are connected with your own Child within, you can more easily connect with your physical children on the emotional level that they need. But when you are disconnected from your own Child in any particular area, you will likewise remain unavailable to your physical children in the same area. You will lack the ability to truly hear them, and all your attempts to connect will not work.

Becoming a True Adult for your own Child is the most effective thing you can do to become a better parent for your children. I tell clients who ask me to work with their children to come to my office themselves instead. As parents work individually and with each other, they begin to see their children's behavior transform miraculously, even without any direct involvement of the children in the process. Doing the work of Inner Alignment is the quickest path to becoming enlightened parents with happy and emotionally intelligent children. For a demonstration of the power of Inner Alignment in families, I invite you into a session with my clients Jaclyn and Mark, and their children.

Jaclyn and Mark's First Session:
Resentment and Resignation

Jaclyn and Mark are a married couple struggling to raise their two young children while keeping their relationship strong and intimate. They came to me because they'd gotten stuck in a pattern of resentment and resignation in their relationship. This has created a stressful, negative emotional environment that can't help but erode intimacy for couples with children.

For their first session, I've invited all members of the family, including 10-year-old Kyle and his sister, 8-year-old Sarah. I don't typically have children present in sessions because, as I've noted, the emotional work done by each parent with their own inner Child is more impactful than anything they could do with their physical children. But at times, I do invite children in for the first session with their parents to show them clearly that even the Big People—their parents—need and can get support for difficult issues. In addition, children have already been exposed to their parents' issues at home, either directly or indirectly, and can always feel when something is not right, even if they don't understand it. Knowing that their parents are addressing the issues that have been impacting the family can validate, calm, and relieve the children, and can help the whole family's process.

When the family enters my office, Jaclyn and the children sit on the couch and Mark takes an adjacent chair next to Jaclyn. Jaclyn is the first to speak.

"I just don't know what to do," she says, sighing deeply. "Kyle and Sarah fight with each other all the time." She glances at her husband and then back at me. "Kyle gets upset with me sometimes when I need to give Sarah extra attention. He had me all to himself before Sarah came along…. He should understand that there's not a lot of time, and because she's younger, she needs more from me. And Sarah's always upset that Kyle picks on her."

Jaclyn looks down and then back up. "My husband Mark is so tired from work that he doesn't want to deal with their behavior. His only remedy is telling them to knock it off, which doesn't help. I work full time as well, and barely make it home with enough time to make dinner for all of us, so I'm pretty tired, too."

Jaclyn pauses, looks down again, and shakes her head. I glance at Kyle and Sarah, who are both looking down with their hands folded across their laps, sitting very still. The room has become silent as we all wait to see what will happen next.

I stay with the silence for a few more seconds and then, making eye contact with Jaclyn, I say, "Of course you would be upset and frustrated over Kyle and

Sarah fighting so much. And, it's especially difficult when you barely get home in time to fix dinner."

I pause. Jaclyn resumes speaking, her voice increasing in intensity. "Yes, and I also feel so angry with Mark for not helping more with the kids. He seems to have given up and left everything in my hands. I feel so alone, even though I'm surrounded by my family. I just don't know what to do."

Jaclyn stops, glances at her husband and her children, and then looks down at the floor. Before I can reflect her Child's feelings back to her, Mark takes a deep breath and begins to speak.

"Look, honey, I don't think you know how hard it is for me at work. I love you, and I love Sarah and Kyle, but I'm just so tired of coming home late, after fighting traffic every single night, to the kids shouting and chasing each other… to you flying off the handle, shouting at the kids…" He pauses, takes another deep breath, and lets out a long sigh. "I just want some peace and quiet. I feel like I'm going crazy sometimes, so I just…" He looks straight ahead. "I just shut down and watch TV, not only to cut out some of the noise, but just to zone out and get some peace."

As Mark is speaking, Sarah starts fidgeting with the doll she brought and Kyle starts thumping his heels against the couch. Jaclyn is staring straight ahead. Once Mark finishes, both children stop moving and sit still.

Feeling deep empathy for this family's predicament, I reflect back Mark's struggle. "After working such long hours and fighting traffic, to then come home to all the screaming and fighting, it makes sense, Mark, that you would just want to relax and zone out. It certainly makes sense that when you don't know what else to do to make things right, you'd just shut down and watch TV."

Maintaining my own healthy separateness, I'm able to get Mark's Child's experience without opinion or reaction. This helps to create a sense of safety for everyone in the room. While still deeply feeling Mark's Child, I look over to see Kyle and Sarah staring at their dad. Jaclyn looks over at her husband, while Mark's eyes remain focused on me. He smiles and speaks.

"Ron, it feels good to hear you say that. I have to admit, this is going differently from what I expected… which was that I'd be criticized for shutting down and leaving Jaclyn to deal with the kids alone." He pauses, looks at his wife, then at his kids, and again at me. "But you do seem to understand. I want to help Jaclyn, but I don't know what to do. I guess I feel kind of lost."

"Mark," I reply, "it makes sense that you'd expect to be criticized for shutting down and leaving Jaclyn alone to deal with the kids because you know they need you. And even though you want to help, it's hard enough just to deal with your hard day and the traffic, much less the chaos at home. How painful and frustrating it must have been to feel blamed when you simply didn't know what to do." Mark lets out a sigh of relief.

Now I turn back to Jaclyn to reflect what she'd said before Mark spoke. "Jaclyn, it also makes sense to me that you'd be angry at Mark when you felt he wasn't really taking care of Kyle and Sarah while you were trying to make dinner."

Jaclyn looks at me and brushes a tear off her cheek. Placing a box of tissues within the couple's reach, I continue. "It makes sense, Jaclyn, that you would feel angry and alone, even when you are surrounded by your family, because you haven't known how to ensure that Mark hears you and understands your feelings."

For a few moments, we all sit in silence. Then Jaclyn glances at her husband and speaks in a soft voice, as if to herself. "Mark, I guess I never realized that you feel lost… and alone… like I do. I mean, I always thought you just wanted to shut us out… that you wanted to be alone." A warm and comfortable feeling permeates the room as some of the tension the family arrived with is eased.

Making It Personal

As you read about Mark and Jaclyn, ask yourself if, like them, you have ever felt alone in your own family. If your answer is yes, know that you have plenty of company. It's often the case that family members suffer in alienation and never talk about it, each one thinking that no one else is experiencing what they are. It is also common for family members not to say anything about their feelings out of fear of creating a chain reaction of conflict that will only lead to more suffering.

To get the most out of this session with Jaclyn and Mark, I invite you to recall a specific conflict or troubling interaction you've experienced in your own family, currently or in the past. It might involve your own children or you as a child growing up in your family of origin. Then, follow what happens in the session with your own situation in mind. Referencing a specific scenario from your own life will help you to see how I AM Training can bring clarity and understanding to your own challenging family situations.

To strengthen your own inner alignment, keep your Child's Journal and True Adult Log close by. Writing your Child's expression and True Adult's observations as you read along with the session will add greater meaning and value to your experience.

After a few more moments of comfortable silence, all eyes turn toward me. I begin by speaking to both Jaclyn and Mark. "When each of you spoke to me, you shared your feelings, including your frustration and struggle with feeling lost, and even alone, in your family. All of those immediate, feeling responses come from an experience of life that I call your Hurt Child."

Hearing my words, Sarah and Kyle begin to giggle. I smile at them as I continue addressing Jaclyn and Mark, introducing the concept of the Little Adult as a Child in coping mode, and explaining how reactive thoughts and actions are always expressions of a Little Adult. I then introduce the True Adult, and explain how a True Adult can become aligned with the Child for healing and guidance.

Suddenly, Mark is smiling again. "Ron, after I told you about feeling frustrated and confused, you said I made sense, and you didn't criticize me. Is that what you mean by a True Adult?" I nod, and Mark, still smiling, leans back in his chair and looks at his wife, who is also nodding. Jaclyn extends her arm, placing her hand in Mark's hand. I look over at the children to see them grinning at their parents.

"I feel more connected to Mark now," Jaclyn says. "We've actually been feeling the same way... confused, lost, lonely... without even knowing it."

I look at Jaclyn and Mark, and then over at the children, who look back at me, their eyes wide with interest. I smile at them and turn to address their parents.

"Earlier, when I responded as a True Adult to each of you, without judgment or opinions, you both felt a sense of relief. Now, I'm going to invite each of you to give yourselves—your Child within—the same benefit, by being your own True Adults."

Jaclyn Becomes a True Adult for Her Child

I begin with Jaclyn. "I'd like you to think of a specific incident over the last week—a family interaction that upset you."

Jaclyn thinks a moment and then speaks. "The other night, Mark had just gotten home, and Kyle and Sarah were arguing over who got more dessert." She pauses to look at her children. Kyle stifles a giggle and Sarah clutches at her doll.

"I tried to settle the kids down and then brought some dinner into the living room for Mark where he was watching TV. I asked him to handle the kids, because I was tired and needed some help. He shook his head like I was a nuisance and then yelled at them from his chair, 'Knock it off and listen to your mother!' Then he just started scarfing down the dinner I brought him, and continued watching TV."

Jaclyn looks down and continues. "At that moment, I felt so angry. I shouted at Mark to start being a *real* father. But without so much as looking at me or turning down the volume, he snapped back, 'You sound just like the kids!' And to make things worse, he actually turned the volume up!"

"I stormed back into the kitchen where the kids were eating and demanded they go upstairs to bed, right away. I'd had it! The kids went quietly, but later when I tucked them in, they didn't even want a goodnight kiss. Then I went to our bedroom, sat on the bed, and cried. I felt like the kids hated me, that they were blaming their father's yelling on me. I thought what a horrible father Mark was and felt angry at him for being so unresponsive to me. I even felt angry at the kids for not wanting me to kiss them goodnight." Jaclyn cries softly as she speaks.

She wipes her tears with a tissue Mark hands to her, shifts in her seat, and continues. "Then I got mad at myself for blaming Mark, because I knew how tired he was. I was afraid I'd gone too far by telling him he wasn't being a real father. I decided that I wouldn't ask Mark to do anything anymore; I would just handle the kids myself."

Jaclyn stops here. I recognize her words as a direct expression of her Hurt Child's feelings and her Little Adult's reactive thoughts and plans for action. This is a good time for Jaclyn's True Adult to be available, so I begin to coach her.

"Jaclyn, I invite you to sit in my chair." I stand up and Jaclyn moves hesitantly into the chair I've been occupying. I take another seat next to her. "Imagine that it was your Child who just spoke and is now sitting in the chair across from you. Begin to reflect back, in her words, all of your Child's feelings and reactive thoughts regarding what happened. Call her Jaclyn, little Jaclyn, or a nickname she had growing up. You can call her by any name that feels right."

"I'm going to speak to my Child just like you did with Mark and me, right?"

I respond, "You're exactly right, Jaclyn."

She begins, "Jackie, what happened last week with Mark and the kids was very painful for you. It makes sense that you felt resentful and angry at Mark for being so focused on the TV when you needed his help. He's your partner, and you felt like he was leaving *you* to carry most of the weight and responsibility. And then, of course you felt hurt when Kyle and Sarah didn't even want to kiss you goodnight."

Jaclyn pauses, puts her hands down on her knees, and looks at the floor. "It makes so much sense to me that you went into the bedroom and cried. You felt so hurt and sad... and angry... and isolated... because you felt so cut off from your family."

After a moment of silence, Jaclyn turns to me. I motion for her to switch seats and she does.

Her Child now speaks. "Yes... it was so hard. I hate that feeling. I want to be a good mother to Kyle and Sarah and a good wife to Mark. I just don't know what to do. I feel so overwhelmed and... lost sometimes." She pauses and looks down. Lifting her head up, she stands up and moves back into her True Adult Seat.

Sitting down, she turns to me and asks, "Ron, what do I say now?"

"Begin by saying back what you feel is the most notable thing your Child said."

Jaclyn turns back toward her Child and says, "Jackie, you feel really overwhelmed and confused, and that's why you were so angry with Mark and sad about the kids."

Turning to me, Jaclyn says, "Ron, it sounds like I'm letting my Child off the hook... like my True Adult is making excuses to justify my Child's behavior."

I reply, "You're not agreeing or disagreeing with your Child, but rather acknowledging her experience and how she makes sense based on that experience. When you do so, she hears, sees, and feels that you care about her feelings. Only then can she feel safe enough to open up to you further."

Jaclyn leans back in her chair, releases a deep breath, and smiles. "I think I'm getting this. I do feel a sense of relief. By not judging myself, I'm already feeling better."

"Yes, you are getting it, Jaclyn. And this is just the beginning. You've now experienced a Child–Adult Conversation, which lets you know that your Child feels safe enough to speak with you as a True Adult. Now, let's give your Child another chance to respond. First, sit silently. Again, receive her experience before you switch seats to let her speak."

Jaclyn gazes ahead for several seconds before she switches. Her Child then begins to speak.

"It's so nice to have you to talk with me about this. It's been so hard for me. I know we all love each other very much, but it gets very upsetting and confusing sometimes. And I just don't know what to do or who to turn to, and then I guess I just get angry and distant from everyone." She sits silently for several moments before switching to her True Adult Seat.

True Adult: "It makes sense, little Jackie, that you get pretty down at times when you feel really alone. And then you get angry at Mark when you think you have a partner who isn't doing his part." Jaclyn pauses for a moment. When she speaks again, her voice is louder. "Yes, Jackie, it makes sense that you would decide that you can't count on Mark at all, and that you would just ignore him and handle everything on your own. And that if he's going to cut himself off, you'll cut him off, too. It makes sense that you just figured, if you can't beat 'em, join'em." She hesitates. Instead of continuing, she stops and turns to me. I motion for her to switch seats.

Child: "It feels so good that you understand me. I can feel you... really here for me... and that's something I've wanted my whole life." Jackie's tears fall in silence as she allows herself to feel truly heard and supported by her True Adult.

After this heartfelt moment, Jackie stands up and moves back into her True Adult Seat. I then say, "Jaclyn, you might want to continue this Conversation with your Child on your own, or with me in a future session. But for now, I invite you to sit silently, receiving a sense of your Child and everything she has shared with you. You may even get a sense of the difference that your presence as a True Adult is making for her right now. Ultimately, this process of receiving will become effortless."

Jaclyn sits silently, staring intently at the chair in front of her. A look of deep compassion forms on her face as she nods slowly and knowingly to her Child. Then she turns to me. "Ron, that was very special. I was truly separate from my

Child, and she felt my presence, respect, and support. I feel such reverence for her, and even for myself."

As I watch Jaclyn settle into her new, powerful sense of inner connection, I notice Mark's eyes are welling up with tears. He wipes them, letting out a sigh as they continue rolling down his cheeks.

Mark's Turn to Be a True Adult

Mark leans back in his chair, looks up at the ceiling, and begins speaking in a shaky voice. "I remember that night, too.... I mean, I remember so many nights like that. But that night, when I yelled at the kids to knock it off and then turned up the volume on the TV to drown out Jaclyn's demands..." Mark glances at his children, at Jaclyn, and then straight ahead.

"First of all, I'd had a horrible day at work, and I was dog-tired. When Jaclyn told me to be a *real* father to my children, whom I adore, I felt so damn angry! Doesn't she understand, after all this time? I mean, we've been married 14 years now. I work hard to provide for our family, to put food on the table, to pay the mortgage on time. Doesn't she get it?" He pauses, clearly confused by his wife's words. "And then, when she stormed out of the room, I felt so angry and hurt! I did what she wanted me to do. When I yelled at the kids to knock it off, they did. And then she puts me down for it. I just don't get it. I never will."

Mark stares at the floor. "I remember feeling angry and hurt, and then I thought, *what's the point?* My family ... my home ... it's supposed to be a place where I can rest and forget about all the insanity at work—just relax, for Pete's sake!

"Then, yes, I started feeling guilty for not spending more time with the kids—except on Sundays, my only day off. I started wondering if maybe Jaclyn was right, that I wasn't such a good father. But I resented her for not asking me more about my work—she's always so wrapped up in the kids. And then, right away, I felt guilty and selfish for even thinking that way."

Mark pauses and shakes his head slowly, back and forth. Silence fills the room. He continues, "I remember feeling so tired at that point. So tired of work, so tired of the kids fighting and Jaclyn yelling. Tired of… well… all of it. That's when I turned the TV volume up, just to shut the world out. I had to go into another world, a more peaceful one."

Mark stops and sits in silence. He doesn't look at anyone. Kyle and Sarah sit stiffly and look at their father. I turn to Jaclyn's True Adult and say in a soft voice, "Jaclyn, I'd like you to take a different seat now so Mark can take the True Adult Seat." I turn to Mark. "I invite you to take the True Adult Seat now, Mark, just as Jaclyn did, and respond to your Child as a True Adult."

Mark sits down in the therapist/True Adult Seat and looks back at the empty chair he just left. I remind him: "Simply reflect back what your Child just told you, without agreeing or disagreeing with his feelings or reactive thoughts. If what he said makes sense to you, given his perspective, tell him that, too."

He begins speaking in a soft voice. "So, little Mark, you had a lot of feelings and thoughts about that evening." Mark pauses and looks at me for encouragement. "Is that what I should do, Ron?" I nod with a smile, and Mark continues to address his Child. "You were tired after work and upset that the kids were fighting again. It makes sense how angry you felt after you yelled at the kids to knock it off, and Jaclyn shouted angrily back at you. And here you thought you were helping her!"

He pauses again. Leaning forward slightly, Mark continues. "It makes sense that you would feel hurt and angry when Jaclyn made the comment about you not being a real father, because you were trying to help, and she didn't get it."

Mark sits up straighter now, like an adult who is finding his place, ready to be available for a hurting child. "It makes so much sense that you judged Jaclyn for putting you down and being so demanding. You felt that she didn't understand, after all these years, how hard you work to pay the bills and the mortgage, to put food on the table. It makes so much sense, little Mark, that you didn't feel appreciated by your wife."

Mark pauses, exhales slowly, and continues, "It's easy to see how you started to feel guilty, thinking that maybe you don't spend enough time with the kids, that you should be doing more… and that you aren't a good father."

Mark closes his eyes and nods to himself. Then he opens his eyes, leans forward, and continues to reflect, his volume rising slightly. "You think you should be doing more, but you don't know what to do or how to do it. So how could you not feel confused and guilty when you believe you're supposed to know how to make everything right?"

Mark's face brightens with his new understanding, and he nods supportively to his Child. "It makes so much sense that not knowing what to do and feeling put down by Jaclyn when you're doing your best… you'd just shut down in front of the TV to block everything out and finally get some peace. What else were you supposed to do at that point, when you didn't know what else to do, except to tune everyone out?" Mark turns, looking at me for guidance.

"You're seeing his world more clearly now and beginning to get how he makes sense, Mark. Now, let's find out what he wants to say to you in response."

Mark switches into his Child's Seat and takes a moment to settle in. "Exactly! What else was I supposed to do? I feel like whatever I do isn't what she wants. And I'm struggling with the same kind of crap at work. Then I finally come home just to find more of the same. You bet I finally check out. I do what I can, and then I just can't take it after a while. So you're right… thank God for the TV!"

Switching back to his True Adult Seat, Mark replies to his Child, "I get it, little Mark. After doing the best you can, when your best doesn't seem to be good enough, you and the TV work it out together. That makes a lot of sense to me." Mark sits up straighter in his chair and nods as his face softens.

I say, "Mark, give your Child the opportunity to have the last word, even if he is silent. Then, when your Child is ready, you'll end in your True Adult Seat to receive him in silence. You may even sense the difference your presence is having for him."

Mark nods and switches to his Child's Seat. "I have to say, it feels really good to actually be understood for once in my life. It's just getting too hard to be the bad guy all the time. I could use a lot more of these kinds of Conversations." Looking intently now at his True Adult Seat, he says, "I'm ready for something different... very different." He takes an extra moment in silence, continuing his steady gaze at his True Adult.

Mark switches seats again. As a True Adult, he is now silent as he sits up straight, looking intently toward his Child's Seat. After several moments, he nods once and then slowly turns to me, then to Jaclyn, the kids, and back to me.

Noticeably calm now, Mark says, "Ron, I feel this sense of relief... of relaxation. I haven't felt this way in a long time. I don't know... maybe ever."

"Mark," I begin, addressing him as a True Adult, "I want to acknowledge that the relief you are feeling is the result of your Child finally having the experience of being cared for by a True Adult—You. You have become the True Adult your Child has longed for. That connection is what I call *your ultimate relationship*, the one you are, right now, developing with yourself—with your Child. It is this relationship that will lead to all your other relationships being more joyful and fulfilling."

With a new, energized tone, Mark replies, "I must say, Ron, I can believe that now. I'm feeling very different, and I think it has something to do with what you're talking about."

Jaclyn chimes in, "You do look different, Mark," and then says tenderly, "It's really nice to see you this way, honey."

Mark appears to be savoring Jaclyn's words.

Kyle then jumps in. "Yeah, Dad, you look great."

On his heels, Sarah, leaning sideways on the couch, says sweetly, "Yeah, Daddy."

Mark smiles warmly at the children, responding to their love for him.

As the family connects on this new level, I am deeply moved. A timeless moment passes, and then all eyes turn to me. I begin to wrap up the session.

"Before we complete our session today, I'm going to give you an assignment to do at home before the next time you come in."

Kyle and Sarah chuckle, and Kyle blurts out, "Mom and Dad have homework!"

Jaclyn and Mark look over at their children and smile.

I respond, "Yes, you're right. We're all learning!"

I then introduce the Inner Alignment Chart and explain to Jaclyn and Mark how they can each use it when they are triggered and need to establish separateness from their own Hurt Child and Little Adult. With the Chart, they will be developing themselves as objective True Adults, better able to handle the upsetting interactions that occur in their family situations.

Jaclyn says, "Ron, I know this is our first session, and we have a long way to go, but…" She looks at Mark, then at Kyle and Sarah, and then back at me. "I feel for the first time, in a long time, that it's possible for us to be a real family again."

The session is over, and the family prepares to leave. They thank me in chorus, and I'm delighted that they have taken a big step toward establishing harmony in their family.

Your Turn:

Your Own Conversation

In this activity, you will once again complete an Inner Alignment Chart, this time for a family issue, as directed in part A. Then, in part B, you will use your Chart to have a spoken Conversation with your Child, instead of writing out the Conversation in your Child's Journal, as you did in previous chapters. You'll move to level 3 of skill building by adding sense-making commentary to your True Adult response.

A. *Chart Your Family Issue*

Fill in an Inner Alignment Chart about an issue you have with a person in your family. This person can be a spouse, child, parent, sibling, or anyone close enough for you to consider part of your family. If you don't have issues in your current family, use any unresolved issue from your family of origin.

Download the template for an Inner Alignment Chart from my website (InnerAlignmentMethod.com) and fill it in according to the following steps.

FILLING IN YOUR *INNER ALIGNMENT CHART*

Step 1: The Incident

Briefly describe an upsetting interaction you had with someone in your family. This can be an argument or any interaction in which things didn't go the way you wanted them to go, and you were left with uncomfortable feelings. Keeping it brief, 1 to 3 sentences, strengthens you as a True Adult.

Step 2: Hurt Child's *Feelings*

These include your Hurt Child's spontaneous feelings about the interaction, such as anger, sadness, etc.

Step 3: Little Adult's Reactive *Thoughts*

These include judgments of yourself, the other person or persons, or both.

Step 4: Little Adult's *Actions* Imagined and/or Actual

Describe what your Little Adult imagined doing—either at the time of the incident, or later, upon reflection— and then ultimately did to cope with the upsetting situation.

B. *A Conversation with Your Child—Level 3*

In this activity, you will be using your Inner Alignment Chart from part A to support you in having a back-and-forth dialogue between your Child and you as a True Adult. Again, you will be using your Chart, switching seats each time you verbalize an item listed under each category, as you did in chapter 9. Now, however, add sense-making commentary when reflecting back to your Child what he or she has said. You've practiced using sense-making commentary when writing Conversations in your Child's Journal. Now, adding it to your spoken Conversation brings the full power of transformational listening to your experience.

The addition of sense-making commentary marks the third level of skill development in having verbal Conversations with your Child. Your Conversations are now more likely than before to elicit exponential healing, by taking you back to a time in your past when the wounding originated. Such revelations can be unsettling when they come up, so I advise you to always have your empowerment notebooks with you when practicing a level 3 Conversation. Then, you can deepen and integrate the experience by writing about it.

A fourth level of skill in these Conversations happens when you no longer need a Chart to guide you, because the dialogue in the Conversations happens spontaneously, in the moment. As you've seen in the training sessions, my clients have Conversations without a Chart because I am present as a coach, replacing the need for a Chart. For now, I recommend that you continue filling in a Chart to use as your training wheels, to support you in having spoken Conversations with your Child. For the times when you don't want to take your chart into a Conversation with your Child, remember that writing down your Child's feelings and Little Adult's reactive thoughts in chart form is valuable on its own.

Here are the directions for using your family-issue Inner Alignment Chart to create a back-and-forth dialogue, adding the new element of sense-making commentary, as follows.

LEVEL 3: READING YOUR CHART, SWITCHING BACK AND FORTH, AND ADDING SENSE-MAKING COMMENTARY

1: Set up two chairs and begin in your True Adult Seat

Establish your separateness from your Child by simply taking a moment in silence. Enjoy being unburdened by your Child's feelings and reactions regarding the specific incident.

Switch to your Child's Seat.

2: Read the incident

As your Child, read the incident out loud to your True Adult. Take a moment in silence to experience having expressed yourself to a safe and interested Big Person.

Switch to your True Adult Seat.

3: Reflect back what your Child said

As a True Adult, begin by silently receiving what has just been shared with you. Then respond, repeating back what your Child said about the upsetting incident. Take a moment to silently be with your Child before switching.

Switch to your Child's Seat.

4: Read your first feeling

As your Child, begin by basking in the experience, as you are able, of hearing your True Adult reflect back to you about the incident. Now, let yourself connect to the first feeling word in your chart so that you feel it. Then speak it to your True Adult by using the word *I.* For example, "I feel . . ."

Switch to your True Adult Seat.

5: Reflect back your Child's feelings

First, receive the words your Child has spoken and then reflect back the feeling word by using the pronoun *you.* This time, ***add sense-making commentary,*** as you are able. For example, if your Child expresses anger over a family incident, you might reflect back by saying, "It makes sense that you'd feel angry, because you believe you were treated unfairly."

Switch to your Child's Seat.

6: Read your next feeling word

Again, as your Child, and as you are able, bask in the experience of being seen, heard, and responded to by your own True Adult. Then, look toward your True Adult and, reading from the Chart, say, "I feel . . ."

7: Continue switching back and forth

Express one Chart item at a time and switch seats to reflect the item back. After going through the feeling words, go to the next step: Little Adult's reactive thoughts. As a True Adult, continue to add sense-making commentary, if able, when reflecting back each reactive thought and action. For example: *Jerry's such an idiot.* True Adult: *It makes sense you think Jerry's an idiot, because he insulted you in front of everyone.* Then move on to Little Adult's actions. For example, *I walked away as if it didn't bother me.* True Adult: *It makes sense that you'd walk away as if it didn't bother you, because you did not want to risk things getting worse.*

8: Complete reading from your Chart

Use this back-and-forth format until all items have been read and responded to.

Partner variation

The back-and-forth dialogue of this chart activity can also be accomplished by having another person respond as a True Adult to your Child.

Here's how to do it: Instead of switching seats yourself, have a partner sit opposite you. Begin with step 1 on your Chart, the incident. Reading as your Child, go through all four steps. For each step, your partner reflects your words back to you. For example, if you read *I feel sad*, your partner says back, *You feel sad.*

Your partner is not likely to use sense-making commentary in his or her reflection, unless you instruct him or her in how to do it, as sense-making commentary is a more specialized listening skill. Still, the simple process of listening and reflecting can be very powerful, because your Child always wants to be seen and heard by a safe and reliable Big Person.

Tip: It's not a problem if you as a True Adult or someone else responding to your Child as a True Adult is inaccurate in the sense-making commentary, because your Child can always clarify what is accurate. For example, "Actually, I walked away because I was embarrassed."

Take the time to write in your Child's Journal to express feelings that may have come up during the activity, both comfortable as well as uncomfortable. Also, write any observations and insights you have about your Child's experience in your True Adult Log. The deeper healing you are now doing with your Child may be further integrated when you journal about your experiences.

▲

What's Next...

In the next chapter, Mark and Jaclyn return for a second session, this time without their children. In their second session, Mark experiences the exponential healing power of a Child–Adult Conversation to resolve a wound that has been at the root of the couple's current family issues. As a result of their Child–Adult Conversations, both Mark and Jaclyn gain a bigger-picture perspective and are thus empowered as True Adults to make more effective choices for greater peace, love, and intimacy in their relationship.

CHAPTER 12

FAMILY RELATIONSHIPS: EXPONENTIAL HEALING

In families, the buried wounds of the parents impact their children, who then grow up in the shadow of those wounds. Parents who did not have a True Adult consistently present and available for their own Child when they were growing up can't help but pass their wounds on to their children. I AM Training allows you to go right to the source of the original trauma, providing your inner Child with a much-needed True Adult. This enables you to heal your Child's wounds and thus free your children from carrying the burden of a painful legacy.

In their second session, Jaclyn and Mark discover how Inner Alignment helps break transgenerational patterns through exponential healing. You have seen how exponential healing is an accelerated, permanent healing of past wounds that transcends time and results in *true* change. With exponential healing, the wounds of the past remain in the past, no longer interfering with your life. You are then free to make new choices from a bigger-picture perspective, which I call *True Adult Clarity*.

Let's enter the session and see how exponential healing leads to this new perspective of True Adult Clarity. Then, I will show you how you can add a section to your Inner Alignment Chart for discovering and recording new True Adult perspectives that were unperceivable when your Little Adult was in charge.

Mark and Jaclyn's Second Session:
A Family Transformed

Mark and Jaclyn arrive for their second session, this time without their children, and sit across from me on the couch. They both look anxious for our session to begin. After I invite them to share, Jaclyn looks over at Mark, frowns, and turns to me.

"Ron, after our last session, we took the kids out to dinner and enjoyed ourselves like we hadn't in years." Jaclyn pauses and looks at Mark, who smiles slightly, and then continues. "The next several days continued to be incredible. The kids didn't have one argument, and Mark and I spent private time together every night after the kids were in bed. One night, we talked for hours about how we'd first met and started dating. I mean, everything seemed so new.

"Then we hit a snag. Last night, Kyle was picking on Sarah for bringing her doll to the dinner table, and Mark had just arrived home from work. I didn't want to bother him, so I took the kids up to Sarah's bedroom and tried to do what you showed us—to be a True Adult with them.

"It felt uncomfortable at first, but I told them I was going to listen to each of them talk about any feelings and thoughts that had come up at the dinner table. I also told them to listen as each other talked. Kyle said, 'You mean just like you and Dad did with that man, Ron?'

"Sarah started first, complaining that Kyle was mean and saying she would never play with him again. Sarah cried as she talked, hugging her doll the whole time. Kyle just sat there looking straight ahead. I listened to everything Sarah said, then reflected it all back as best I could—just like you did with Mark and me in our last session.

"I said, 'Sarah, of course you'd be angry with Kyle for making fun of you. You know that you deserve for him to treat you kindly and respectfully. It makes sense you'd feel hurt when he makes fun of you, because it never feels good when someone makes fun of us. And, you love your brother, which makes it feel worse.' Right then, Sarah popped off the bed and threw her arms around my neck—I was so surprised!

"Then I turned to Kyle, who was standing with his arms folded, looking down. I said, 'It's your turn, Honey, to share.' He glanced over at Sarah, then fixed his eyes on me and just poured his heart out. He said he was angry that Sarah got more attention because she's younger and a girl, and that he was scared to tell me or Mark about feeling so angry. He also talked about feeling bad for picking on her. He shared about a recent incident at school when some kids laughed at him and called him names for saying he likes playing with his sister.

"I waited a moment and then reflected back what Kyle had said, just as I'd done with Sarah. I felt so much compassion for him as I told him it made sense that he was feeling angry that Sarah gets more attention than he does, because it seems unfair. And how I got how hard it was for him when kids teased him about playing with his sister.

"When I finished, Kyle slowly walked over to me and, without saying a word, gave me a big hug. Then he jumped on the bed and hugged his sister. She beamed and immediately handed him her doll. Then the most wonderful thing happened... both kids jumped on me, and all three of us fell into a giant hug!

"I got the kids ready for bed and tucked them in with lots of hugs and kisses. I was so excited to share what had happened with Mark that I rushed downstairs and quickly took his dinner into the living room where he was watching TV. I told him every detail of what had happened with the kids, raising my voice over the TV and hardly taking a breath.

"Then I looked at him . . . and I froze. He was just sitting there, staring angrily at the TV. He picked up the remote control, muted the TV, and said in a loud voice, 'Well, Honey, I'm glad you had so much fun playing shrink with the kids while I nearly starved to death!' Then he reached for his food and turned the TV volume back on, even louder."

Mark sighs deeply and Jaclyn continues. "Ron, I was overcome with mixed emotions. I felt so confused, angry, hurt, sad.... Then, well... I just snapped. I told him that if he really loved his kids, he would be proud of me for being a True Adult with them. But he just sat there, eating and watching TV, like I wasn't even there!

"Then I really lost it. I screamed at him for not caring about the kids, not caring about me, not caring about our marriage... not caring that we just started this therapy process. I was livid, and it was all I could do to restrain myself from picking up his dinner plate and throwing it in his face!

"He got up without a word and stormed up the stairs. He didn't even take his plate to the kitchen. I was still so angry that I turned off the TV and dumped the rest of his food in the trash, right along with his plate. I went out into the backyard and sat in a lawn chair, thinking, *What have I done... that a perfect week could end this way? It's the last time I share anything with that self-absorbed... TV addict!* I just felt so confused and alone."

Jaclyn stops there and leans back in her chair, her face flushed. Mark sits silently, looking down. After a few moments of silence, I reflect back to Jaclyn, using sense-making commentary, the feelings and reactive thoughts she has shared. When I'm finished, I acknowledge Jaclyn for having been a True Adult, so beautifully, with Kyle and Sarah. I emphasize that to the degree we are able to be a True Adult for ourselves, we can then be a True Adult for others.

I see that Jaclyn's Little Adult is still looking worried and tense, so I take the opportunity to share with both her and Mark a key principle of I AM Training. "Jaclyn, I want you to consider that whatever you experience—the arguments and fights, the anger and sadness—all of it, no matter how unpleasant—is all perfectly facilitating your healing and growth. In short, *nothing is ever wrong.* You'll begin to see that events are arranged by the Infinite Children who are all in communication with each other. Your Children, like all Children, create a kind of divine choreography to expose buried wounds that have been blocking the truth of who you both are. Only when those wounds are brought into the light and your painful feelings are experienced, can they be healed, freeing you to live a more authentic and fulfilling life.

"Of course, it doesn't feel that way when you're in the middle of a fight, like the two of you were last night. It takes experience to know in the moment that conflicts are always an invitation to self-discovery, evolving you to a higher quality of life. As you practice I AM and see how everything that happens moves you forward, it becomes easier to see in each moment that *nothing is ever wrong*."

Putting the Past in the Past:
Exponential Healing

I look over at Mark who seems lost in thought. He looks at me, his eyes now brimming with tears, and suddenly explodes. "Well, it certainly seems wrong, what Jaclyn did! She didn't even ask me to join her with the kids, to be part of listening to them.... I mean... I wish I had been there for that!"

Mark glares at Jaclyn, her mouth open and eyes wide with surprise at his outburst. He looks back at me and continues. "Ron, in our last session you trained me to be a True Adult for my Child, and it felt good. But Jaclyn doesn't want me to be there with the kids. It's like I don't exist. She comes downstairs after leaving me alone and hungry, gives me a plate of cold food, and expects me to be thrilled that she just had such a great time with the kids—*without me!*

"I was so hurt when she told me how all three of them hugged. She never invited me to be a True Adult with the kids. I felt left out, like I'm just in this family to bring in the bulk of the income and cover the bills." Mark stops, visibly shaken by his own words.

"In the last session, Ron . . ." Mark's voice is now quivering with emotion. "You heard how Jaclyn said to me, *Try being a real father*. But then... when there's an opportunity, she leaves me out. I was so angry at her, but at the same time, I felt guilty for feeling like that about the mother of my children. I love Jaclyn... but I felt confused, so I just shut down, and then I went upstairs to bed."

Mark pauses, looks down, and shakes his head slowly from side to side. Jaclyn covers her face with her hands. I move the box of tissues closer to her and sit in silence. She takes a tissue and dabs her eyes, then looks at me and nods.

I turn my attention to Mark and reflect back to him, "How painful and hurtful it must have been for you not to be included in this major family interaction when you were home and had the ability to be part of everything." Mark nods as Jaclyn reaches over and takes his hand.

I let a few moments pass and then continue, "Mark, I would like you to sit in my chair now and, as I just did, be a True Adult for your Child." I move, and Mark takes my chair.

I begin to coach Mark. "As you know, Mark, all the feelings and reactive thoughts that you were just expressing came from your Child. Now, he gets to hear you reflect back what he shared, as you did in our last session. This time, be open to receiving any memories that your Child might want to bring to you."

Mark hesitates before replying. "But Ron, I don't remember things that happened in my childhood."

"That's okay; you don't need to actively recall any memories. Your Child will bring them to you at the perfect time as you remain open and available to him."

Mark's face relaxes. He turns toward the empty chair where his Child now sits. He takes a few moments and then begins to address his Child. "Little Mark, of course you would feel angry about feeling left out of the conversation with the kids, especially when you finally know what to do." Mark takes a breath and steadies himself. I nod encouragement and he continues.

"How could you not be angry hearing Jaclyn describe the love and closeness she had shared with the kids while you were left alone and hungry? Of course it would hurt you to hear how they all had a big hug together—without you. How alone you felt in your own family, as if you were only the breadwinner and nothing else."

Mark pauses and reaches for more tissues. He continues. "It makes sense, little Mark, that you felt left out and blamed Jaclyn for not inviting you into such a meaningful encounter with the kids. And it makes sense that you felt guilty about judging Jaclyn when she was just trying to help them. And then you judged yourself for getting angry with her, thinking you'd been selfish."

Mark pauses, shaking his head from side to side. Suddenly, he sits upright, and with his voice increasing in volume, continues addressing his Child. "Marky, buddy, all your feelings and everything that happened last night, it all makes so much sense to me!" He pauses again, his eyes now wide with intensity. "It makes sense, because when your mom got divorced for the second time, she gave all her attention to your half sister and brother, Kathy and Stevie. While you sat alone and watched TV night after night!"

Mark stops, not knowing where to go next.

It's clear to me from what he has already shared that painful memories are beginning to surface. I can feel that Mark's Little Adult could use some guidance from me. "Mark, just let your Child respond to the significant things you just said to him."

Mark switches seats to allow his Child to speak. As he begins, I can hear in his voice the emotion of a young child who is finally being heard. "She gave Kathy and Stevie all her attention, because their dad—my stepdad—had just moved out. But *all* her attention? What about me? I needed attention, too. At least Kathy and Stevie had each other. It was even worse when my own dad left.... Mom never even sat down to talk with me about it. I lost *two* fathers—and I was sad, too."

Mark's Child begins to sob as he continues, "Watching them all together... I felt so alone." He sobs for several moments.

Mark slowly stands up, takes a handful of tissues, and moves into the True Adult Seat. After some silence, he compassionately addresses his Child. "I'd forgotten all about that, Marky buddy. It must have been so hard for you when your stepdad left and your mom gave you no attention. You were never able to talk with her or anyone else about it. You haven't even thought about how hard that time was in all these years."

Mark turns to me. "I'm not sure what to do now. Should I just switch seats?" I nod, and he follows through.

Mark's Child, now feeling totally supported by a True Adult, responds with intensity. "You bet I never thought about it! I was doing my best not to think about it by watching TV all the time. I was trying not to hear them all talking as if I wasn't even there. How could they do that? How could my mom act like I was invisible? I was just a little guy myself and I had already lost my own dad. Then I lost my second dad, too. But nobody talked to me, even after I lost *two* dads! It's like I deserved to lose them." He starts sobbing again.

Mark stays in the Child's seat for several more moments, tears running down his face. Then he slowly stands up and switches seats.

Now, as a True Adult: "Marky buddy, I'm so glad you're talking to me about this. It's so huge. You were just a little guy when your dad left, without anyone talking with you about any of it. And then it happened all over again. But it was even worse this time because when your mom finally did talk about it, it wasn't to *you*.... You weren't included even though you were right there."

Mark switches seats again, this time to his Child's Seat.

"Thank you. It feels so good that I can express my feelings and that you hear me. It's hard to hold them in all the time. Watching TV gets me through the stress, but it's still really painful. The pressure just keeps building up, but at least talking to you... somehow... I feel relieved." He gazes at the seat of his True Adult for several moments.

After moving to the True Adult Seat, Mark looks over at Jaclyn, and then turns to me. "That was intense—how the memory of my mother abandoning me came out of nowhere." Mark tries to gain some equilibrium, but he is clearly shaken.

"That's often how it happens, Mark," I respond. "Your Child will bring to you what he needs you to hear to free him from the pain he's carried for so long."

"I could see myself when I was young, sitting on a sofa in the family room and watching cartoons all alone." Mark is now connecting even more deeply to this core wound from childhood.

Gently, I redirect Mark back into the Conversation with his Child.

He turns and addresses his Child directly. "You were sitting there watching cartoons by yourself, hearing your mother at the kitchen table with Kathy and Stevie. She kept telling them how much she loved them and that they would be okay, that *their* dad loved them and always would. But she never told you that *your* dad loved you when he left. How could you not feel so hurt and alone? You were completely left out, as if you weren't part of any family at all."

Mark's eyes fill up with tears.

I notice Jaclyn reaching over for more tissues and wiping away her own tears. I am deeply moved, and I remain available for whatever comes next from Mark's Child.

After a few moments, Mark switches to his Child's Seat and exclaims, "Wait a minute! Jaclyn and the kids... it's like she's my mom with Kathy and Stevie. I never thought of it that way, but that's exactly how I felt last night, when I was sitting in front of the TV, and Jaclyn was upstairs with the kids... the same as back then with my mom, and Kathy, and Stevie! I felt left out then, and I still do now. I felt my mom didn't love me, because... because I reminded her of my dad... and he left her. She hated him, so she hated me!"

Mark is quiet, staring down for several moments.

I too am silent, listening for the guidance that I rely on from my own Child. When it feels right to me, I gently say, "When you're ready, I'd like to speak with your True Adult."

He nods and switches seats.

I now address Mark in his True Adult Seat. "That was a pretty powerful experience for a young child to go through, wouldn't you say?"

"Oh man! It was really brutal. How could a mother do that? How could she blame her son for how his dad was? I wasn't my dad. I didn't even spend much time with my dad, but she still blamed me."

"You might want to say that to little Mark."

"Right." Mark nods and turns to his Child. "How horrible that must have been for your mom to blame you like you were your dad. It makes sense you've always felt so out of place, like you don't really belong, no matter where you are. You always feel like that's just the way it is, and there's nothing you can do about it."

Mark moves to his Child's Seat and begins speaking immediately. "None of it was my fault! I hardly even knew my dad, so how could I have been like him?"

True Adult: "Marky buddy, you're seeing that none of it was your fault. You felt like your mom treated you as if you *were* your dad, but you hardly even knew your dad at all. It makes sense that you've always felt so uncomfortable around your mom… it was like she cut you off the day your father left her and didn't love you anymore. After that, you felt like an outsider."

Child: "Yeah! And I feel the same way when I get home from work and see Jaclyn with the kids, like I'm not really a part of my own family. It's like Jaclyn and the kids are the real family, and I'm… I'm… I don't know…"

True Adult: "Little Marky, I so get it. You feel like you're not a real member of your own family. It's like you're the breadwinner… and you're not a bad guy, so they keep you around. But you never feel that you have the same importance as Jaclyn and the kids."

Child: "Right. Like I'm not really that important. So I make sure I work hard and earn enough money to pay the bills… so they'll let me stay around. Growing up, I was always afraid that one day I'd finally be kicked out. That's why I kept so quiet and watched TV all the time, so they'd have no reason to kick me out. And, I had to numb out so I wouldn't worry about everything."

True Adult: "It makes so much sense that now you do the same thing, automatically, every day when you get home. You go right to the TV as soon as you can to numb out. But now, you tell yourself it's because you're tired from work. And you *are* tired from work, because at work you feel the same way. You feel like you don't really belong there, either."

Mark turns to me and says, "Ron, I can feel that Marky is getting tired. I think this is a lot for one day."

"It is a lot, Mark. Change seats and let your Child have the last word to complete the Conversation. Then, when your Child is finished, come back to your True Adult Seat and silently sit with your Child and what the two of you have created together in this Conversation."

After switching, Mark sits quietly in his Child's Seat for a few moments and then speaks to his True Adult. "Thank you for getting that I'm tired, and that all this was a lot to go through today." He sighs and continues, "I feel like a ton of weight has been lifted off of me. And I'm actually feeling a whole lot better than I can ever remember."

Mark switches back into his True Adult Seat, sits silently, and looks straight ahead for several moments. He is letting his Child integrate the experience of having had a True Adult available to him in the way he has always needed. After a sigh of relief, he turns to Jaclyn, smiling and nodding his head. Jaclyn responds with a warm, loving smile.

Turning to me, Mark says, "Ron, I have this feeling of wholeness right now. It's like… I've found a missing piece of myself."

Mark has no further words. He turns toward Jaclyn who reaches out to give him a hug. She wraps her arms around him and whispers audibly into his ear, "What a courageous man I have. I love you so much."

With eyes closed, they hold each other tightly for a long moment. Our session is now over.

True Adult Clarity

As you followed Mark's Child–Adult Conversation, you saw how his connection with his Child had the power to bring old wounds to the surface for healing and integration. As a result of his exponential healing, Mark was able to view recent events from a bigger-picture perspective and see that Jaclyn's actions were not aimed at him personally. He could then see other options for responding to similar situations and choose an option from the vantage point of his new perspective, which I call *True Adult Clarity*.

Let's recap how I AM Training brings you to a state of True Adult Clarity, giving you options and choices unavailable to you in Little Adult mode.

It begins with your willingness to connect with your Child. Listening and reflecting back, as you've learned to do, establishes trust and develops your relationship. In the exponential healing that occurs in a Child–Adult Conversation, you discover how emotional reactions to the people in your current life are simply the stirrings of old wounds from childhood. By traveling back in time to revisit your painful wounding experiences, you provide a True Adult where one was desperately needed. You become clear that your undesirable feelings and reactive thoughts, based on those experiences, formed a constant undercurrent that still impacts all your interactions.

As it becomes clearer that the feelings of a Hurt Child and the reactive coping methods of a Little Adult have been running your life based on the past, you find yourself separating from those feelings and thoughts. You recognize that nothing is personal and that, as a True Adult, you are no longer powerless. This frees you from feeling like a victim in your life. Your new awareness and objectivity free you from the trap of repeated painful conflicts, because you finally see that *it's never about what it seems to be about*. It's *always* about your Child's wounds.

Once you're connected with your Child, you have the power to transform experiences that, in the past, would have left your Child feeling mistreated and powerless. For example, before his I AM Training, Mark would react as though he was a powerless child and Jaclyn was his mom. Since his Child–Adult Conversations, Mark recognizes that nothing is ever personal. As a True Adult, he knows he has the power to effectively communicate with Jaclyn if something isn't working for his Child.

The Inner Alignment Chart is a tool that supports you in continuing to develop your True Adult's ability to maintain your separateness and objectivity, leading to clarity and power. It can also guide you in the back-and-forth dialogue of a Conversation with your Child.

Your inner relationship deepens over time. When you gain solidity as a True Adult and can connect reliably with your Child, more old wounds automatically surface to be healed. A new perspective on upsetting events and painful conflicts then becomes possible. Increasingly, you look through the eyes of a True Adult and see the truth, rather than the false, programmed reality your Little Adult had been living by. You could not have had this perspective when you were required to react as a Little Adult in order to survive. But as a True Adult, you can now make new, more effective choices from the perspective of True Adult Clarity.

Mark experienced True Adult Clarity in his realization that Jaclyn was not trying to exclude him, as his mother had done in the past. From this new perspective, he could see that Jaclyn had simply wanted to give him some peace and quiet by taking the children upstairs. With such True Adult Clarity, he can now respond differently if the same situation were to occur again. A new option for Mark might be to postpone his dinner, grab a snack, and follow Jaclyn and the kids upstairs. He would then be a part of the family interaction, and not feel excluded, which is what his Child had longed for.

As you have come to see and hopefully experience, the connection you make with your Child through I AM Training can literally change the past as you experienced it. Your future, no longer bound by history, is then filled with new possibilities for you to live in the truth of who you are.

Your Turn:

Standing in True Adult Clarity

You can develop True Adult Clarity by extending one of your previously completed Inner Alignment Charts to include the True Adult Clarity Chart. This chart contains two new steps: step 5: *True Adult Big-Picture View* and step 6: *True Adult Options for Action*. A template for the True Adult Clarity Chart can be downloaded from my website: InnerAlignment-Method.com. If you choose, you can put your Clarity Chart information in your True Adult Log.

Follow the directions below:

FILLING IN YOUR TRUE ADULT CLARITY CHART

1: Begin with a recently completed Inner Alignment Chart or fill in a new one.

2: Then use the Chart to have a spoken Conversation with your Child, adding sense-making commentary when you are moved to do so. You may need to follow the steps as described in chapter 11. Regardless of whether or not memories come up for exponential healing, the Conversation is often the key for you to gain a new perspective of clarity and choice.

3: Next, fill in these two new steps, either on a True Adult Clarity Chart or in your True Adult Log: step 5, True Adult Bigger-Picture Thoughts, and step 6, True Adult Options for Action. Write as a True Adult, this time not reflecting back your Child and Little Adult. Rather, let yourself connect to the bigger-picture perspective, guided by your Infinite Child. This perspective will just come to you; you do not even need to recognize that it's coming from your Infinite Child.

Follow the chart example below regarding the incident Mark worked with in his Child–Adult Conversation in my office. Note that, similar to the way Mark's True Adult spoke with me about his Child during his sessions, Mark also writes about his Child in the Chart, just as you have been learning to put

True Adult/therapist notes in your Log. This strengthens separateness while creating the experience for his Child of having a supportive Big Person on the scene.

Mark's Inner Alignment Chart		
Step 1: Incident – Jaclyn is a True Adult with the children and settles their argument without me as if I'm not home.		
Step 2: Hurt Child's Feelings	**Step 3: Little Adult's Reactive *Thoughts* (usually judgments of self or others)**	**Step 4: Little Adult's *Actions* Imagined and/or Actual**
I feel Angry	I'm not valued.	**Imagined:**
	I don't matter.	Yelling at Jaclyn!
I feel Resentful	No one cares about how I feel.	**Actual:**
		Shutting down
I feel Hurt	Jaclyn is selfish not to include me with the kids.	Watching TV
I feel Sad		Ignoring Jaclyn
	How dare she judge me, saying that I'm not a real father!	Storming off

After having the conversation with his Child, Mark was capable of discovering a bigger picture, This new perspective was what allowed him to see how Jaclyn's Child made sense. This helped him begin to understand that nothing is ever personal.

He filled in the new steps, 5 and 6. First he recorded his True Adult's thoughts based on the bigger picture. Next, he recorded his True Adult's options for action, based on the bigger picture:

Mark's True Adult Clarity Chart	
Step 5: True Adult Thoughts Based on the Bigger Picture	**Step 6: True Adult Options/ Choices Based on the Bigger Picture**
What happened with Jaclyn and the kids was filtered through my Hurt Child's past experiences. My Little Adult made all the same interpretations with Jaclyn and the kids that he did as a child with his mother and half siblings. He thought that the way he was treated was personal, when in fact it was not. I see now that his mother never worked out her own issues with his dad, so she took them out on little Mark. Jaclyn was just trying to take care of the kids, so Marky could have some peace and quiet after work. She was not choosing to leave Marky out of the valuable interaction she had with them. She probably didn't know she'd be having those conversations with the kids until they happened in the moment.	*Option #1:* I could use the tools I'm learning to address my Child's upset. Then, as a separate True Adult, I could work things out with Jaclyn. If I couldn't get separate right away, I'd work with my Child until I was separate enough to go upstairs and join her with the kids. *Option #2:* Given that I didn't know in advance that Jaclyn was going to have a Child–Adult Conversation with the kids, I could have just worked with my Child on the feelings that were already stirred up for him—being tired, resenting his job, etc. Then I'd get my own dinner from the kitchen and enjoy relaxing until Jaclyn came downstairs. *Option #3:* After being triggered by hearing about the interaction Jaclyn had with the kids, I could either work with my Child's feelings on my own or have Jaclyn support me in having a Conversation with my Child.

By getting practice in writing out your newly acquired True Adult Clarity on an extended Chart, you will find yourself reacting less and less from your Little Adult's drive to survive at all costs. Your Hurt Child will be freed from such "protective" domination, and your Child of the Infinite will be able to guide you in the most profound experience of life, a relationship with your infinite source of knowledge and wisdom.

Let's recap the structure of the new power you have to raise the quality of the rest of your life. Your Hurt Child is the source of your feelings. Without the presence of your True Adult to properly address those feelings, healing and resolution cannot occur. Your Coping Child reacts to the void by attempting to address the feelings of your Hurt Child. However, your Coping Child lacks the power to make things right, especially without the requisite clarity—the ability to see the big picture—to effectively take care of your Hurt Child's feelings, both within and with others.

Anytime you have an uncomfortable reaction to someone or something, your Child is experiencing the painful absence of a True Adult and thus needs you to step in to address your Child's feelings for resolution. Once you do so, your Child no longer needs to go into Little Adult coping mode. Instead, your Child feels taken care of and moves forward naturally.

Therefore, whenever you feel the stirrings of reactivity, remember that it's best not to speak or act until you have taken at least a moment to connect with your Child. That way, not only do you avoid continuing to recreate your Child's painful past, you bring in True Adult power to clear the past and make things right for your Child.

▲

What's Next...

In the next chapter, I share stories from both my clients' lives and my own to illustrate what it looks like to live as a True Adult in your everyday experience. In the Epilogue, I briefly reflect on the implications of a future society being led largely by True Adults, specifically in the arenas of business, education, and the environment.

For a moment, try to imagine a world led by True Adults, guided by the Children of the Infinite. Is it possible?

I think it is.

Part IV

LIVING
YOUR ULTIMATE
RELATIONSHIP:

Inner Alignment and the Realm
of the Children

CHAPTER 13

TRUE ADULT: FROM SURVIVING TO THRIVING...AND EVER EVOLVING

Life as a True Adult is a wondrous adventure. You no longer merely survive in the trap of Little Adult reaction, endlessly repeating painful experiences from the past. Instead, you thrive in your new relationship with yourself, enjoying clarity, guidance, and the intimacy you've so longed for.

In this chapter, you will hear stories of what it's like to live the promise of life as a True Adult, both in your relationship with your Child and with the Children in everyone. You will see what life can be like when you are guided by your Infinite Child to step outside your assumed limits and find creative solutions to everyday challenges. Your reactions to life's stresses fade—frustration and anxiety, for example, give way to ease and inspiration. Effectiveness and productivity increase, and joy radiates from within, spreading to everyone around you. Life is rich with purpose and direction. The Infinite Child you are has finally arrived.

As an emerging True Adult, you are on an accelerated path of development and evolution. The tools of I AM Training, and the relationship with yourself they make possible, give you the ongoing ability to upgrade your life in every way.

Are you ready to start living the promise of life as a True Adult? Are you ready to shift from surviving to thriving… to evolving into the person you truly are? If so, here's where you're headed.

True Adult Evolution

Looking back on the work you've done in this book, you can see that you have been on a developmental path, leading you to becoming a True Adult. First, you learned how to listen to and receive your Child in a transformational way.

Then, by writing in your empowerment notebooks and using the Inner Alignment Chart, you quickly separated as a True Adult, able to become objective about your Hurt Child and Little Adult and distinguish the survival methods of your Coping Child/Little Adult. This helped your Little Adult to relax, quieting the noise inside your head.

Simultaneously, you were having Child–Adult Conversations that built trust, healed old wounds, and solidified your bond with your Child. You began to discover, as a True Adult, your ability to acquire a bigger-picture perspective of your Child's experience. Such a perspective empowers you to choose the most effective options to best care for your Child while strengthening your relationships with others. In short, you've achieved what few have. With ongoing practice, you'll continue developing a solid and intimate relationship with yourself— your ultimate relationship. This is a great accomplishment.

As you advance in your training, your channels will continue to open and your Infinite Child's guidance will flow through to you as a True Adult. Eventually, you will become well established in a profound relationship with your Child of the Infinite, experiencing magic and miracles as ordinary occurrences in your everyday life—your extraordinary life.

But the True Adult path doesn't usually unfold in such a smooth or linear fashion; each of us progresses in a way that is uniquely our own. Nonetheless, as we progress, we travel along a continuum of growth between Little Adult and True Adult—from surviving to thriving—shifting back and forth between the two as we evolve.

When you are driving your car, how often do you need to adjust the wheel to stay on course? If you don't pay attention to the necessary adjustments, you know you would have a rough ride and potentially serious consequences on the road. However, just as paying attention to your driving avoids accidents, becoming more aware of your feelings, judgments, and actions, as you do in I AM Training, ensures that you avoid upsets in your life.

I don't think we can ever experience being a True Adult 100 percent of the time, but as you establish and deepen your relationship with your Child, you find that your forward movement along the continuum is more consistent. The more you connect, the more you evolve, leading you to a rapid and accelerated path of development that becomes a way of life. You increasingly experience life on the True Adult side of the continuum, choosing your actions rather than being run by Little Adult programming. When you do have Little Adult moments, you transform them by using your Inner Alignment tools and stepping in as a True Adult, giving your Child what he or she needs to heal, grow, and evolve.

So far, we have focused on developing your True Adult by creating a relationship with your Child, facilitating the healing of your core wounds. This has led you to achieve clarity and the ability to choose more effective actions. In this chapter, the focus shifts to the possibilities that exist for you as a True Adult, both in alignment with your own Child and with the Children in everyone, leading to a life filled with meaningful and fulfilling interactions.

Living in Not Knowing

As a True Adult, you develop the capacity to empty yourself of preconceived ideas and receive wisdom from your inner and outer experience. You practiced this ability to "not know" through the skill of transformational listening, which allowed you to receive your Child's past wounding experiences without judgment or agenda.

Living in a state of not knowing may seem counterintuitive, believing as we often do that wisdom requires us to already know about everything. Little Adults are perpetually trying to analyze and figure things out, hoping to feel more confident and prepared to protect their Child. But with Inner Alignment, wisdom comes from the Child of the Infinite in the living moment, not from what we already know.

Getting comfortable with not knowing—welcoming it as a way of life—frees you from clinging to any one perspective or belief and allows you to greet new ideas with interest and enthusiasm. This becomes even more essential when your connection to your Child expands, and you start receiving guidance from your Child of the Infinite. This takes you beyond the limitations of what you already know or think you are capable of.

The Infinite Child is always guiding us to re-open our minds and to realize we are not to be limited by what we already know. Magic is everywhere, especially within us, in the form of our Child of the Infinite. Life provides the training, always giving us opportunities to receive with greater clarity that *the answer lies within*.

The following story is one example of how I let myself be guided in going beyond my limits. It is one of many examples of how my Infinite Child continually teaches me, freeing me from limiting thoughts and beliefs about what is possible.

Infinite Child Push-Ups

As a martial artist, one of the ways I stay fit is by doing push-ups on a regular basis. One day, the idea came to me to do them in a different way. I had done push-ups both on my fingers and on my knuckles before, but this time I was inspired to try them on the tips of my fingers. At first, it seemed too preposterous an idea for my rational mind to even consider. But recognizing what was clearly a firm request from my Infinite Child, I decided to go for it.

I began by getting down on my knees and putting my fingers and thumbs on the carpet, bent at the top joints. Then I leaned forward to add body weight. Again, it seemed impossible to extend my arms into a push-up position.

You can do it if you're willing to trust me and totally embrace that it's possible, I heard my Child say.

On my first attempt, I collapsed immediately. Pushing myself back up into a kneeling position, I heard the words of my Infinite Child once again. *You can do this if you totally embrace that it's possible and follow my guidance, not your programmed ways of thinking.*

By letting go of what I had thought was possible, I found myself moved to a deeper place of trust in my Child's guidance. I poised myself on my knees, ready to make it happen. Once again, I put my fingers and thumbs on the carpet, bent at the top joints, and leaned forward. This time, I was able to lift and hold my entire body in a push-up position—supported by my toes, fingertips, and both thumb tips.

Then my Child said, *Now do a push-up.*

I could hardly believe I was holding my body weight on my fingertips, much less that I could move up and down in that position. But I focused, went for it, and then the impossible happened: I successfully did a full push-up. I jumped to my feet, excited about my new ability.

My Child exclaimed, *Now do five more!*

Okay, I can do this, I responded, rubbing my hands together in preparation. I got down onto the tips of my fingers, thumbs and toes again, and proceeded to do five full push-ups. "I *did* it!" I yelled, jumping up when I finished.

Over the next few days, I continued listening to my Infinite Child's guidance to discover that I was capable of virtually anything I wanted to accomplish. At the end of four days, I was able to do 25 fingertip push-ups in a row. Once again, out of my willingness to free myself from limiting thoughts and beliefs, my Child took me to a new level of success, beyond what I thought was even possible.

True Adult as Coach

True Adults are receptive, but they can also take an active role by intervening on behalf of their Child when needed. This is similar to how a parent intervenes to support a young child who is facing challenging circumstances. In the role of a coach, your True Adult can provide encouragement and support in the moment, when there's no time for a Child–Adult Conversation, or when all that's needed is some True Adult backup.

For example, if your Child is experiencing fear or self-doubt about his or her ability to perform a certain task, you might say as a True Adult to your Child, *You can do this! Stay focused … that's good … you're okay … stay with it!* Keep in mind that as a True Adult coach, you are not forcefully urging yourself to try harder, which is the case in most instances of Little Adult coaching. Rather, True Adult coaching frees up your Little Adult and welcomes in your Infinite Child, so you can reach your as yet unrealized potential.

As a True Adult coach, you are better able to work with tough challenges. The following story illustrates how my client Lois stepped in as a True Adult and coached her Child to stick to an exercise program for staying healthy and fit.

Inner Fitness Coach

When Lois first came to see me, she'd been dealing with a weight problem for many years and was, at the time, 50 pounds overweight.

"When I hit middle age, I started piling on the pounds," she told me during our first session. Now in her 60s, Lois was afraid of "going downhill quickly" if she didn't do something soon.

Working with her Child, Lois' Little Adult was able to relax and her True Adult was able to discover and heal the underlying wounds that related to her weight. She acquired a level of healing and bigger-picture clarity, bringing forth new options: to cut down on Little Adult emotional eating and make better food choices. This allowed her body to release the 50 extra pounds. Along the way, Lois was also inspired to begin an exercise program to help her maintain her weight loss. But it wasn't easy for her in the beginning. "As hard as I try, I can't seem to stick with an exercise program," she lamented during one of our sessions. As Lois continued to deepen her relationship with her Child, she was moved to start a new cardio workout routine of climbing stadium steps at the local college track. Her goal was to walk up and down 42 steps 10 times, and get it done in 30 minutes.

During her first time out, she encountered her Little Adult's need to take over; her True Adult was not yet present and in charge in this category of her life. "By my fifth set," she told me, "a voice in my head started freaking out. It was saying things like, *It's too hot... You're going to pass out or have a heart attack! You aren't breathing right! Stop doing this right now!*

"I almost stopped, but I could feel my excited Child still wanting to run up and down the steps and finish! Suddenly it became clear that the voice in my head was my Little Adult. I recognized it by the panicky tone, telling me I was about to croak and insisting that I stop no matter what! But the minute I got separate, I knew I wasn't really in danger—it was just my Little Adult running her old, protective program: *I can't do this.... It's not going to work out.... I don't relate to being truly healthy and in good physical shape.... I don't get to feel good about myself.* But the reality was that I was completely okay, and my Child wanted to run!

"The minute I assured my freaked out Little Adult that a True Adult was here, she relaxed and stopped trying to protect my more adventurous Child. I could then feel my Child's fun energy, and it gave me the boost I needed to complete my routine."

Following her breakthrough, Lois returned to the college stadium on a regular basis, keeping up her routine and even picking up speed as she moved up and down the steps in record time. Now she was able to manage her process from the perspective of True Adult Clarity, drinking plenty of water and being mindful of extreme temperatures, her breathing, and anything else her Child of the Infinite might bring to her in the moment.

"My Child is thrilled to have so much fun getting in shape," Lois said to me. "I now have the best possible workout coach helping me to reach my goals—my own True Adult!"

True Adults in Addiction and Recovery

A True Adult steps in to support the Child in a variety of challenging daily life situations. However, when one's True Adult is absent, one's Little Adult is required to come up with coping methods to distract from and avoid the painful feelings that are the reminders of past traumas (PTCM). Distractions can be as seemingly benign as spending too much time on the Internet, texting, or watching television, or as consequential as eating too much sugar, too many unhealthy foods, or too much food, or compulsive shopping, gambling, or sex. There can also be more externalized methods of distraction, such as verbally or physically abusing oneself or others, to avoid feeling one's internal pain.

Anything can be used to avoid one's pain, and can become harmful depending on how or how much it's used. It is not about one's behavior in itself, but rather the motivation behind the behavior that meaningfully informs us about ourselves or others.

A common attempt to avoid one's pain is through the abuse of alcohol or drugs. My clients with substance abuse issues who are involved in 12-step recovery groups, such as Alcoholics Anonymous (AA), find they have an additional sponsor in their own True Adult. The following story shows how, when faced with the temptation to use a substance as a means of numbing painful feelings, a True Adult can step in and make all the difference.

True Adult Stops the Craving

Paul had been trying to remain abstinent from alcohol and drugs for many months before he began his I AM Training. Participating in a 12-step program for almost two years, he had been "white knuckling it" in between "falling off the wagon" all too often.

He had been drinking, smoking marijuana, and using cocaine from the time he was a teen until his Child began to experience, at 30 years of age, having a reliable relationship with him as a True Adult. No longer having regularly scheduled sessions with me, he is now living his life in relationship with his Child. When he came in recently for a check-in session, he told me about how I AM Training was helping him to stay sober and still enjoy his social life.

"After getting clean, I didn't go out with any of my old friends who still drank and used." he told me. "As recommended in my 12-step program, I avoided them, even though I'd done so much work to heal the wounds that had led me to numb my pain with substances. But I missed my old friends and wanted to go out and socialize with them again.

"About three months ago, I decided to go out to dinner with my friend, who is a moderate drinker. I told myself I'd be fine, that it really wasn't a problem—even though I'd been warned not to hang out with friends who drink. But I didn't want to keep avoiding my friends who were only social drinkers.

"Before dinner, my friend ordered a beer. Beer had always been my favorite and I noticed a strong impulse to get one myself. I sat there at the table, really wanting a beer. Just then, I recognized my Little Adult's voice, nudging me, *Go ahead and just have one...* At that moment, it became clear that my Little Adult was in automatic reaction, moving into the coping strategy he had come to rely on for so many years. I was able to separate myself from that old me—my Little Adult—and continue to bring in my True Adult presence.

"Because of my training in Inner Alignment, I was getting to know my Child better and discovering his relationship to alcohol in a way that I hadn't realized.

A nice cold beer in a frosty glass was always my anxious Little Adult's reliable, comforting friend. As a True Adult, I saw what was going on as I watched my friend take that first sip, some of the frothy head lingering for a moment on his moustache as he lowered his glass.

"I paid close attention as my Little Adult started to fall into his old alcohol-created mind–body experience to numb his Hurt Child's pain. It all made great sense to me. I noticed how my Little Adult had created a whole alternative world where he could relax and trust that everything was okay. It was a child's attempt to do my job when I hadn't yet arrived on the scene. Only now I knew it was really *his* pain that I was feeling, not mine. All my Hurt Child needed was for *me* to be present and available for him.

"Almost instantly, my interest in having the beer evaporated. It was shocking—like I'd replaced my craving for the beer with what my Child *really* needed, a present and receptive True Adult. I didn't have to order that beer, even while I watched my friend enjoy his. I was amazed that I didn't even think about it for the rest of the evening.

"I have found that I can still enjoy my friends who are social drinkers. Oh, and some of my friends have told me that when they go out with me now, they don't drink as much as they normally do. Ron, you did tell me that it's not just our actions that impact others, it's who we are being. I'm discovering that as I keep healing my wounds, I have a powerful impact on the people in my life, just by being me—a True Adult in relationship with my Child."

Authentic Self-Expression

As a True Adult, you discover your authentic self-expression and are able to bring it forth. This is because your Infinite Child is half of who you are. When you as a True Adult, your Infinite Child's partner, are present, your full self is engaged in a truly enlightened experience of life.

As you as a True Adult allow your Child's full expression—your authentic self, you are a natural contribution to others. At the same time, you find that you are more appreciative of the contribution that others are to you. The following story illustrates how you contribute to others the most when you are aligned within and committed to your Child's deepest truth, and you express yourself authentically

Being True to Yourself

I was attending a seminar and sitting front row center in a room filled by over a thousand people. On stage, a panel of highly acclaimed professionals engaged us with their knowledge and expertise. I found one of the panel members' remarks deeply moving. Without thinking, I started clapping as I leapt to my feet. I could hear others applauding too, but soon realized that no one else was standing; I was the only person in the entire room standing up and clapping enthusiastically.

At what could have been an embarrassing moment, I considered sitting down again, but when I checked with my Child to make sure he felt strongly enough to continue standing, I received an instant response—*Yes!* I continued standing and clapping, trusting that because it felt so right, it *was* right. Soon I noticed others had joined me. When I turned around, I saw the entire room standing and applauding as whole-heartedly as I was.

Later, when audience members had an opportunity to speak with the panelists, I joined the crowd gathered around one of the speakers. Suddenly, he stopped midsentence. Looking directly at me, he said, "I have to tell you, it was incredible to see you standing up alone and clapping in a room full of a thousand people. I could tell you didn't care if anyone joined you. But they did, and your leadership energized the whole room!"

Others chimed in with their agreement, some thanking me for standing strong and expressing myself regardless of what others were doing. Their comments confirmed to me that by simply listening to my Child and expressing his truth, I had been a contribution to everyone.

I continue to discover every day the difference we can all make in the world, simply by being true to ourselves. I am often moved, sometimes to tears, when I experience people expressing themselves authentically, whether in a personal or witnessed interaction, or through the performing or fine arts, a speech, sports, or a scientific or technological breakthrough. In every aspect of life, there are countless examples of people ushering in their Infinite Child… a gift to us all.

Connecting to the Realm of the Children

As you move along the continuum of development from living all too often as a Little Adult to becoming more and more a True Adult, you start noticing that you are naturally plugged into the Realm of the Children. You find yourself increasingly able to relate to all people with ease and even love, regardless of the circumstance. You no longer feel threatened by people in authority positions who used to appear to you as the Big People of your past. Instead, you see everyone as an extension of your own Child. While remaining present with your Child, you are also available to receive and get how others with whom you are interacting make sense.

In your Child's world, no one is bigger than you. In other words, as a True Adult, you experience yourself as the CEO of *The (Your Name) Corporation*. You no longer suppress your natural expression, and instead freely feel, say, or do whatever is inside of you as a True Adult, who sees the bigger picture. You receive any negativity others send your way as free training and an opportunity to learn more about your Child and all of humanity.

This constitutes a shift in your ultimate relationship that is based on a fundamental principle of life as a True Adult: True Adults acknowledge all the Children. They treat the Child within all other people as they would their own Child. When you are connected with the Children, your life becomes an exciting experience of relationship with everyone you come across. Life gets richer and more interesting when you see that the Children are arranging all that goes on for everyone's greatest benefit and growth.

True Adults are always watching for the Children's divine choreography. Information comes not only from your own Child but from the Realm of the Children, a magical place where synchronicity abounds and miracles occur. A True Adult is guided by such choreography toward rapid evolution and an extraordinary life.

The following story illustrates how True Adults connect freely to both their own Child and the Child in others, inviting even the most mundane of circumstances to become meaningful and enriching.

Children Flying Together

I was seated on an airplane, ready for takeoff, when I overheard the passenger across the aisle nervously joke to the flight attendant that he might be needing a barf bag. He was making light of this being his first time flying, in spite of the fact that he was 40 years old. My Child felt an immediate connection with the Child in this man, and so leaning over, I struck up a conversation about what I'd overheard. He told me he was joining his wife and children who'd left days before on a family vacation. He'd stayed home, as he always did, because of his fear of flying. But, at the last minute, he'd gotten up the courage to get on a plane and join them after all.

I shared with him that even after countless flights, for me, flying was magical, like a spectacular Disneyland ride. He seemed interested, so I told him that my favorite part of the flight is the takeoff, because it reminds me of the acceleration of a fast and powerful car. He responded excitedly, remarking that he, too, loved the feeling of acceleration in his own fast car.

After we shared stories of our driving adventures, I told him that I, too, used to be afraid of flying, until I learned that flying is statistically safer than is driving a car. Hearing my words, he seemed to relax. Later, when we hit some mild turbulence, he gripped his arm rest and mumbled quietly to himself. I then shared about the discomfort I'd had with turbulence before I learned that most turbulence is akin to bumps in the road.

As we chatted and the ride became smoother, a growing confidence and lightness became visible on my new friend's face. After we landed, he thanked me for helping him through what could have been a traumatic experience. He added that he could easily see himself flying in the future, no longer missing out on valuable time with his family.

Inwardly, I thanked my Child for so clearly guiding me to connect with another person's Child. I've learned that no encounter is a coincidence; there was a reason why we were sitting near each other. The transformative experience we created together, that made such a difference in the life of this man and his family, was deeply moving to me, and it added to my appreciation of how the Children are always facilitating us—arranging circumstances for the benefit of everyone's evolution.

Manifesting Your Dreams

The more you connect with your Child to heal your wounds, the more you open the channels for your Child of the Infinite to flow through you. As you've learned, having Child—Adult Conversations further connects you to all the Children. Over time, you find yourself in relationship with everyone and everything. Sensing the presence of a True Adult, the Children of the Infinite communicate valuable information and guidance through your Child to your True Adult. Then, when you attempt to manifest your dreams—get a new job, complete a creative project, begin a relationship—the Realm of the Children will aide you, through your own Child of the Infinite, to manifest your desires.

This choreography of the Children is what manifests the people, resources, and events you need—a business or showcase opportunity, a happenstance meeting with the perfect romantic partner—to bring about your desired outcome.

As you shift energetically by clearing the wounds that have been in your way, you open yourself to an exhilarating path. Your Child of the Infinite is able to bring you what you need, including connection to the Children who join you in a new dance. Your dreams manifest, often without any conscious effort, and the outer world increasingly matches and supports your inner desires.

As a result of healing your Child's old wounds, programmed messages such as *I don't deserve…*, *I'm not good enough*, or *I don't get to have what I want* cease to exist. All that is left is the magical cycle of your Child of the Infinite, connected to the Realm of the Children, flowing through your receptive True Adult and back into the world. Through such relationship with life—what I call, *making love with life*—you find that the quality of your inner experience continues to deepen, and is increasingly matched by the quality of your outer experience.

Living in a state of not knowing, True Adults are always open and available for opportunities to further develop themselves, and to succeed at whatever they pursue. Think of a parent who sees his young child expressing a gift or talent, like dancing, doing science projects, or playing sports, and guides that child by engaging her in activities that move her. You as a True Adult do the same with your inner Child, seeing the potential for supporting him or her in bringing forth those unique gifts and talents. At the same time, you as a True Adult receive your Infinite Child's guidance in concert with all the other Children, leading directly to the expression of that gift or talent.

Once your inner alignment is strong and solid, you find yourself living the life you want and choose to live. This is the secret of the Law of Attraction, the popular notion that you attract your strongest desires by focusing on them over time. By healing your wounds and coming into alignment with your Child, you set up a powerful energetic grid that has the universe—the Children—supporting you in your endeavors. Because all the Children are connected, your alignment with your Child automatically aligns you with all the Children, who feel the energetic oneness that we all are.

Inner alignment is what makes miracles possible, as the following story about my client Laura, who manifests her dream job, exemplifies.

Inner Alignment Leading to Outer Alignment

Laura was a partner in the international Fortune 500 company where she'd worked for a number of years. Unhappy with the infighting and backstabbing going on in the upper levels she'd reached, she mentioned in session one day that it would be nice to work for a specific, different Fortune 500 company. Some months later, when she was more seriously considering leaving her current company, she heard about an opening in the company she had expressed interest in. Finding the timing meaningful, she was compelled to have Conversations with her Child regarding such a big life decision.

Her Child guided her to pursue the possibility. After several interviews, she shared with me in session, "I've been offered a vice-president position in the new company," she reported excitedly. "The problem, however, is that the position only pays half my current salary. I really don't know what to do. I feel so ready to leave my current job, and I've been drawn to this particular company for some time. It's just too interesting that they have an opening for this high-level position at the perfect time for me. But it's such a big decision, and there's no way to know if I would even be happier there. Even if I could know for sure, I don't know if I can accept living with half the pay that I'm accustomed to."

I listened and replied, "Laura, have you considered the possibility of getting the job at the pay level you've been accustomed to?"

"We went through that," she responded, defeat creeping into her voice. "They said it was the salary allotted for that position, and that they couldn't change it."

"Laura, your relationship with your Child connects you into the quantum realm, no longer limiting you to reality as you've known it. It actually is possible for you to get the job at your current salary level."

In session, I invited Laura to have a Child–Adult Conversation regarding the situation. After speaking with her Child, she turned to me and said, "Ron, I bring so much to the table—I'm *absolutely* worth getting the pay I'm getting right now!"

"Laura," I explained, "again, when you are in relationship with your Child of the Infinite, you are no longer limited by normally agreed upon conventions. New possibilities open up as the Children sense an energetic shift and rearrange the playing field. In that new reality, the Children take you beyond what appear to be limiting rules, like a specific salary allotted for a position."

Laura returned to negotiating the job offer, again asserting her desire to maintain the salary she'd been receiving in her current position. "Everything was different as I communicated from my Child's truth about what I was worth," she told me later. "They reconsidered my counteroffer, and then agreed to match my current salary. It was a miracle . . . I am just thrilled!" She then added with a note of reverence, "It never would have happened if I hadn't aligned with my Child first, and then been available for the Children to align with me, in everyone's best interest."

A year later, Laura let me know that not only did she love her new position, she'd also been given a raise and a sizeable bonus.

Trusting the Children's Wisdom

As if choreographing an elaborate dance, the Children of the Infinite are choreographing life, from a vast network of intelligence and guidance. While it may not appear so when events occur, this network is used by the Children to wake us all up as True Adults and evolve us.

The experience of my client Sharon illustrates how the Children choreograph situations to bring about the greatest growth for all. After training with me in Inner Alignment for a few months, Sharon shared the following story.

Choreography for Healing

Sharon received an e-mail from her colleague who taught in the same department at a community college. In the e-mail, her colleague vented about her students, using offensive language to describe their behavior. She mentioned one student in particular who had complained about unfair treatment after receiving a poor grade.

Sharon was shocked by her colleague's attitude toward her students, many of whom Sharon knew from her own classes. "I was really upset by this communication," Sharon told me. "I thought of shooting her back a nasty reply, and then going to our department head and telling him what she'd said. But I recognized my Little Adult was being triggered, so I decided to hold off. Instead, I worked with my Child about her reactions. It turned out to be a great opportunity to discover some old wounds and heal them. Later, when I checked in with my Infinite Child about what to do with my colleague, it still felt right to do nothing. So I trusted that the Children knew what they were doing."

The next day, Sharon received another e-mail from her colleague. In it, the other teacher apologized for having unloaded her frustrations on Sharon, explaining that she'd been under unusual stress.

When her colleague acknowledged, in her own way, that she was, in essence, being run by a wound and not being intentionally offensive, Sharon replied to her by phone. She engaged in transformational listening with her colleague, after which they explored possible ways to deal with her challenging student. By the end of the conversation, the two had forged a new, positive working relationship.

"As I continue to develop as a True Adult," Sharon said, "I recognize more and more that when someone is upset and venting their feelings, it's best to check in with my own Child, who is connected to their Child. Like all Children in pain, my colleague just needed to be heard, and so the Children choreographed our coming together."

Dealing with venting colleagues and coworkers isn't easy for anyone. When an incident arises, as it did for Sharon, a common Little Adult strategy is to avoid expressing any negative reaction in an attempt to preserve the relationship. To do nothing and let it go feels easier and safer than to say something you might later regret. Some might see this response as "being nice" by letting the offender off the hook. However, such a decision often results in resentment, which ultimately damages the relationship anyway.

"Being nice" is a common strategy for Little Adults, given that they have no access to their Infinite Child or to the healing of their underlying wounds. As a True Adult, you do have access, not only to your own Infinite Child, but also to the Realm of the Children. Receiving guidance from all the Children, you can say anything to anyone, regardless of how potentially devastating the content of the communication might seem. This is because your truth is offered with the respect that all Children deserve, making that truth feel good—even a gift—to the receiver.

True Adults are guided to action by the inner alignment they have with their Child of the Infinite, rather than by what their Little Adult might think should be done. They know that nothing is ever wrong and that we are all in training, each interaction an opportunity to grow and evolve.

The answers do lie within. And the truth does live in the Realm of the Children.

Inner Alignment on the Road

If you drive a car, or have ever driven, it's likely that you have experienced being cut off by another driver. If so, you probably experienced some strong feelings—perhaps shock, fear, frustration, anger, rage, or powerlessness. It's also likely that you had a few Little Adult reactive thoughts as well.

Remember, as a True Adult, everything is facilitation. Whatever you feel and think as a result of such a violation, while valid, it is actually more about the stirrings of feelings about historical violations.

While there are countless benefits that you gain by working with your Child on traumas from history, I will share with you a couple that specifically impact your driving experience. A number of my clients have noticed the same types of changes that I experienced after working with these deep feelings.

Freeway Facilitation

For years after I began driving, it was not that uncommon for me to be cut off by another driver. One time I experienced an especially dangerous incident that required me to hit the brakes and swerve to avoid the other driver. This sent me into a fishtail and the danger of colliding with oncoming traffic. While I emerged unscathed, my anger and frustration, along with my fear of a future, more serious incident motivated me to have a Conversation with my Child about the experience. I knew that having a Conversation would lead to the underlying wounds that had left me energetically vulnerable to such occurrences. After several Conversations with my Child and the subsequent healing of those wounds, I was free from my Little Adult's automatic reactions. This opened me to receive the guidance of my Child of the Infinite.

After those conversations with my Child, it became increasingly rare for me to be cut off. The next time it did happen, it was a minor incident. I realized that my Child had been trying to tell me all along, before each incident happened, how to prevent being cut off. However, I hadn't yet known how to recognize his communication. Remember, each Infinite Child is connected to all the Children who choreograph life to assist us in evolving our connection with ourselves and one another.

On a couple of occasions over the following several years, I had experiences of actually hearing my Child in time. In both situations, I noticed a thought as it popped into my head. *Look over to your right. That guy is about to speed up and cut in front of you. When he speeds up, just slow down and it will be fine.* Because I was able to hear my Child and follow his guidance, I continued to enjoy my comfortable driving experience. A moment later, I wasn't surprised to see someone ahead of me get cut off by the same driver.

Many years have passed since I've had even one incident of being cut off. My guess, given how Inner Alignment works, is that I have healed and learned what I needed to in that category, no longer requiring the Children to choreograph such experiences for me.

Celebrating the Children

As your ultimate relationship evolves, your increasing ability to be separate from your Child allows you to have a deeper connection with your Child. Likewise, you begin to experience a profound state of *oneness* with all of life, retaining your individuality while embracing a deeper connection with everyone around you. You celebrate the sacred interweaving of your uniqueness with the rest of the world. Your life becomes filled with reverence, gratitude—even ecstasy—the natural result of being fully who you are in every moment.

It's natural for True Adults to want to celebrate their connection with each other when they feel it, such as at a concert when people come together to share their love of the music. Perhaps you've experienced a sense of union and oneness while attending a performance by your favorite rock band, jazz or classical ensemble, or any type of live musical event. Unfortunately, that feeling of oneness is too often dismissed solely as an effect of the music itself. The truth is that the music is merely a vehicle to discovering and experiencing the joyous connection of all our Children. As a True Adult, you are free to express your oneness openly. Rather than being a rarity in your life, it becomes a common occurrence to celebrate your connection with the other Children.

The following story of my concert-going experience is one example of the countless ways we can celebrate our oneness with other Children.

True Adult Oneness

I am at a concert at the Greek Theater in Los Angeles with my wife, Patti. It's intermission and I am standing outside the restroom waiting for Patti to emerge, watching the faces of fellow concertgoers as they pass by. I'm feeling a sense of our shared humanity beyond the musical experience we've been enjoying together.

I find myself moved to look into the eyes of the people walking in my direction; I notice some looking back at me with curiosity, while others are clearly uncomfortable with my direct gaze. Still others are not looking directly at anyone, keeping their eyes to the ground. While I sense some are having their own personal experience, I feel sad for those who seem trapped in their own worlds when the music has been an invitation for us all to feel connected.

Before long, I hear an annoyed and fearful inner voice say, *What the heck are you doing? You're being weird and making people uncomfortable; it's inappropriate. Stop looking at everyone!*

I recognize the signals that my Child is going into coping mode. By staying calm and separate and acknowledging my Little Adult's concerns, I maintain my solidity as a True Adult. I am feeling more fully my Infinite Child's connection to all the Children as I continue to allow myself to be open to experience whatever occurs between me and each person who passes by me.

I continue to smile, open and receptive to everyone. I welcome and celebrate my Child as he lives his truth, moment by moment. I notice my Child has no expectations and is simply enjoying every moment of his experience, including any smiles that are returned. The positive responses grow as I welcome my Child's joy in relating to the Child in each person.

Many times since then, as I've watched the passing faces in the crowds at a concert or other public event, I've felt the freedom to let my love flow through me to each person, taking in each unique response. Sometimes, I'm so deeply moved by these encounters that my full heart spills over and a tear of joy rolls down my cheek.

▲

What's Next:

The Rest (and Best!) of Your Life

You are on your way to discovering how living as a True Adult, aligned and connected with your Child, is a privilege and an honor, and an ongoing, sacred experience. My religiously affiliated clients say that it's as though they are having a direct relationship with God through their Child. You will find that your relationship with your Child of the Infinite invites you into an extraordinary life in alignment with the realm of the Children. This opens you to benefit from the limitless possibilities that the Children choreograph to bring greater love and joy into your life and the world.

By now, you have come to see that I AM Training is the foundation of an actual, *living* relationship, one that grows and flourishes as you give it the attention it deserves. Your participation in that relationship, *your ultimate relationship*, keeps it alive; otherwise, that hard-won bond you have with your Child will fade—much as would any close relationship that isn't nurtured over time.

To help you maintain and deepen your inner relationship, I've made additional information and activities available for you on my website (InnerAlignmentMethod. com) to support your ongoing practice.

An additional opportunity to add tremendous power to your process is my workbook that you will soon find a link to on my website. It includes easy tools that you can use anywhere, at any time, to quickly get separate from your Little Adult's reactions. You will also find a range of activities to incorporate into your practice and life and further resources to speed up your healing process and your personal evolution. The workbook is designed and arranged to enable you to set up a supportive structure for your day to day experience, rapidly upgrading your quality of life in all areas.

Regularly using the tools and activities of I AM Training will support you in furthering and deepening your profound relationship with your Child of the Infinite and the Realm of the Children. I wish you success and enlightenment as you take that next leap forward into the True Adult power that is your Child's birthright. Once you do, I promise that the miracles of *your ultimate relationship* will unfold for the rest—and best—of your life.

EPILOGUE

THE PROMISE OF YOUR ULTIMATE RELATIONSHIP

I magine for a moment what it would be like to live in a world full of True Adults. No one would ever be lost in feelings of victimization, either by themselves or by others. Widespread understanding of the connection and choreography of the Children would keep relationship challenges to a resolvable minimum. People would realize that the way we treat others is simply indicative of the way we treat ourselves. Everyone would recognize that they have the ability to transform their negative reactions into positive experiences that strengthen and deepen their relationships. And, they would see how this is fundamental to true success.

No matter what your life circumstances are, you have great power to impact your world. The more time you spend in your own Child-Adult relationship, the more your eyes will open and you will see what the Children see, hear, and feel. It's an astounding revelation for my students as they move into their personal power and leadership in all aspects of their lives. It is a truly meaningful, passionate, inspirational and fulfilling path.

True Adults recognize that as every cell of the body is an integral part of the whole, so too is every human being an integral part of our collective humanity.

I like something that Albert Einstein said, essentially describing one's disconnection from others—the world of a Little Adult. He offers a suggestion as to the task of humanity—which I would call the journey toward living as a True Adult.

"A human being is part of a whole, called by us the 'Universe,' a part limited in time and space. He experiences himself, his thoughts and feelings, as something separated from the rest—a kind of optical delusion of his consciousness. This delusion is a kind of prison for us, restricting us to our personal desires and to affection for a few persons nearest us. Our task must be to free ourselves from this prison by widening our circles of compassion to embrace all living creatures and the whole of nature in its beauty."

- Albert Einstein

It's valuable to consider what happens when True Adults, rather than Little Adults, determine the ways in which we do business, educate our children, and oversee our environment—just to mention a few categories of life on our planet.

True Adults... Leading the Way in Business

You have learned, as a developing True Adult that complete satisfaction can only come from knowing yourself and having a direct relationship within. This is key for maximizing your effectiveness as a leader at any moment in your life. True Adult leadership comes from sharing the truth as guided in the moment by your Child of the Infinite.

People in leadership positions set the tone of the business environment, affecting everyone. When True Adults run businesses, conditions are optimal. This is because, like True Adult parents in a family those in positions of influence and authority are always looking at the bigger picture and supporting whatever is needed for alignment. The result is that everyone in the company feels valued, respected, and safe, creating a more cohesive and inspiring team environment. Everyone's best ideas and efforts maximize productivity and in turn, the satisfaction of the recipients of the business' goods and services. The company then profits from their True Adult leadership.

Such a supportive, empowering work environment has a natural, positive impact on company members' personal relationships, as they bring a renewed sense of their self-worth and value back to their families. Reciprocally, such positivity at home returns a happier, more self-secure, and inspired True Adult to work the next day. This mutually beneficial arrangement upgrades the quality of each company member's life, both at home and at work. True Adult leadership always seeks to maximize the greatest good and benefit for all involved. The implications are endless and profound.

True Adults... Leading the Way in Education

When schools are led by True Adult administrators and educators, and overseen by True Adult school board members, miracles happen. Classrooms are filled with happy, vibrant young people who feel safe, cared for, and excited about learning. Each student's Infinite Child within is honored and supported, creating an environment that helps to liberate Little Adults and grow True Adults, maximizing their ability to advance academically, emotionally and socially.

In such a nurturing and stimulating environment, one's uniqueness and creativity, as well as interpersonal relationships, are valued along with academic achievement. Students trust their natural desire to learn and grow, and are not afraid of being judged for their "mistakes." They experience being an important part of a team on which each team member is valued as a whole person, encouraged to maximize his or her skills and talents, and effectively express who he or she is for the benefit of the team. Interpersonal conflicts are recognized as opportunities for healing. As team members grow and learn not to judge themselves, they become more supportive of each other. With such connection to self and others, they develop emotional intelligence, ensuring a future of real success, not one based only on external, Little Adult measurements.

Students learning in a True Adult environment emerge from educational institutions with a solid foundation of self and of their connection to the whole. They possess the True Adult qualities of curiosity, creativity, courage, and leadership. Guided by their own higher intelligence, they are interested in and care about the wellbeing of all mankind—all of life. This leads them to develop into well-rounded, authentic people, capable of achieving true success in the world— personally, socially, and professionally.

True Adults... Leading the Way for the Environment

As a True Adult, we treat everyone and everything as an extension of our own Child. Just as other people are an extension of ourselves, so too is our environment an extension of ourselves. Consider that if one denies the outer environment proper care, the same is happening for that person on the inside. It becomes simple and clear to see the truth of someone's inner world by their compassion and respect for their outer world.

Just as a family run by Little Adult parents is unsafe and uncertain until True Adult parents reinvent the family system, so too must we pay attention to how we care for our home—our planet. We all need clean air, water, and natural food from our earth in order to survive and ensure the survival of future generations.

The benefit of having teams of True Adults in charge of our environment is the inquiry and the exploration of multiple points of view that lead to the best decisions for the whole and a thriving of the planet and all its inhabitants.

When True Adults are aligned with the Children, it is natural to love and respect our Mother Earth, who gives us life and sustains us.

You are one part, separate but equal to the whole
which one might call God.
You are an individual going through the process
of discovering this truth.

All that I can offer you, my fellow traveler, is what I have learned about myself and about life that continues to reveal the preciousness and joy of my every moment. Thank you for being an important part of my journey. It's been said that it takes a village to raise a child. I offer, in addition, that it takes a Child to make that village a truly nourishing place to live. The Children—all of us— need True Adults to accomplish the miracles that will continue to put our world on track and into alignment in every sphere.

You are an important part of our planet's evolution. Now that you have a strong foundation of I AM Training, I encourage you to use it to continue discovering and expressing your unique contribution to the great design that we all are. The Children of the Infinite await your participation. The path is now clear for you to join the Children and start living *Your Ultimate Relationship.*

ABOUT THE AUTHOR

Ron Levy, MS, LMFT is grateful to have discovered the Inner Alignment Method (I AM) and feels blessed to be sharing it with so many more fellow travelers. In his more than 30 year psychotherapy practice, Ron has guided countless clients to discover the key to unlocking the door of their emotional prison of the past and to find, in the process, their Ultimate Relationship.

Ron spent his early years as an elementary and special education teacher, youth group director, and martial arts instructor. He earned his master of science degree in educational psychology at California State University and is in practice as a licensed marriage and family therapist in Calabasas, California. Ron also celebrates the expansion that occurs for everyone when training fellow adventurers through Your Ultimate Relationship/I AM Training seminars.

Ron is a Southern California native and a martial artist of over 40 years. He and his wife Patti, soul mates of 25 years, share their home with their two extraordinary feline children, Navi and Tari. Through every interaction and experience, they rejoice in deepening their connection with all of life.

ACKNOWLEDGMENTS

While the concepts in this book were brought to me through my Child of the Infinite and the Realm of the Children, there are significant people who have contributed to my bringing them to the world.

I would like to give special thanks to Nancy Marriott, Patti Levy LMFT, and Conley Falk for joining me as my writing and editing team. Without your inimitable and specific talents, my message would not have been conveyed as clearly or as well.

Thank you, Nancy, for your staunch dedication to making this project what it is, and for being an exceptional partner, living the I AM Training with us throughout the process of creating this book.

Thank you, Patti, for your relentless commitment to ensuring that my readers have the best, most accurate experience. And thank you for living the I AM Training in every aspect of our lives. The results of your willingness to partner with me so fully continue to enhance my quality of life, and deepen my love for you with every single day that I am gifted to have you as my wife.

Thank you, Conley, for stepping in to assist me in creating a new framework and focus for the book, so that I could accomplish my desire to gift my readers through experience, rather than solely with information.

Thank you to my brother Mark, for your steadfast allegiance to my greatest good, and to my shining most fully and accurately. I live in endless gratitude for having you in my life.

Thank you to my parents, first, for giving me life, and for doing all that it takes to successfully raise a child. Thank you, Dad, for being, as it turns out, the model of the fundamentals of living in relationship with everyone and everything. I live in daily appreciation of the gifts you gave me just by being who you are. Thank you, Mom, for being my model of True Adult listening and presence, from the perspective that all people and beings are valuable and worthy of respect, love and compassion.

To my dear friends of many years, thank you for celebrating life and evolving with me. Andrew Schoenberg, you were my inspiration to teach karate as a vehicle to personal growth and awareness, my first student and ultimately, my best friend and brother. Thank you for a lifetime of acknowledgement and love. My friend and colleague, Catherine DeMonte, LMFT, thank you for the years of beautiful friendship, learning and growing together, and your loving support. Rush White, my dear friend, thank you for your tremendous support of this project. You were there early on with a deep recognition of the value of I AM Training, and a fierce commitment to receiving and understanding it. Thank you my dear friend, Christopher DePalma, for creating with me a magnificent relationship and for living I AM Training with a depth of comprehension that is always inspiring to me. Ron Friedland, my buddy since I was nine, thank you for your contribution and endless support. Thank you, Judi Lirman, LMFT, my training supervisor early in my career, with whom I shared I AM when I first discovered it. You were always supportive and acknowledging of my work, and the first to tell me that I need to write a book on it. Twenty-three years later, here it is!

A special thank you to Mardy DeSanto, for capturing the essence of I AM in the logo image, and for introducing me to Chaz Desimone. Thank you, Chaz, for your many generous contributions, as well as the final logo and book cover design.

While I live in deep appreciation of how we all facilitate one another's evolution through every single interaction, there are a handful of other individuals whom I'd like to acknowledge for the contribution that their simply being who they are has been to me:

My clients—who are also my teachers—past and present; the beautiful people who have participated over the years in my I AM Training groups; my generous readers of earlier versions of this book; my dear friend and colleague Gabrielle Borkan; the creator of Dance Alive (and my cousin), Mariane Karou; and my other dear friends and family: Tahdi Blackstone; Uncle Dan Morris; Jaime Segel Estes; my father in-law, Hyman Troped; Ki Karou; The Dance Alive team; Richard Karou; Barbara White; Robert Thurmer; Mark Doorn; John Kania, PhD; and Bob Fair.

BONUS MATERIALS

1. Further Inner Alignment Tools & Activities
2. Inner Alignment Model: Child and True Adult – A Review
3. Little Adult Reactions at a Glance
4. True Adult Perspective for a Specific Potential Challenge
5. Directory of YOUR TURN Activities
6. Inner Alignment Method Key Teachings: Lines I Live by

1. Further Inner Alignment Tools & Activities

In this book, I've been able to give you only a foundation for what is available for you as a student of I AM Training. If you are interested in building on this foundation, please visit my website. You will find a number of valuable opportunities to further develop yourself as a True Adult, leading to your ongoing evolution, growth, and joyful experience of Your Ultimate Relationship. In addition to Inner Alignment tools, you can also find out about teleclasses and in-person seminars designed to build True Adult muscles and further your knowledge and experience on the path to your extraordinary life. Besides materials that are available to the public, there is a private section of materials—only for my readers—that will expand your capacity for making your life more meaningful and fulfilling. Go to InnerAlignmentMethod.com. You'll find the private, Beyond the Book section in the menu. Your password is THRIVE.

The following easy and powerful Inner Alignment tools are structured to support and assist you in your process of creating an empowered life that you love.

▷   Continuum Check
▷   True Adult Anchoring Statements

▷ True Adult Narration
▷ Child–Adult Meditation
▷ Child Expression
▷ Partner Communication Activity (especially for couples or any two people desiring effective communication)
▷ I AM Meditative Art Piece

2. Inner Alignment Relationship Model: Child and True Adult – A Review

The following summarizes the key structures of the Inner Alignment Relationship Model:

CHILD

The Child is comprised of three aspects: Infinite Child, Hurt Child, and Coping Child/Little Adult. The Infinite Child and the Hurt Child occur as immediate and natural experiences of being. The Coping Child, however, is not actually a true expression of the Child, but rather a reactive attempt to cope with trauma.

Infinite Child is you as you arrived on the planet, attuned to the energetic vibrations of the universe and connected to the oneness of all that is. It is you before you were shaped by the environment and conditions of your life—your early programming. You might call the Infinite Child your soul, your Higher Self, or God Within.

Hurt Child is your Infinite Child's experience of the inevitable pain of being human. Like your Infinite Child, your Hurt Child is timeless, always with you regardless of your physical age, and is felt whenever an internal emotional wound is stirred up by your environment. The Hurt Child is the Infinite Child who is shifted out of alignment by something inharmonious.

Coping Child/Little Adult, while still a Child in essence, is distinct from the other aspects of your Child. It is not actually a true expression of either

Child or Adult, but is rather a reactive mechanism that manipulates your inner and outer environments in order to survive. Little Adult arises in response to your Hurt Child's pain and fear from the absence of a True Adult. He or she is committed to the protection of your being, however misguided the attempt may be. Little Adult dominates your life, obscuring your Infinite Child and, to some degree, your Hurt Child from your view.

You may think of your Little Adult as your dark side, in some respects like an ego. However, Little Adult in this system is a more positive element, doing the best he or she can to ease pain and protect your Infinite and Hurt Child. With the development of your True Adult, your Little Adult, or Coping Child, becomes your assistant by letting you know when there's a problem that requires your attention and presence. You can tell this is occurring by the upset, anxiety, or fear that lets you know you are needed. Once you step in, you increasingly find your Little Adult relaxing because a true Big Person is now on the scene.

TRUE ADULT

True Adult is a receptive state you develop in order to connect with your Child. Your development as a True Adult, heals painful wounds, freeing you from a focus on surviving to that of thriving. You remain open, neutral, and available to your Child, seeing and further discovering the bigger picture of your life's circumstance—the essence of the True Adult perspective. True Adults are on the path of mastery, continually evolving through inner alignment with their own Child and with the Child in others which creates an extraordinary life.

Think of the True Adult as a Zen Master, willing to know nothing and therefore open to learning everything. True Adults are powerful in life because, as if plugged into a cosmic socket, they gain access to the unlimited energy, guidance, and wisdom of the Infinite Child.

3. Little Adult Reactions at a Glance

You know your Little Adult is triggered when you are:

▷ Reacting automatically to people or situations

▷ Rigid and closed off; resistant to change

▷ Aggressive or defensive

▷ Biased or opinionated

▷ Invalidating of others

▷ Judgmental or critical of others or self

▷ Controlling, dominating, or needing to be right

▷ Blaming or shaming of self or others

▷ Anxious and nervous about outcomes

▷ Feeling self-pity and victimization

▷ Fearful

* Signs of Little Adult Activation: Page 56

4. True Adult Perspective for a Specific Potential Challenge

I want to make you aware of a possible scenario that, while fairly rare, has occurred for some people. I want you to be prepared should you happen to encounter such a situation, so you'll know what's going on and what you need to do to create healing and further strengthening of your inner structures.

There are times when one's Child will come forth and express some strong, pent-up upsets and negative beliefs. When you consider that we all tend to harbor such stored up material, it's understandable that a Child might, at times, bring to the surface more of it than we might be expecting. It is helpful to remember that often, a Child's feelings have been withheld for long periods of time, the Child not having felt safe enough to let them out. Until the Child is properly debriefed, the challenging feelings and thoughts that surface are experienced in the same way as they were originally experienced—as the absolute truth.

254

Whether you have had a tendency to get lost in your Child's feelings and beliefs or not, such an experience is a powerful training opportunity. In the moment, you might easily forget that what you are experiencing is a Child's harsh, scary—and basically programmed—world, and not the truth. But for your Child, it will seem as if it is the truth, especially when your Little Adult is making a case to prove it.

Your job as a developing True Adult is to use any or all of what I have made available to you: the information, session examples, and tools in the book, and on my website in the "Beyond the Book" section to develop your separateness and ability to see the bigger picture. This practice is what will free your Child from that painful, programmed history, and the reactivity and recreations that have been ongoing ever since.

In the book, I talked about how we've all been left with negative beliefs created by our early wounding experiences. While the conscious focus varies among people, the core beliefs: "I don't get to be happy; I'm not good enough and I never will be; There's no point in trying; It's all too much for me; I can't ever get it right; I'm confused; There's no one to turn to; etc." are largely the same, underneath, for all of humanity. While there are more and less challenging paths, deep down, we all have a Child who feels pain. This is natural, normal, and very real for the Child; it's the human condition. Keep in mind that Little Adults are always focused on hiding anything others might judge. So when comparing your experiences with others' experiences, it helps to recognize that you are comparing how you feel on the inside to how other people look on the outside.

If you find that what your Child brings up to you is more than you are comfortable working with, it would be valuable to seek professional support, and at the least, support from someone close whom you trust. While such material is challenging for everyone, the fact that your Child is bringing that material to you means that he or she is ready to be rid of these stifling and oppressive wounds so you can begin, with your Child, to create and start living an extraordinary life.

5. Directory of YOUR TURN Activities

The following is a listing of the Your Turn activities found at the end of chapters 3 through 12.

6. Inner Alignment Method Key Teachings: Lines I Live by

The following are key teachings—lines I live by—for your easy reference.

Chapter 1: A Relationship with Yourself

1. By shifting your focus off the other person and putting that focus—not blame—on yourself, you can begin to develop an empowering relationship with yourself: your ultimate relationship.

2. Your Infinite Child is the you who arrived at birth, pure and timeless. This aspect of your Child exists in an energetic reality within which everyone and everything is connected.

3. I AM Training gives you the power to heal your childhood wounds and clear out those unconscious programs so you'll no longer find yourself running endlessly in circles, recreating your painful past. The Infinite Child is a trusted guide pointing you in the right direction, an inner guru connecting you with your deepest truth.

Chapter 2: My Ultimate Relationship

1. Early wounding always involves a painful experience of disconnection from the Big People we depended on and felt especially close to.

2. I've learned that all I have to do is be true to myself. This means listening to my Child and everyone else's Child as they guide us all to the highest quality of life that we are available to experience.

Chapter 3: Child and Little Adult: A Fundamental Misalignment

1. Anytime you find yourself reacting to someone or some circumstance or feeling a negative emotion, the experience is unconsciously reminding you of a time in childhood when you felt cut off—invalidated—by a Big Person.

2. Post Traumatic Childhood Moment (PTCM), refers to the trauma of the past—times when we didn't feel seen, heard, or connected with by a True Adult—being re-experienced in current life.

3. None of a Little Adult's efforts will ever work, because in addition to pushing aside the Child's feelings, all these efforts are those of a child trying to do an adult's job.

Chapter 4: True Adult: The Solution

1. As a True Adult, you become an objective observer of all that goes on in your Child's world. Rather than being entangled in your problems, you become a compassionate witness to those problems.

2. A True Adult never blames anyone for anything, knowing that whenever there is conflict, each individual in that conflict makes perfect sense, and that we are all just doing the best we can.

3. People are more available to new perspectives after they feel that their own perspectives have been validated.

Chapter 5: A Sacred Connection: The Conversation

1. It's amazing what a profound difference you can make as a True Adult, simply by listening to your Child. It means everything to a Child to be shown interest, compassion, and respect.

2. Because you have access, 24 hours a day, to every thought, feeling, and experience your Child has ever had, you are in the position to be the most effective coach/therapist—True Adult—for your Child.

3. The connection between you as an emerging True Adult and your Child will deepen through communication, as does any relationship.

Chapter 6: Healthy Separateness: The Chart

1. As you develop healthy separateness within, you'll find that you have a greater and more natural ability to do the same with others.

2. A first step toward healthy separateness is to distinguish the reactive thoughts and actions of your Little Adult from the feelings of your Hurt Child.

3. Only when your Child's feelings and your Little Adult's reactions are distinct, and no longer merged as one experience, can you emerge as a True Adult, properly address your Child's feelings, and heal.

Chapter 7: Romantic Relationships: Inner Alignment in Love

1. A richly intimate, committed partnership for life is possible; the honeymoon doesn't ever have to end.

2. It is in your relationship with yourself that you do the deepest healing work for creating a profound relationship with your partner.

3. As you and your Child continue to have conversations together, he or she will experience the healing that occurs naturally as the result of the relationship being developed between you.

Chapter 8: Romantic Relationships: Exponential Healing

1. When you're having a negative emotional reaction to someone or something, it's never about what it seems to be about. It's always about something deeper, something buried in the past that is now beyond your conscious awareness.

2. Through exponential healing, the baggage from your past magically disappears, as though the pain had been in someone else's life.

3. Upsets, struggles, and conflicts in relationship are opportunities for healing.

Chapter 9: Workplace Relationships: Inner Alignment at Work

1. When your True Adult steps in and reflects back your Child's feelings and thoughts without judgments or opinions, your Child feels validated, supported, and gotten, and thus relieved.

2. Always be open and receptive to any memories your Child might bring to you. Your Child will guide you to past incidents he or she wants to talk with you about.

3. As you develop your ability to be a True Adult, you'll gain a sense of calm, inner connection, and emotional well-being.

Chapter 10: Workplace Relationships: Exponential Healing

1. As you experience reflecting back your Child's feelings and thoughts, you begin to feel a connection with him or her and the conversation starts flowing more naturally.

2. It's comforting for your Child when you receive his or her feelings while remaining clear that those feelings belong to him or her, not to you, his or her True Adult.

3. As your Child eventually learns to depend on you, he or she will more readily provide you with information, guidance, and insights regarding your issues.

Chapter 11: Family Relationships: Inner Alignment at Home

1. Once you align with your Child and emerge as a True Adult, you are available to be continually guided by your Child of the Infinite to connect to the higher selves of others, especially the young children you may be parenting.

2. When you as a parent are connected with your own Child within, you can more easily connect with your physical children on the emotional level that they need. But when you are disconnected from your own Child in any particular area, you will likewise remain unavailable to your physical children in the same area.

3. Becoming a True Adult for your own Child is the quickest path to becoming enlightened parents with happy and emotionally intelligent children.

Chapter 12: Family Relationships: Exponential Healing

1. In families, the buried wounds of the parents impact their children, who then grow up in the shadow of those wounds.

2. It takes experience to know—in the moment—that conflicts are always an invitation to self-discovery, evolving you to a higher quality of life. As you practice I AM and see how everything that happens moves you forward, it becomes easier to see—in each moment—that nothing is ever wrong.

3. I AM Training brings you to a state of True Adult Clarity, giving you options and choices that were unavailable to you in Little Adult mode.

Chapter 13: True Adult: From Surviving to Thriving . . . and Ever Evolving

1. Getting comfortable with not knowing—welcoming it as a way of life—frees you from clinging to any one perspective or belief and allows you to greet new ideas with interest and enthusiasm.

2. True Adults acknowledge all the Children; they treat the Child within all other people as they would their own Child.

3. As your connection to your Child deepens, you begin to experience a profound state of oneness with all of life, retaining your individuality while embracing a deeper connection with everyone around you.

Epilogue: The Promise of Your Ultimate Relationship

1. It's valuable to consider what happens when True Adults, rather than Little Adults, determine the ways in which we do business, educate our children, and oversee our environment—just to mention a few categories of life on our planet.

2. You are an important part of our planet's evolution.

3. The path is now clear for you to join the Children and start living Your Ultimate Relationship.